IMAGES
of America

MOORE COUNTY

I0806182

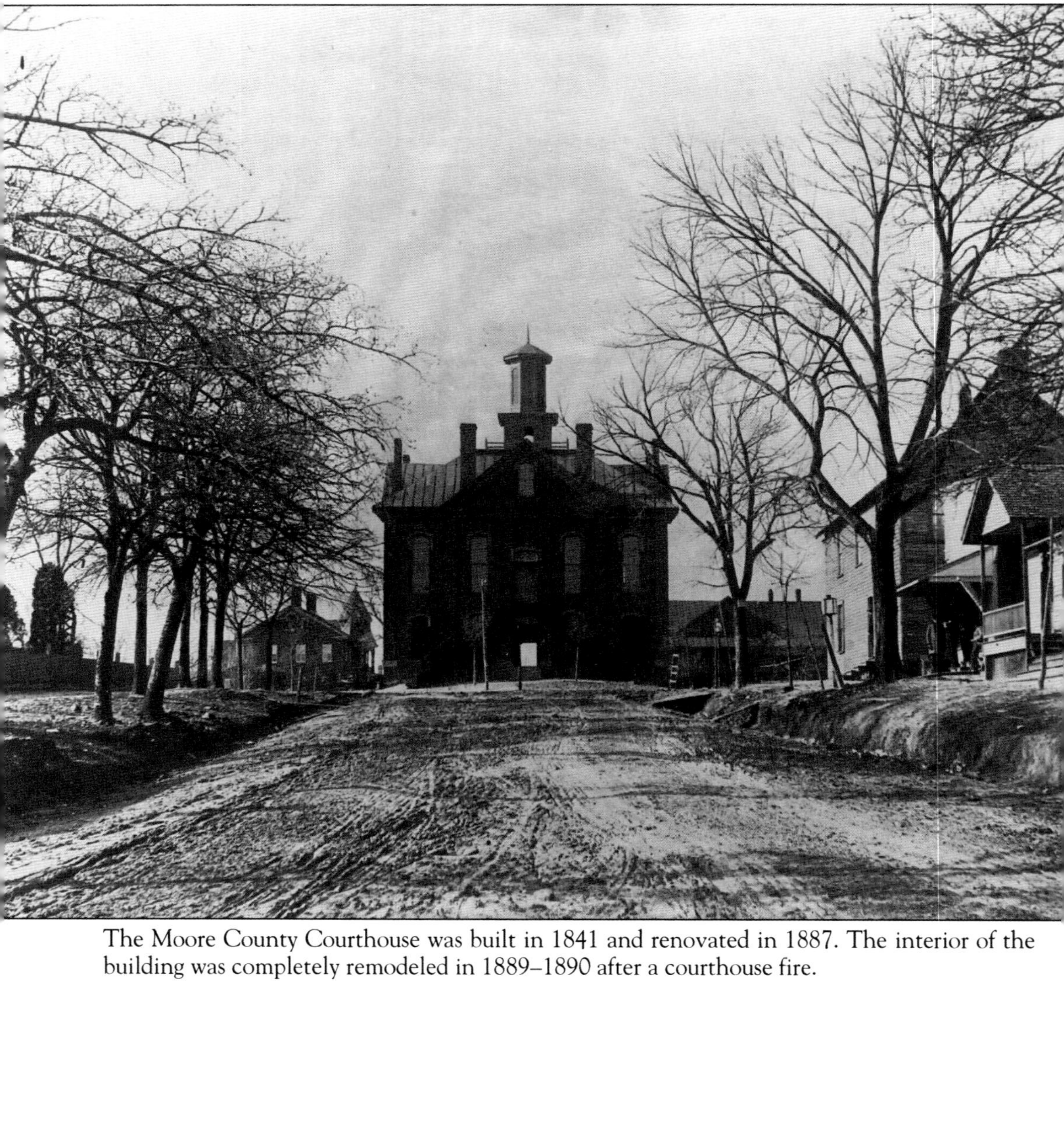

The Moore County Courthouse was built in 1841 and renovated in 1887. The interior of the building was completely remodeled in 1889–1890 after a courthouse fire.

IMAGES
of America

MOORE COUNTY

Richard J. Schloegl

ARCADIA
PUBLISHING

ISBN 978-0-7385-6875-1

Published by Arcadia Publishing
Charleston, South Carolina

Printed in the United States of America

Library of Congress Catalog Card Number: Applied for

For all general information contact Arcadia Publishing at:
Telephone 843-853-2070
Fax 843-853-0044
E-mail sales@arcadiapublishing.com
For customer service and orders:
Toll-Free 1-888-313-2665

Visit us on the Internet at www.arcadiapublishing.com

To Candace Street Simmons

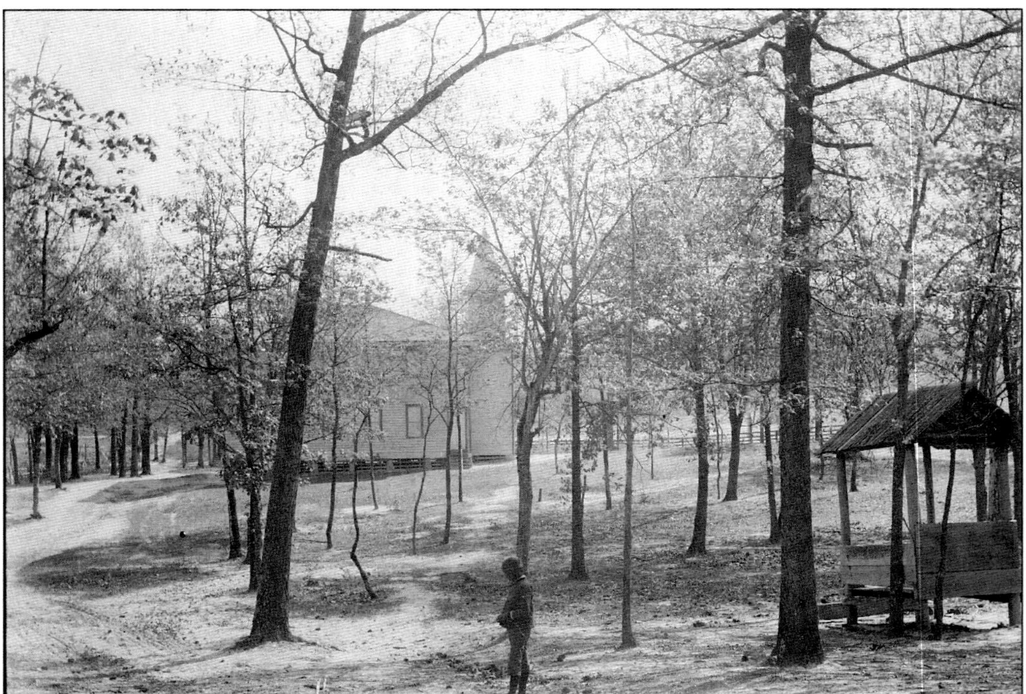

Pictured is the outdoor pulpit at the Bethesda Presbyterian Church and Cemetery. The church was established in 1788.

Contents

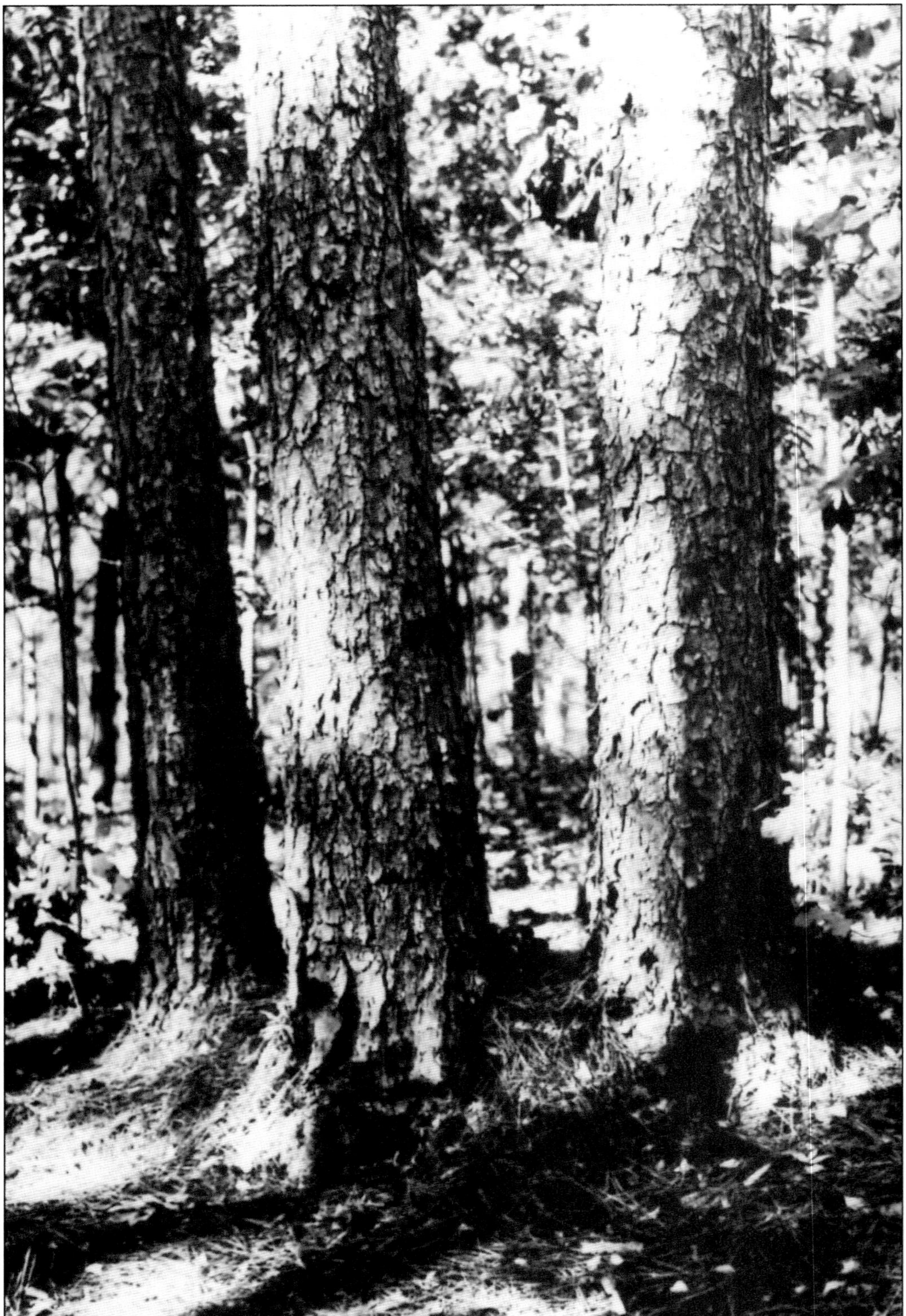

Longleaf pines like these three were an important resource for early developers of the Moore County area.

Introduction

This pictorial history covers a brief but historically significant period in the development of Moore County. The coming of the Raleigh and Augusta Railroad in 1877 marked the beginning of nearly five decades of uninterrupted growth for a region previously known for its isolation. Its roads were poor, and its soil was considered almost worthless by the standards of the day.

But it did have pine trees, and they were amongst the largest in the state. Massive longleaf pines soared 150 to 200 feet in the air and had been virtually untapped as a source of lumber. These trees blanketed the sandhills of North and South Carolina.

The railroad literally brought the trees to market. Shipping points were established along its route and gave rise to the early towns of Cameron, Manly, Keyser, and Aberdeen. Smaller short line railroads were constructed to facilitate movement to the forests' interior.

The resort industry took hold after the forests were depleted. The timbered-over land was inexpensive, and the network of railroads provided transportation facilities for the communities of Jackson Springs, Southern Pines, Pinebluff, and Pinehurst. These towns were to become health resorts known for the medicinal qualities of their water, air, and climate.

The focus of the towns changed in 1897 with the introduction of golf, which became a favorite sport of wealthy patrons from the New England and Middle Atlantic states who soon built commodious winter homes or "cottages" in Pinehurst and neighboring Southern Pines. Golf courses were laid out throughout the county, and by 1907, Pinehurst was the first resort in America to offer seventy-two holes of golf. The internationally acclaimed golf course architect Donald Ross had taken up residence in the village in 1900.

As pervasive as the game of golf was the sport of fox hunting. Its popularity soared, and large estates were established east of Pinehurst and south of Southern Pines. Polo and horse racing were also introduced, and by the early 1920s, Southern Pines was recognized as one of the nation's leading equestrian resorts. Famed novelist James Boyd and his brother Jackson served as joint masters of the Moore County Hounds.

I've tried to present this chronology in pictures. It is by no means complete, but I hope it is an interesting tale.

Richard Schloegl
March 3, 1997

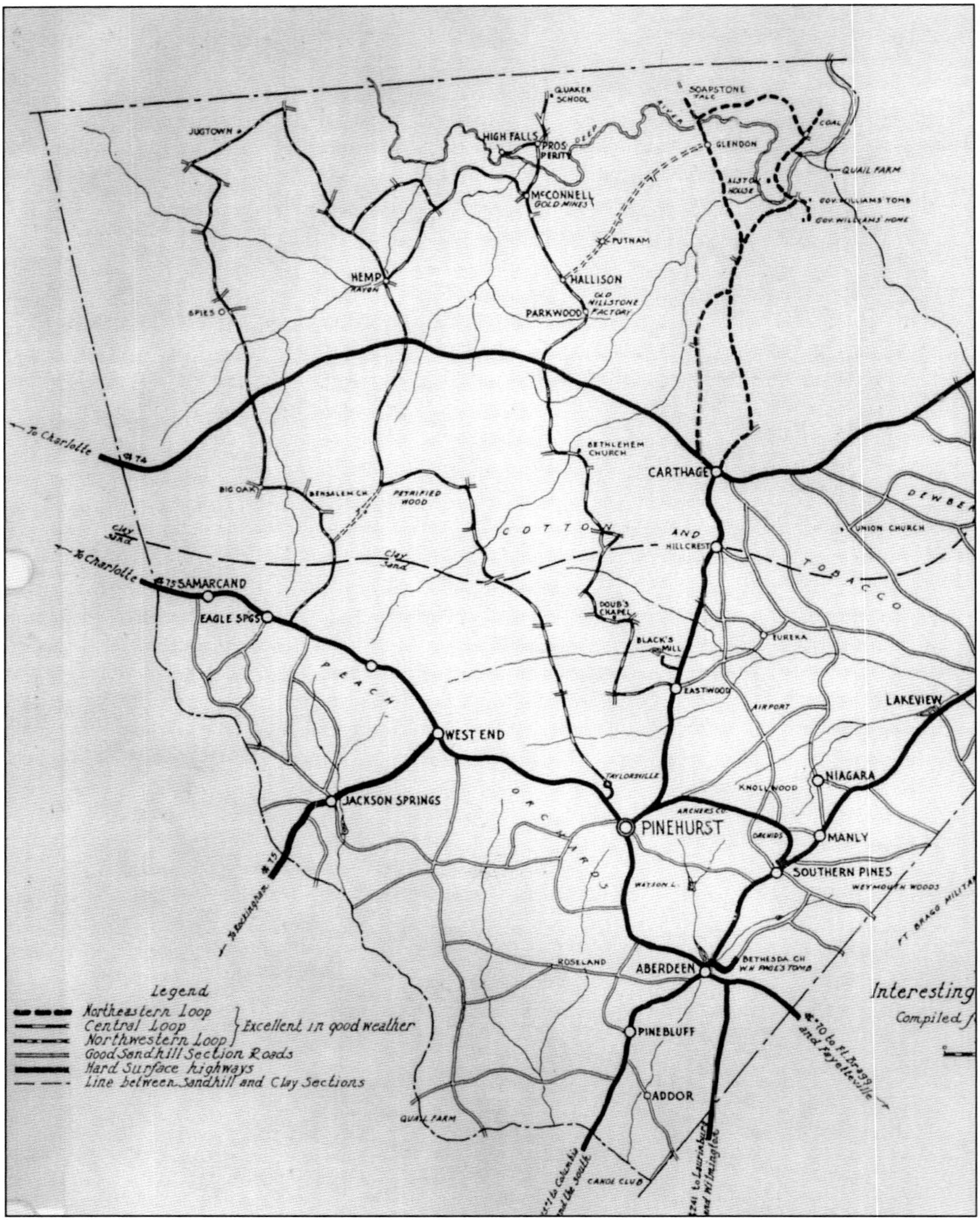

A map of Moore County shows many of its nineteenth-century towns. Moore County was formed from Cumberland County in 1784.

One

THE BEGINNING

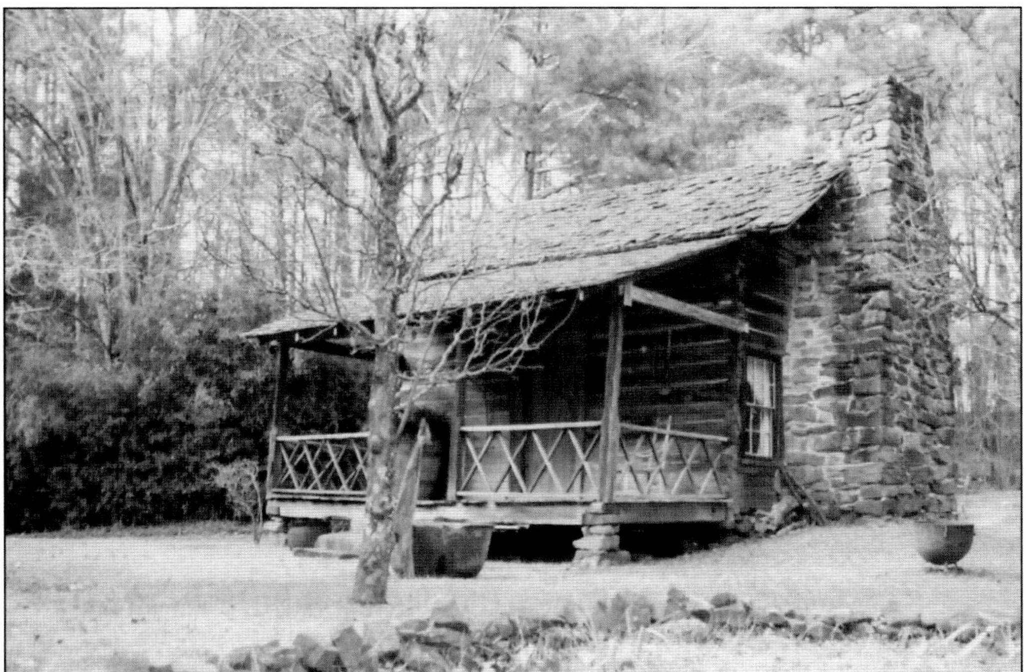

This is a photograph of McLendon's Cabin, built 1760.

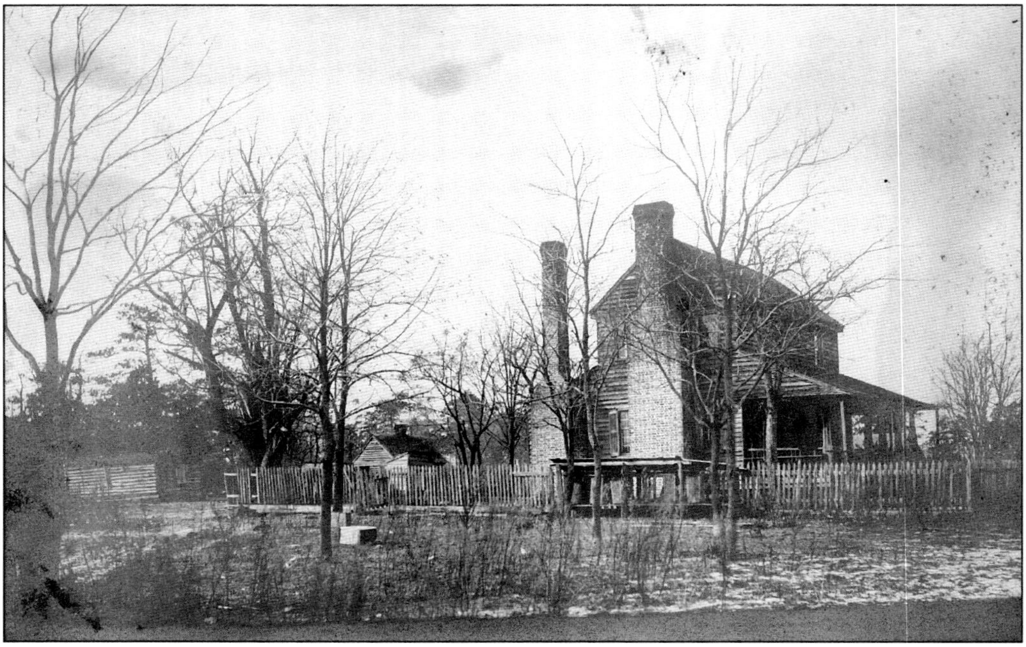

This is the Archibald Blue House, built 1825.

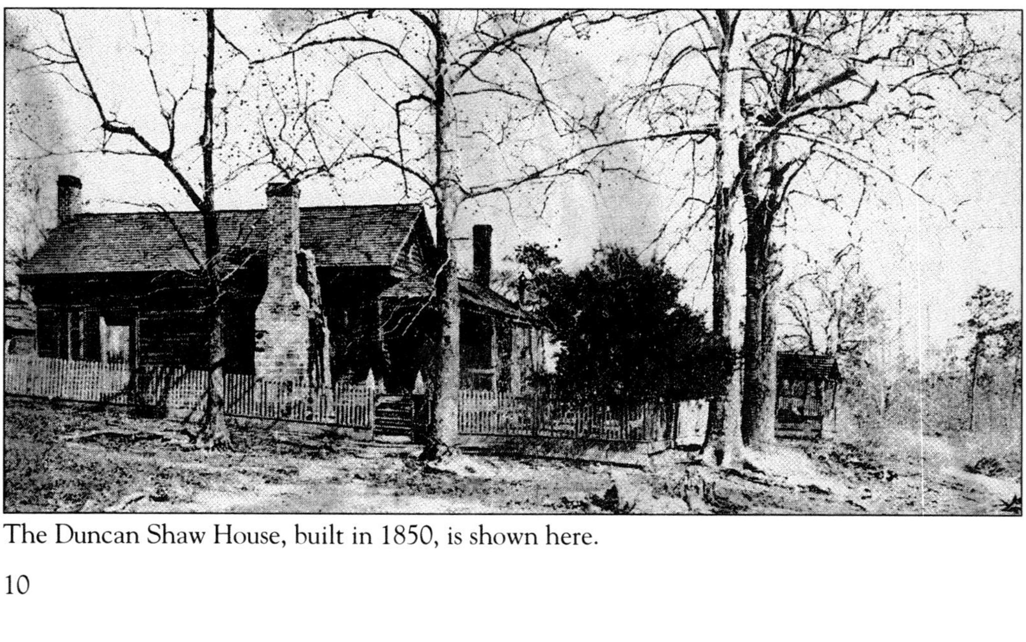

The Duncan Shaw House, built in 1850, is shown here.

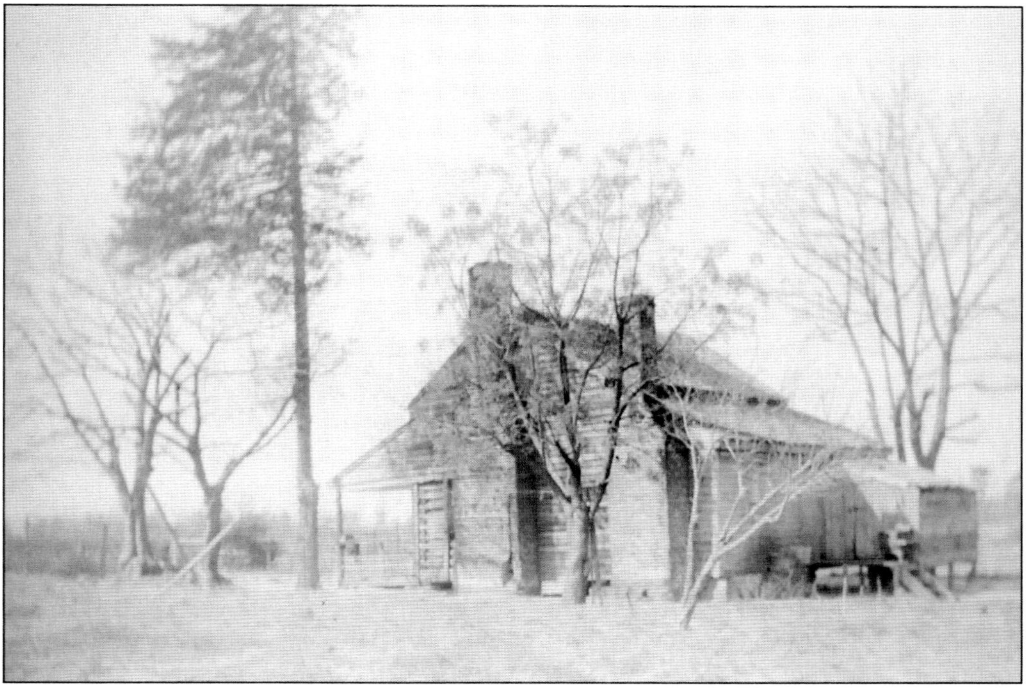

The Solemn Grove Post Office (the John Buchan House) was built in 1800.

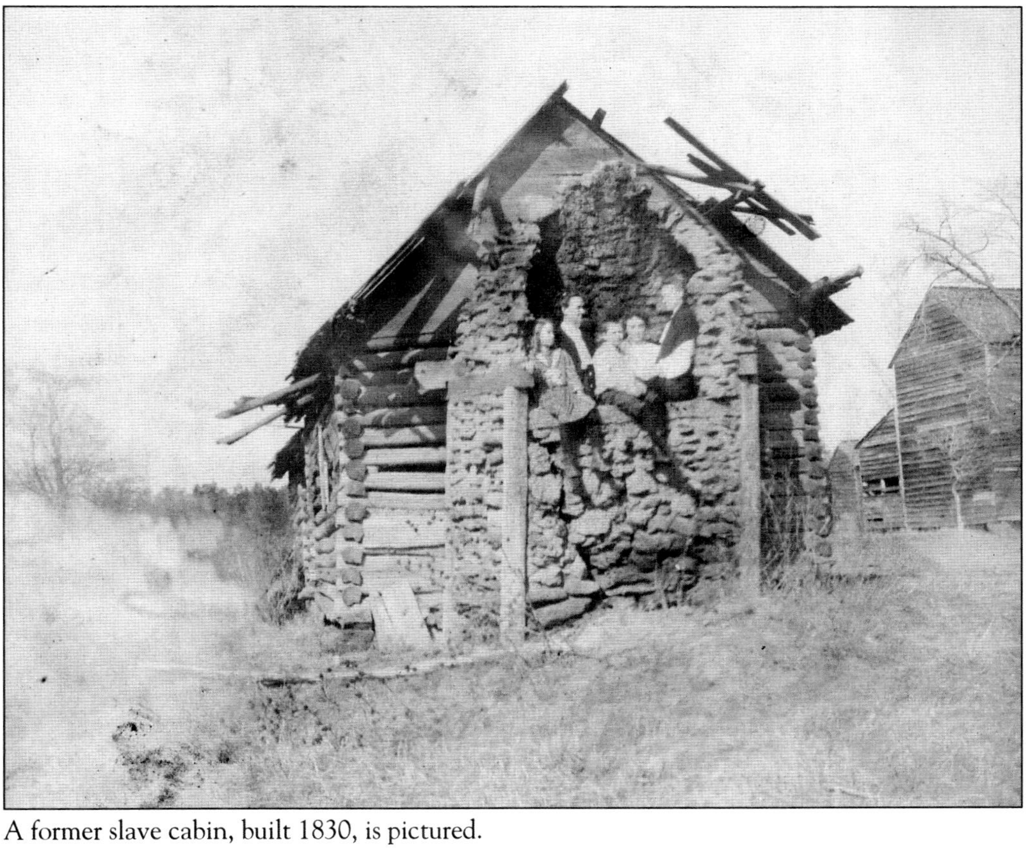

A former slave cabin, built 1830, is pictured.

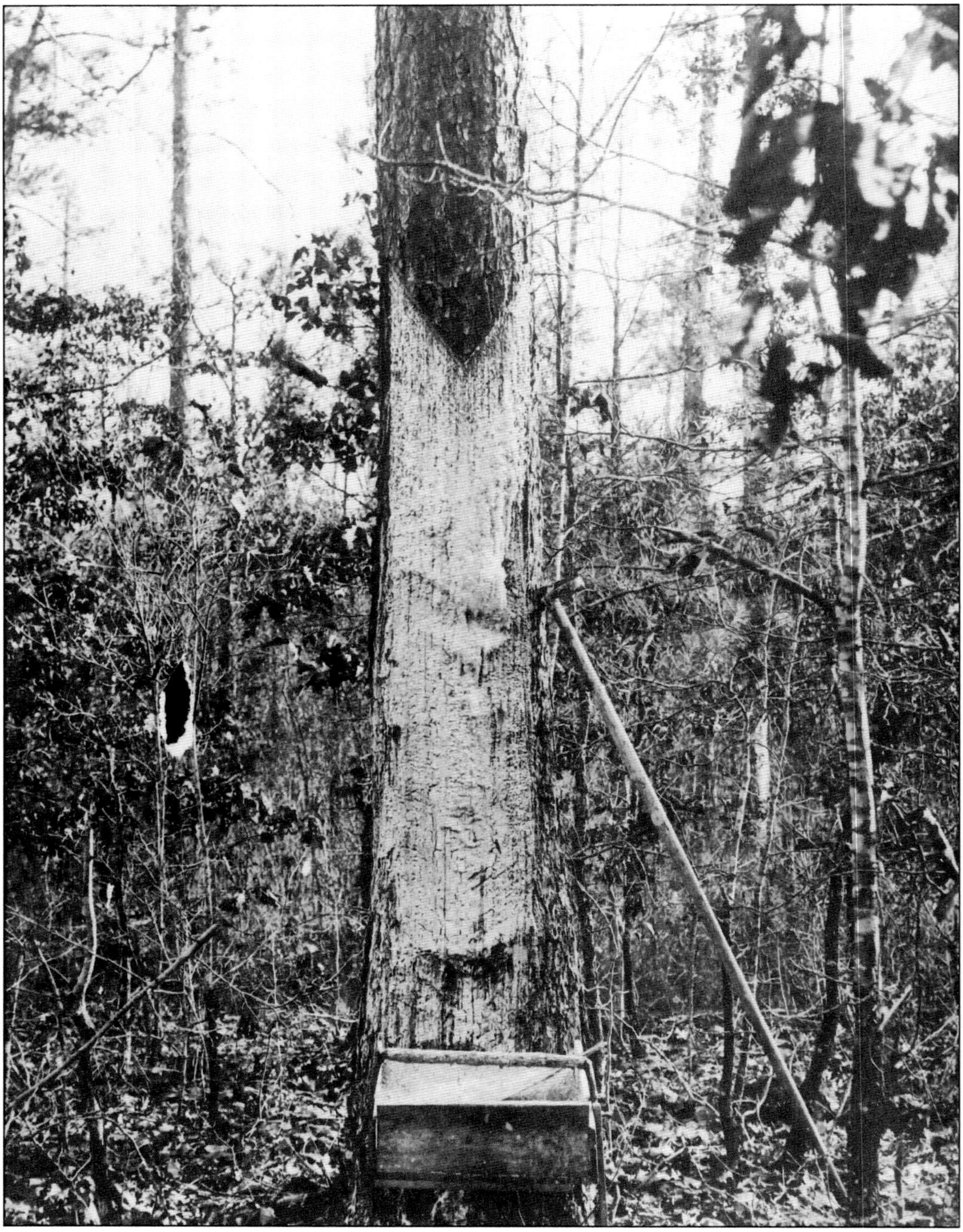

The resin extracted from the boxed pine was distilled into turpentine.

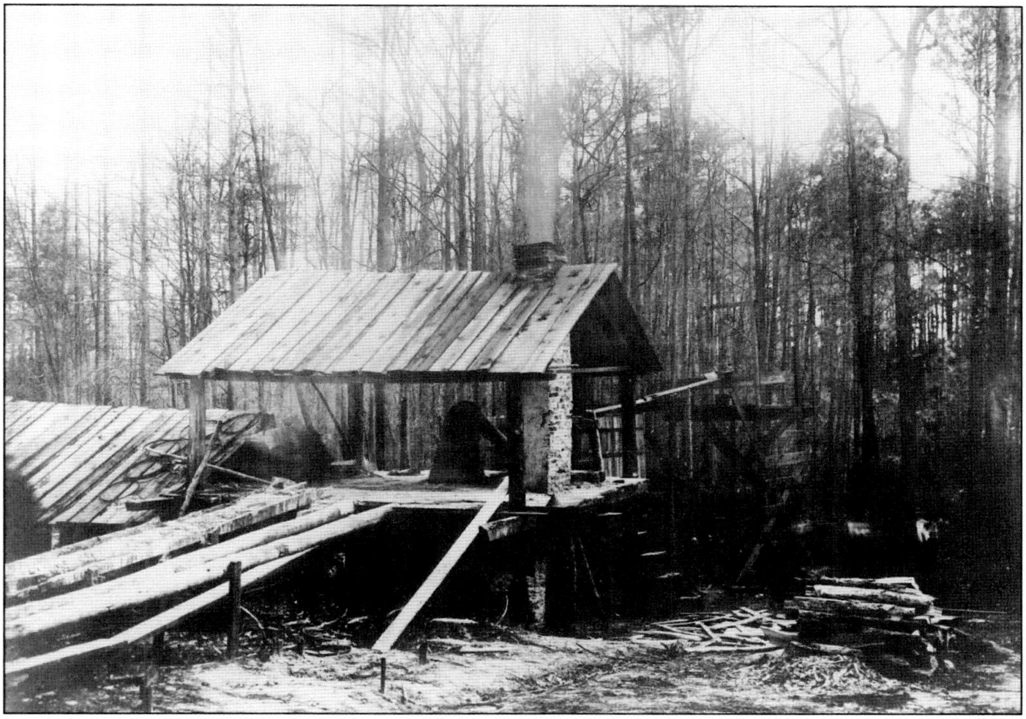

Turpentine distilleries processed the boxed pine's resin.

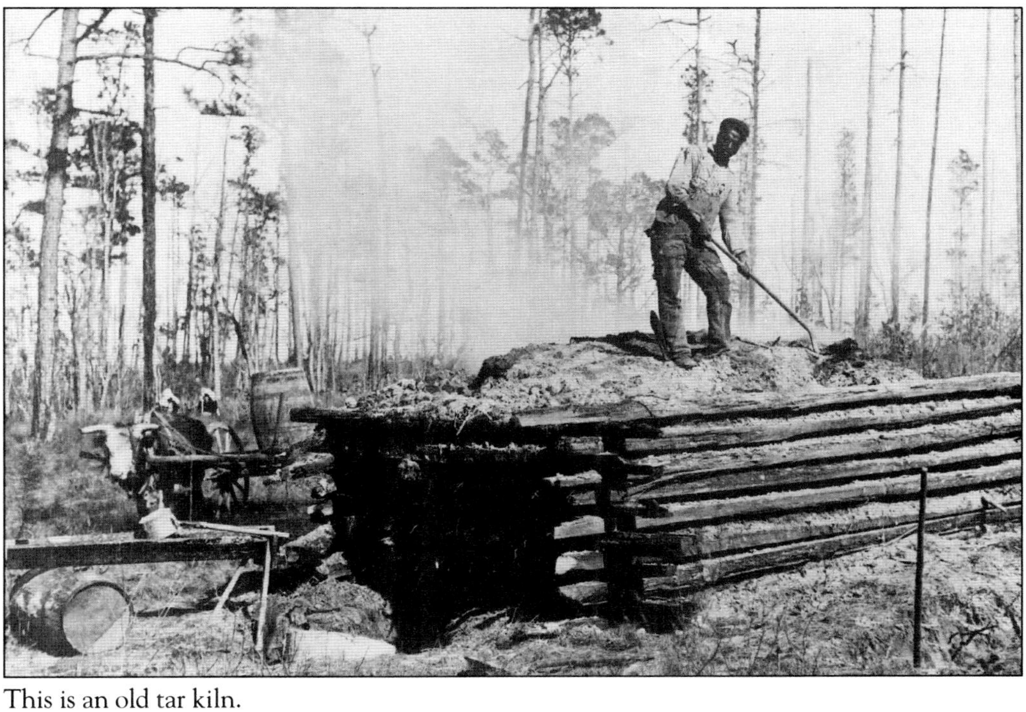

This is an old tar kiln.

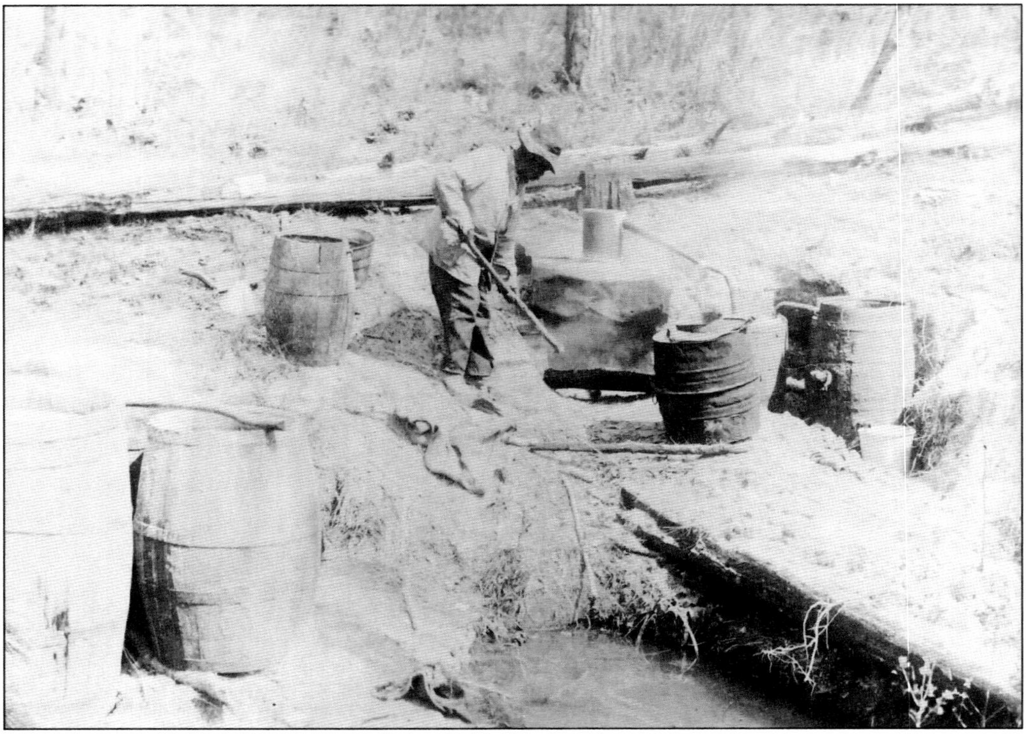

After distilling, the turpentine was stored in barrels such as these.

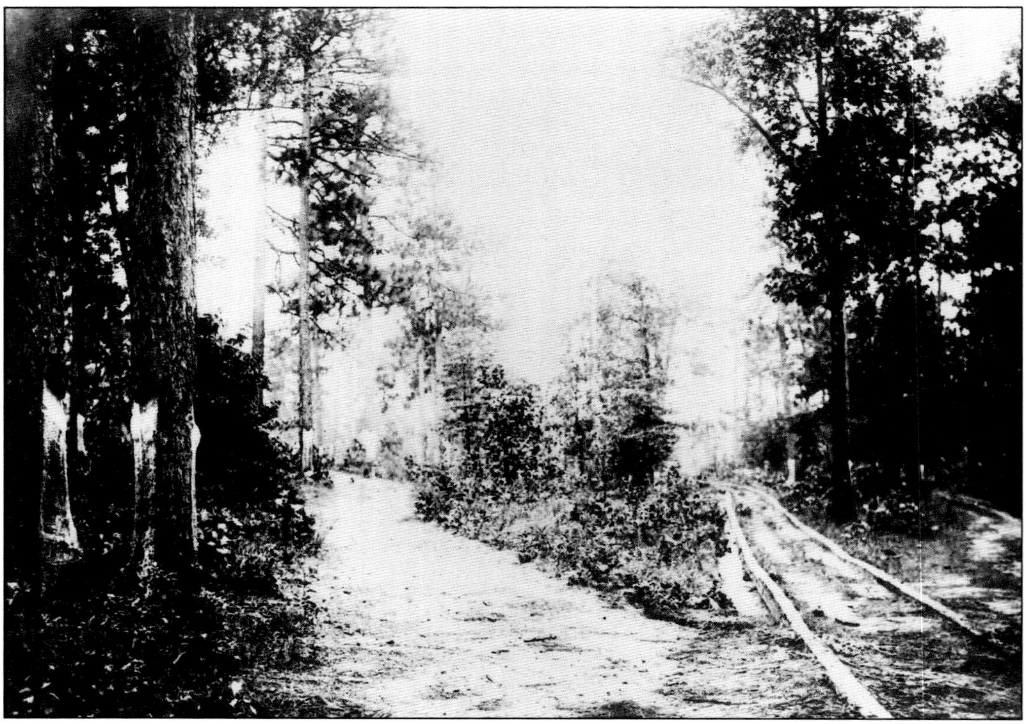

This type of wooden tram was used to transport lumber and turpentine.

Two

The Early Railroad Towns

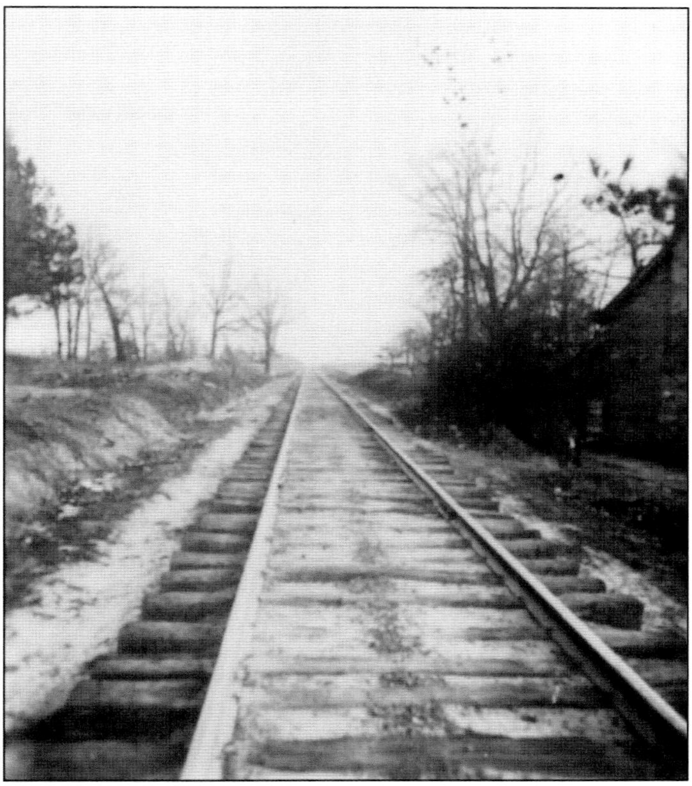

An early 1880s photograph of the Raleigh and Augusta Railroad tracks between Cameron and Manly.

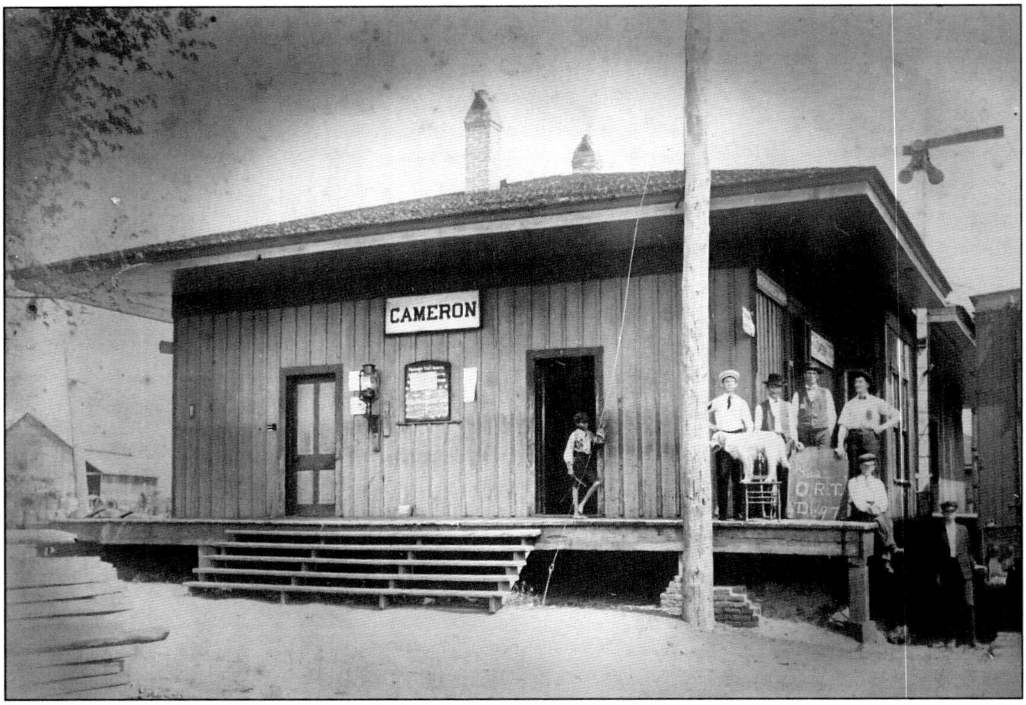

The old Cameron Depot was built in the late nineteenth century. The town was founded in 1875 as the terminus of the Raleigh and Augusta Railroad and served briefly as the principal shipping point for Moore County's early lumber and turpentine industries. It would later become known as one of the nation's leading producers of dewberries.

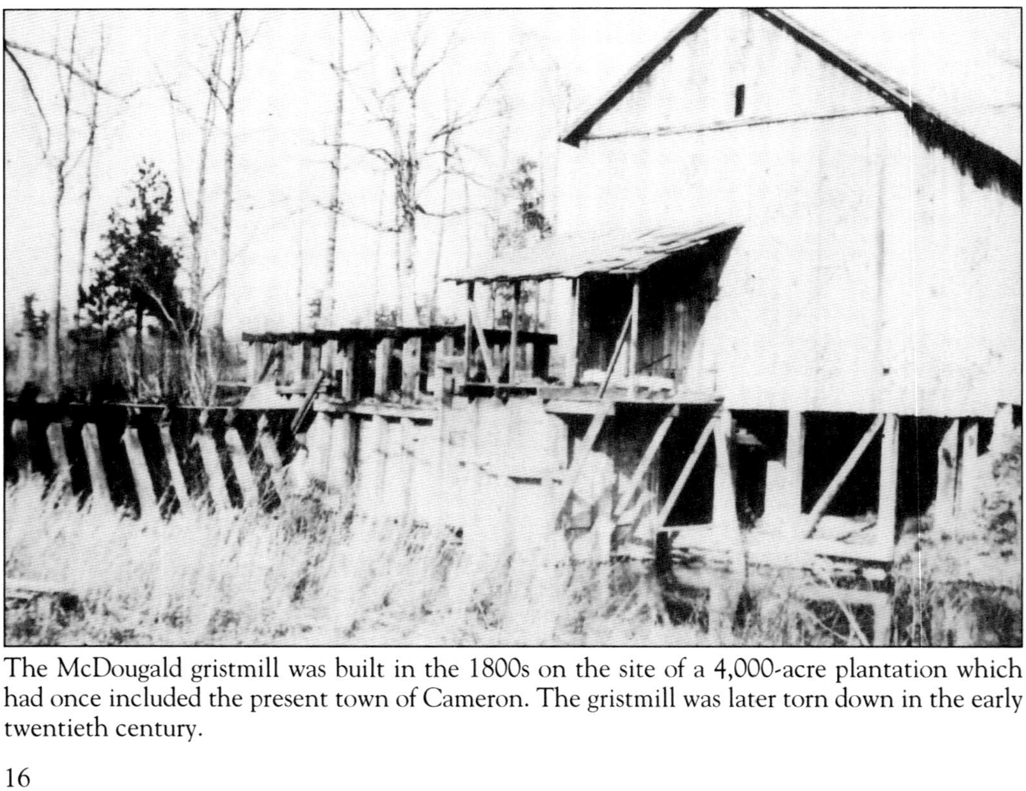

The McDougald gristmill was built in the 1800s on the site of a 4,000-acre plantation which had once included the present town of Cameron. The gristmill was later torn down in the early twentieth century.

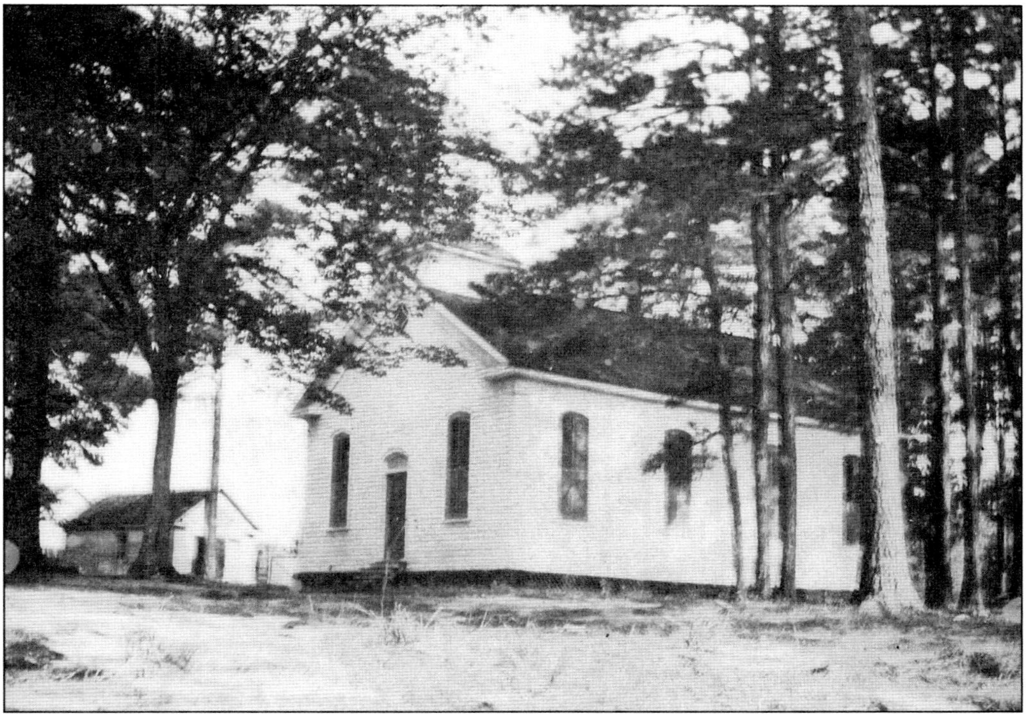

The Cameron Presbyterian Church, built in 1879, is pictured here.

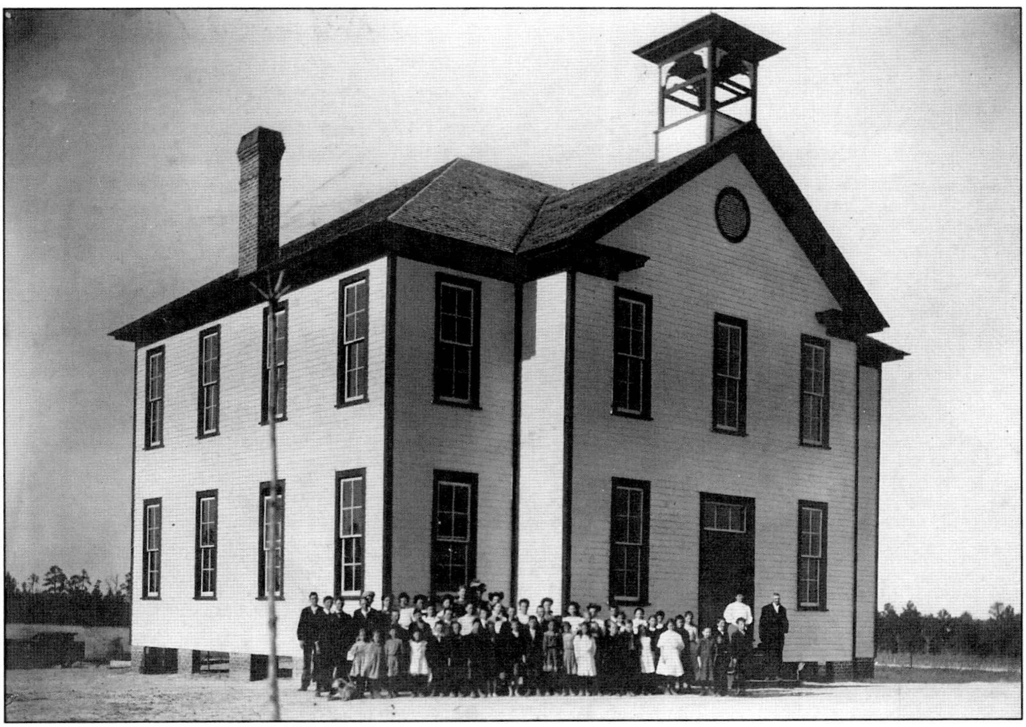

The Cameron Graded School opened in January of 1908 and had two teachers. Pictured is the class of 1908–1909, with teachers Malcolm D. McNeill and Miss Pearl Johnson on the schoolhouse steps.

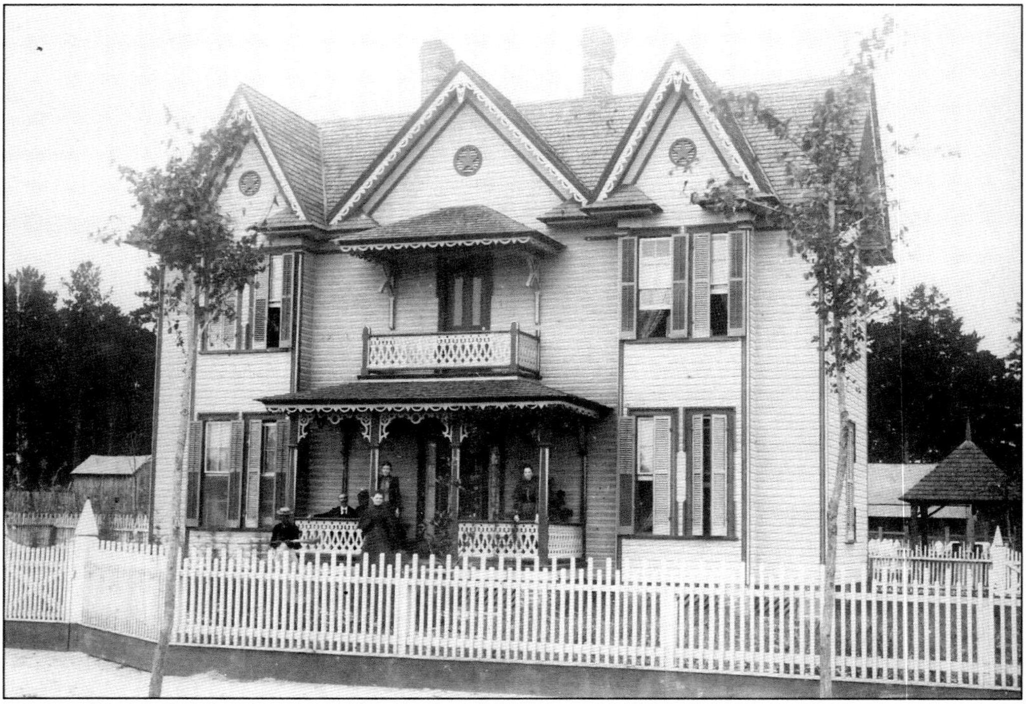

The richly embellished Murdoch McKeithen House was built in 1885 during Cameron's halcyon days as one of Moore County's leading commercial centers. Pictured are Murdoch McKeithen (sitting on the porch) with his wife, Belle Ferguson McKeithen, standing to his immediate right.

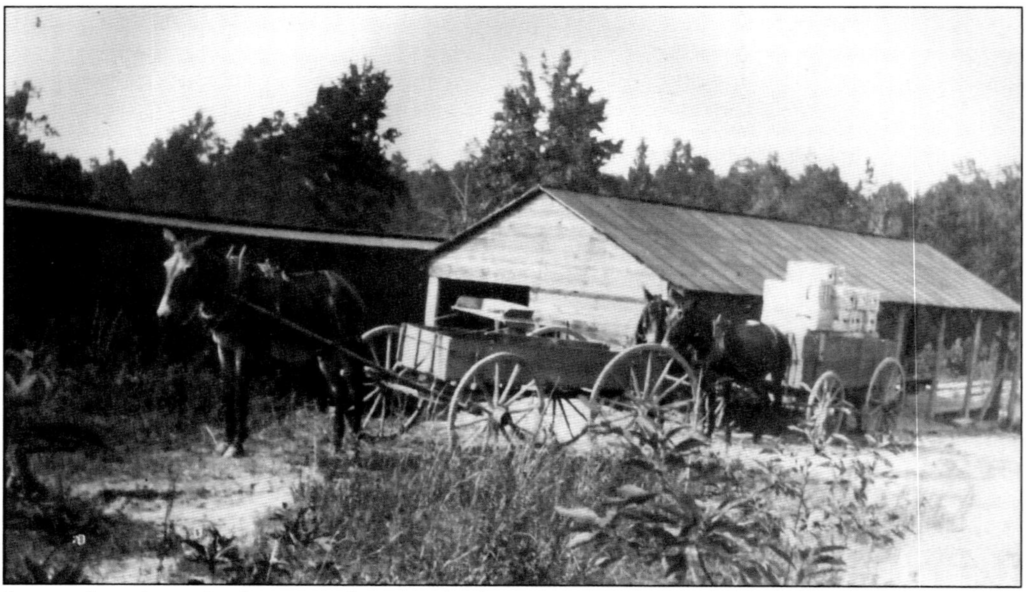

Pictured in the right foreground is a mule-drawn wagon laden with crates of dewberries near the Raleigh and Augusta Railroad tracks. The fruit was introduced to Moore County by H.P. Bilyeu in 1890, and by the early twentieth century, Cameron was known as the "Dewberry Capital of the World." The berries were marketed in New York, Philadelphia, Buffalo, Cincinnati, and Pittsburgh.

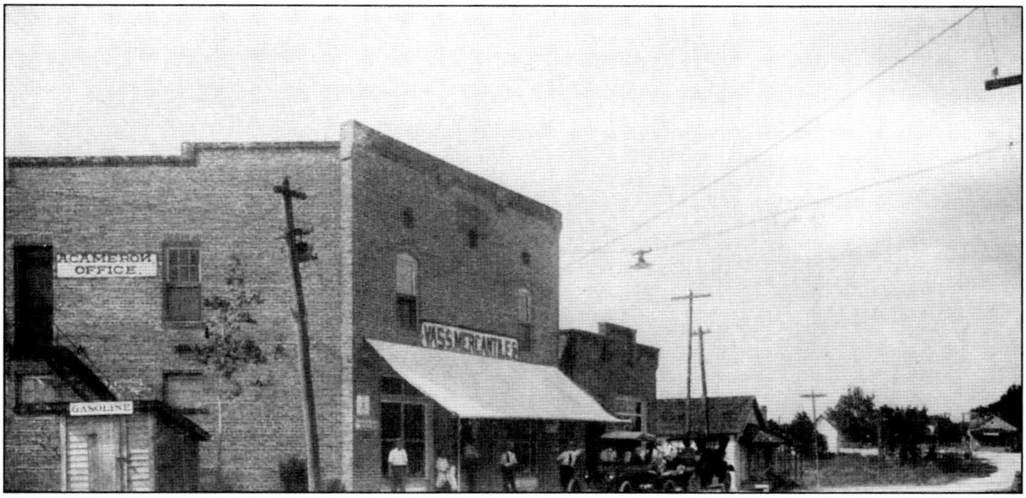

The town of Vass was originally called Bynum, but its name was changed to Winder after the Raleigh and Augusta Railroad passed through the region in 1877. In 1892, the town's name was changed to Vass to honor Major William Worrell Vass, an official of the railroad.

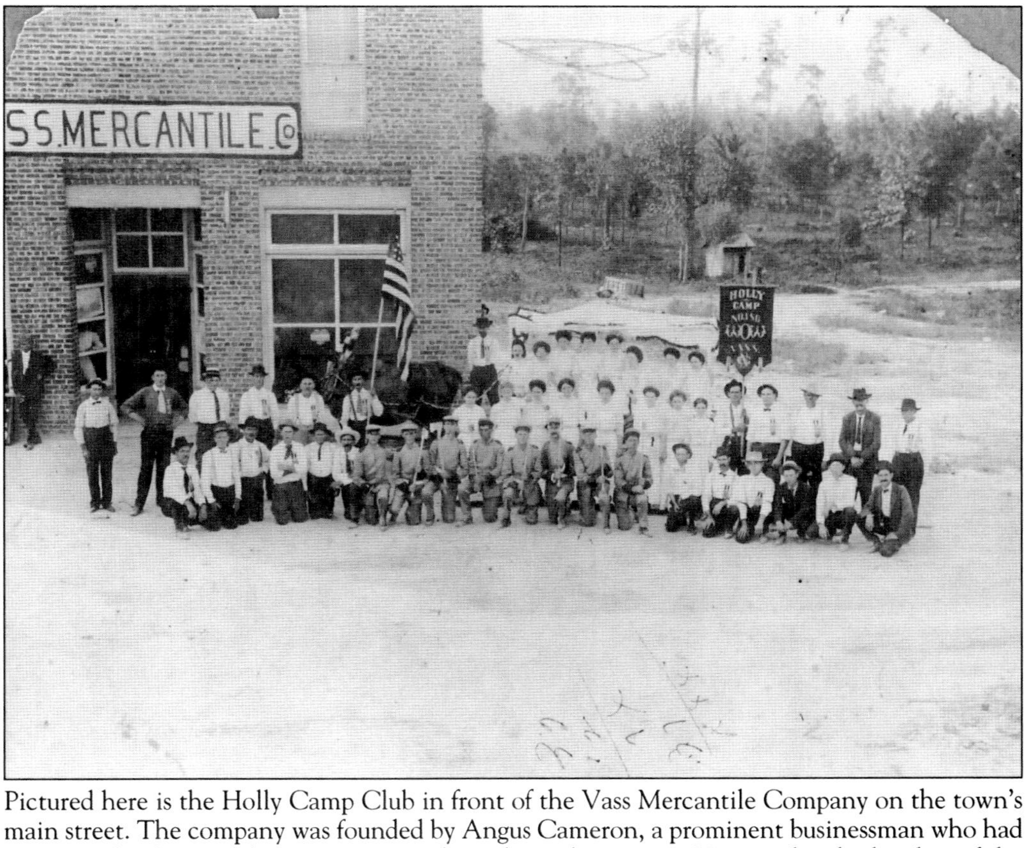

Pictured here is the Holly Camp Club in front of the Vass Mercantile Company on the town's main street. The company was founded by Angus Cameron, a prominent businessman who had extensive lumber and farming interests throughout the county. He was also the brother of the town's first postmaster, John Cameron.

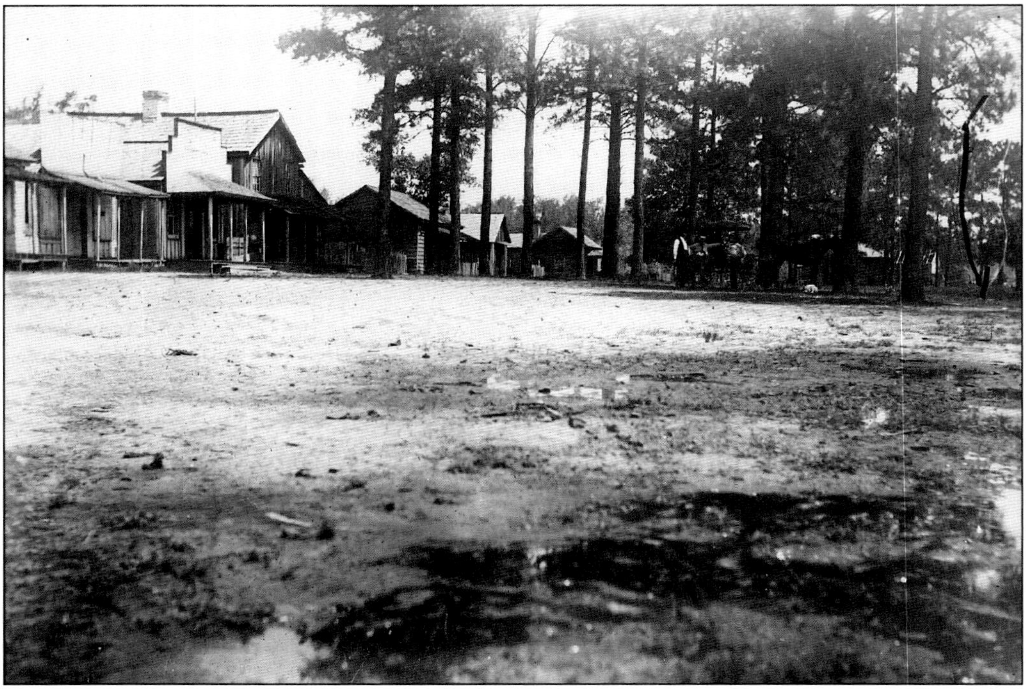

Manly was incorporated in 1879 as a major shipping point for the Raleigh and Augusta Railroad. It had several saloons and was the scene of many violent brawls between workers from the railroad and from nearby lumber yards.

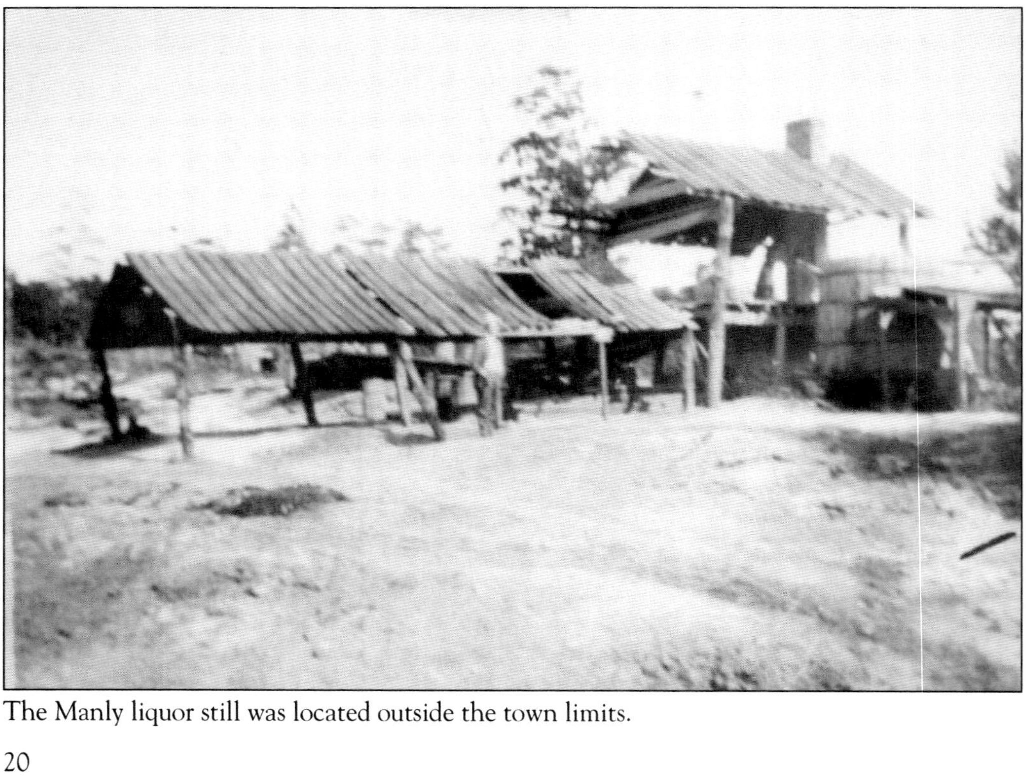

The Manly liquor still was located outside the town limits.

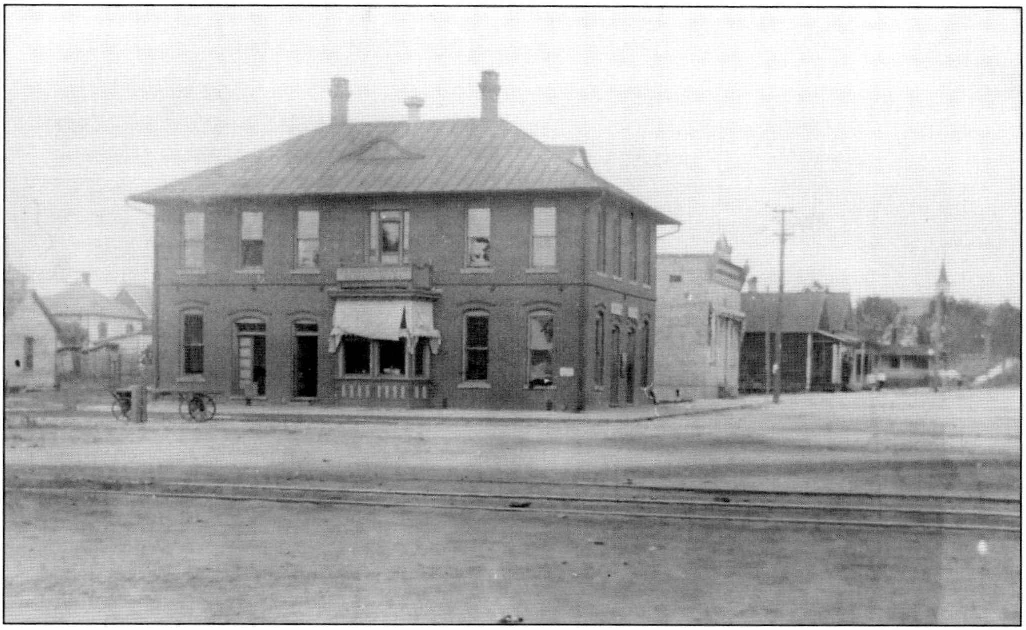

The town of Aberdeen was originally called Blue's Crossing, but its name was changed to Aberdeen in 1887. It became Moore County's leading railroad and industrial center and was also home to three short-line railroads by 1894. Pictured is the handsome Aberdeen and Rockfish Railroad Depot.

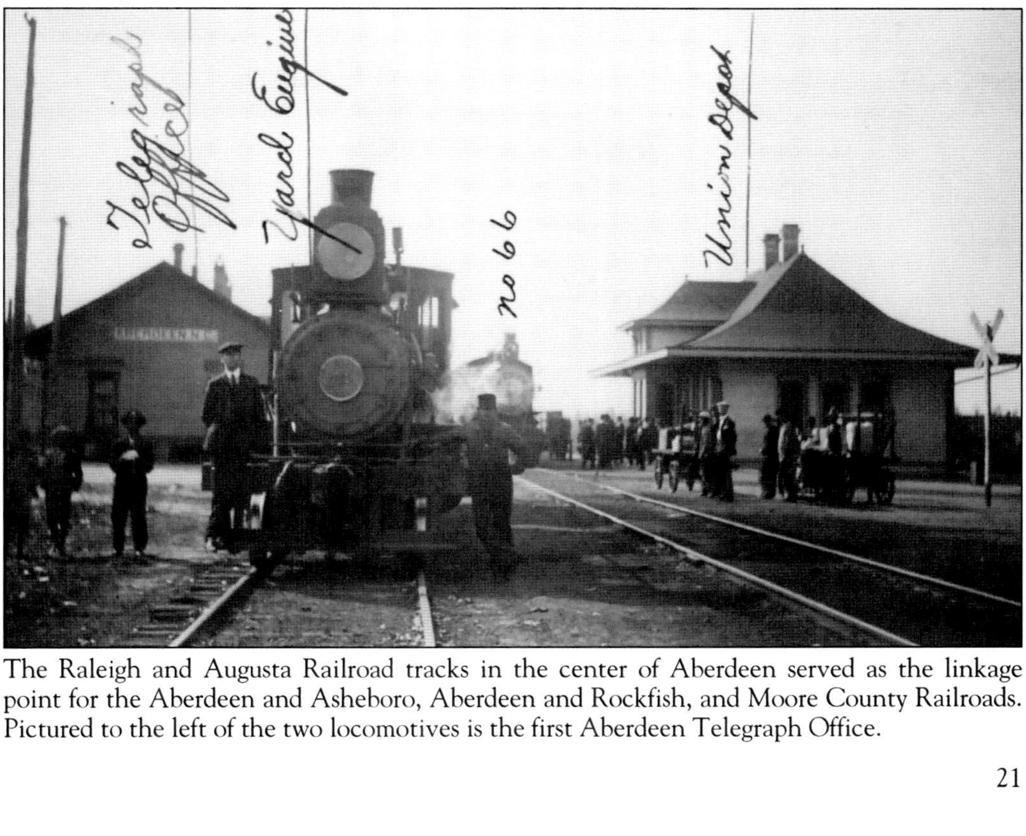

The Raleigh and Augusta Railroad tracks in the center of Aberdeen served as the linkage point for the Aberdeen and Asheboro, Aberdeen and Rockfish, and Moore County Railroads. Pictured to the left of the two locomotives is the first Aberdeen Telegraph Office.

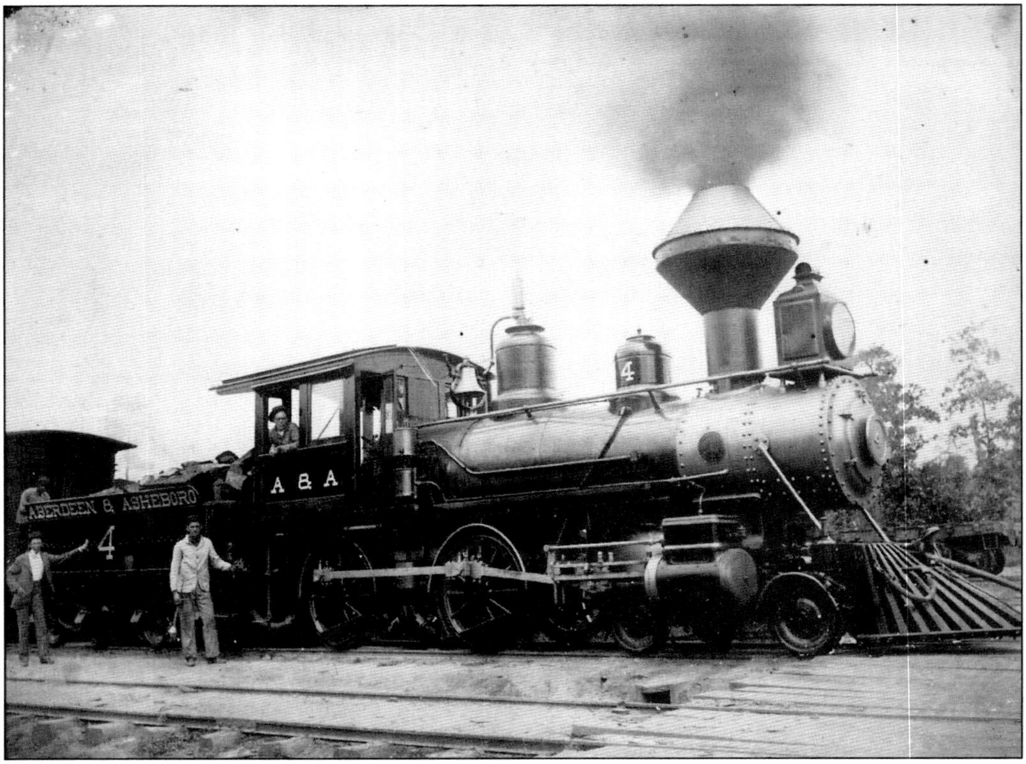

An Aberdeen and Asheboro Railroad locomotive is pictured here in the early twentieth century. The railroad was founded by Allison Page in 1888 as the Aberdeen and West End Railroad and was later sold to the Norfolk Southern Railway in 1912.

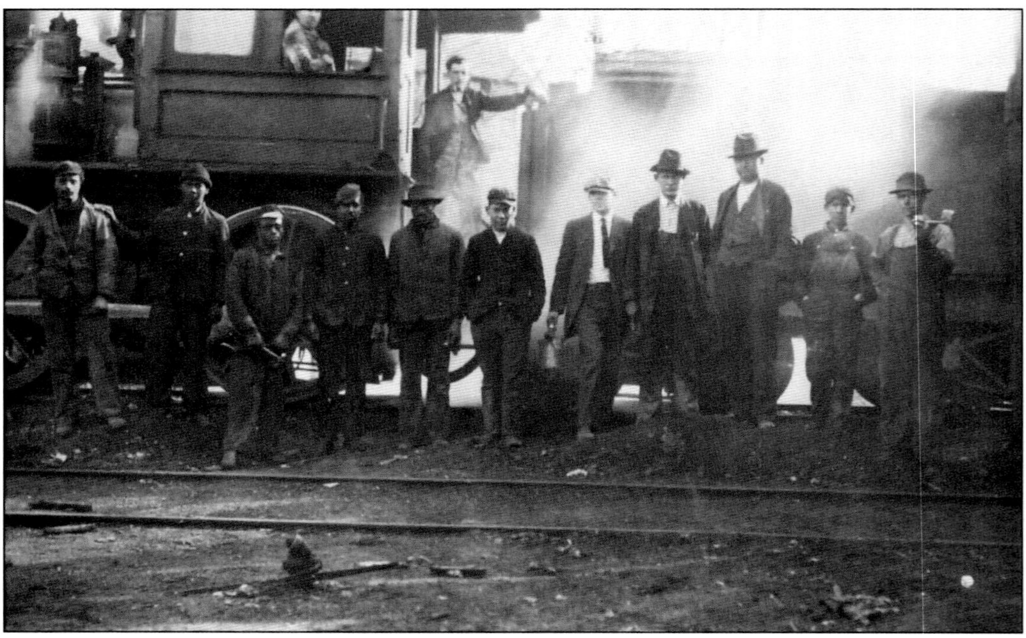

Railroad workers are pictured in front of an Aberdeen and Rockfish locomotive.

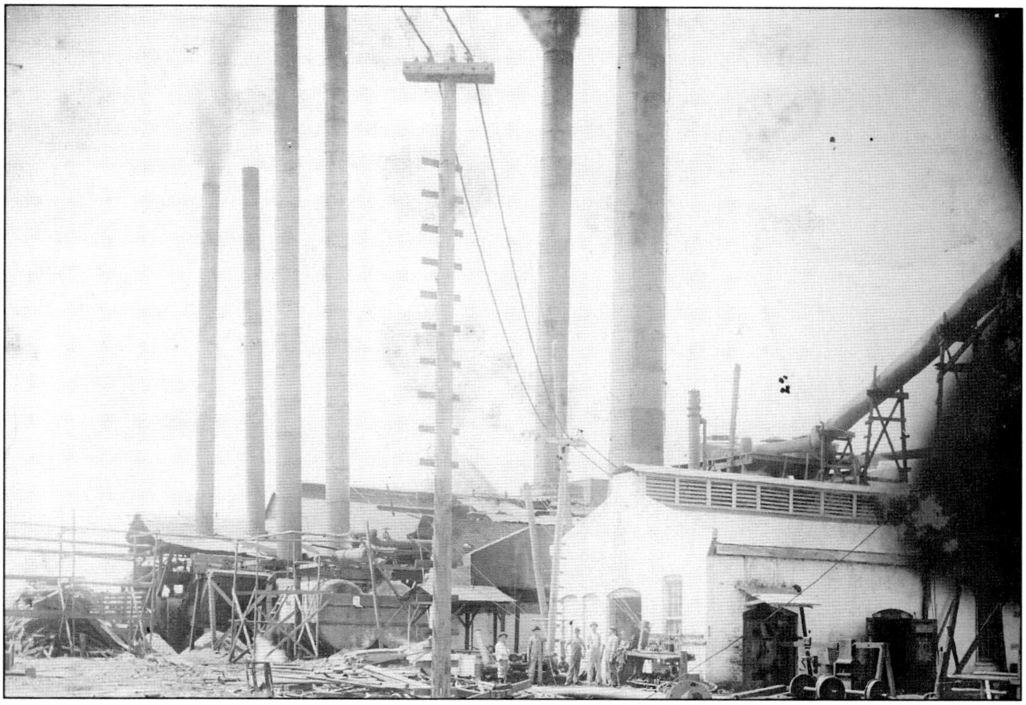

The Aberdeen Sash and Blind Company was one of the town's largest industries. Shipments were made almost daily to Baltimore and New York City.

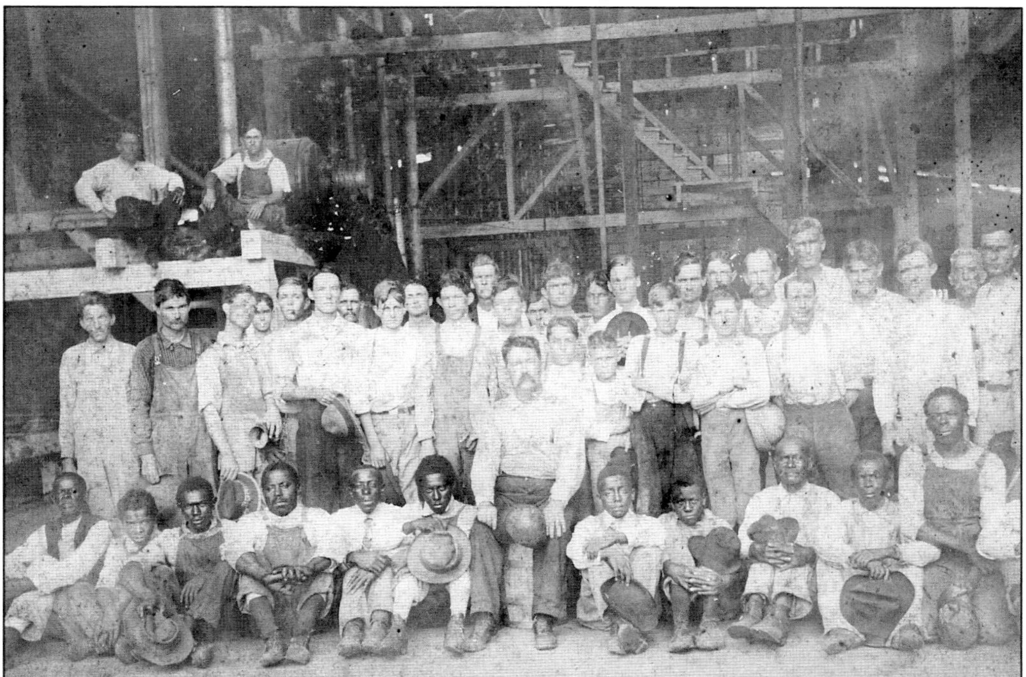

E.E. Brantley and fellow workers at the Aberdeen Sash and Blind Company are pictured here in 1902. Brantley was a history professor who had moved to Aberdeen from Chatham County in 1896.

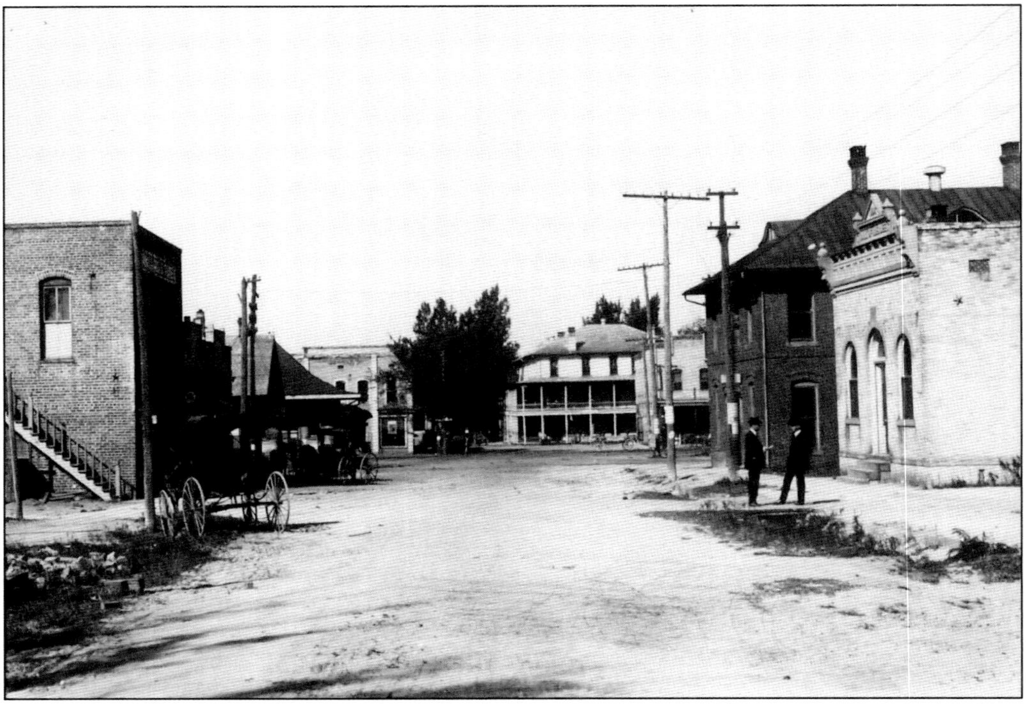

This particular Aberdeen street scene, looking west, shows the three-story Hotel Aberdeen in the background.

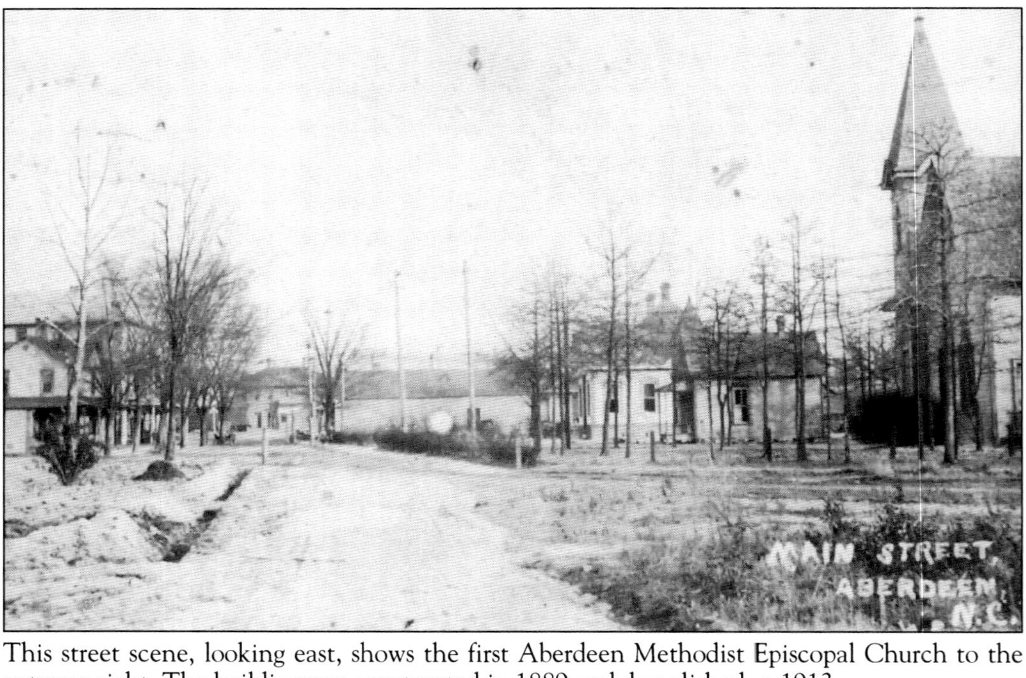

This street scene, looking east, shows the first Aberdeen Methodist Episcopal Church to the extreme right. The building was constructed in 1889 and demolished in 1913.

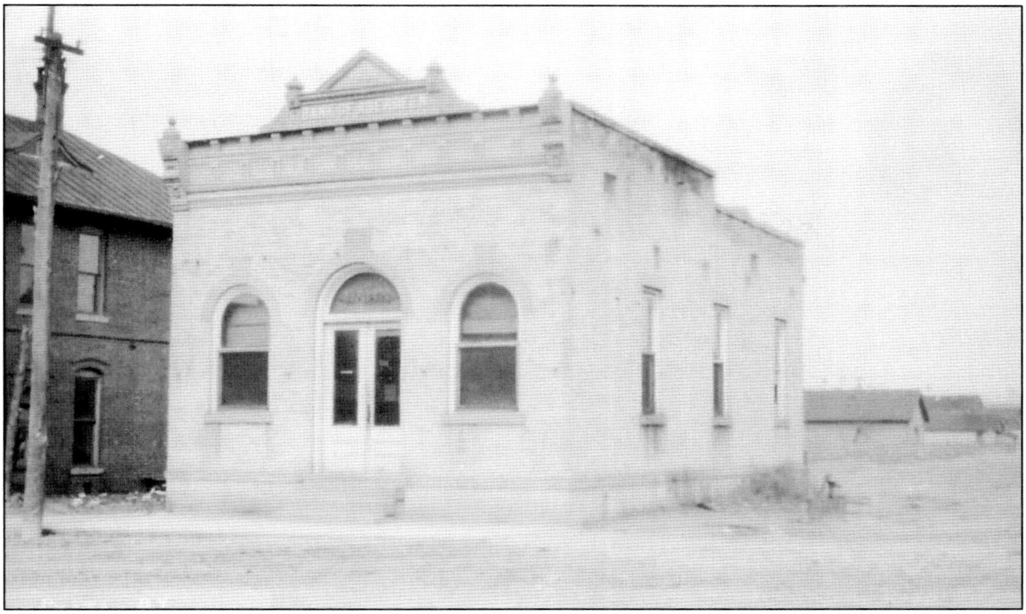

The Bank of Aberdeen was adjacent to the Aberdeen and Rockfish Railroad Depot. It was founded in 1904 by the Page family and John Blue.

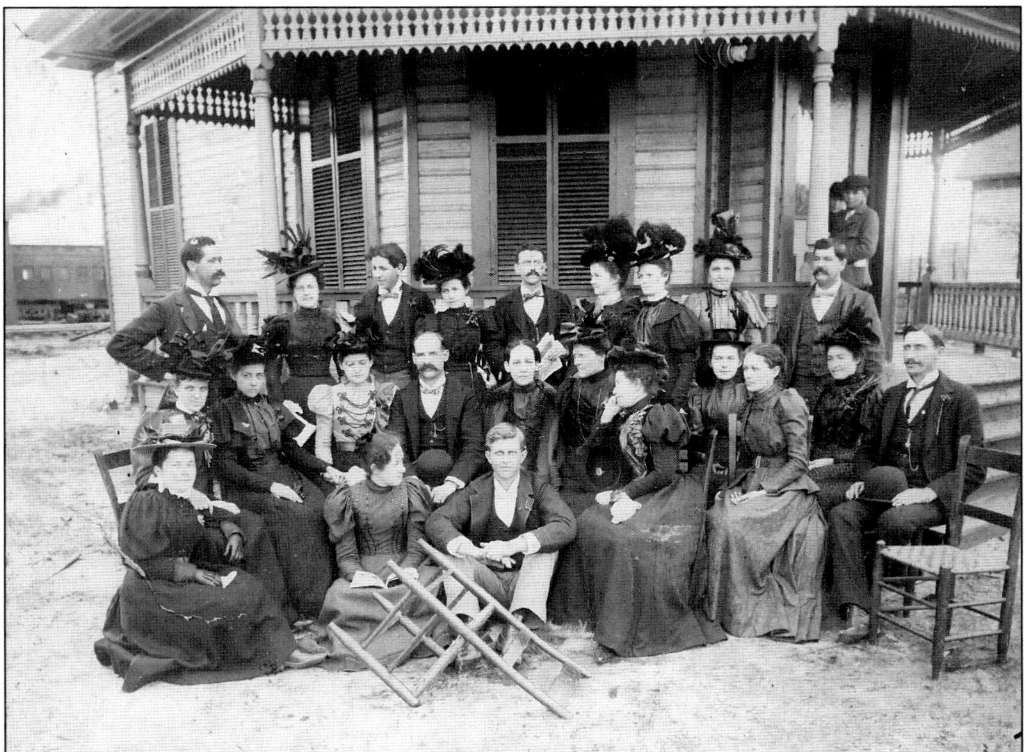

Pictured in front of the town's first library building is the S.A.L. Magrundi Club. The structure was used for a variety of social activities.

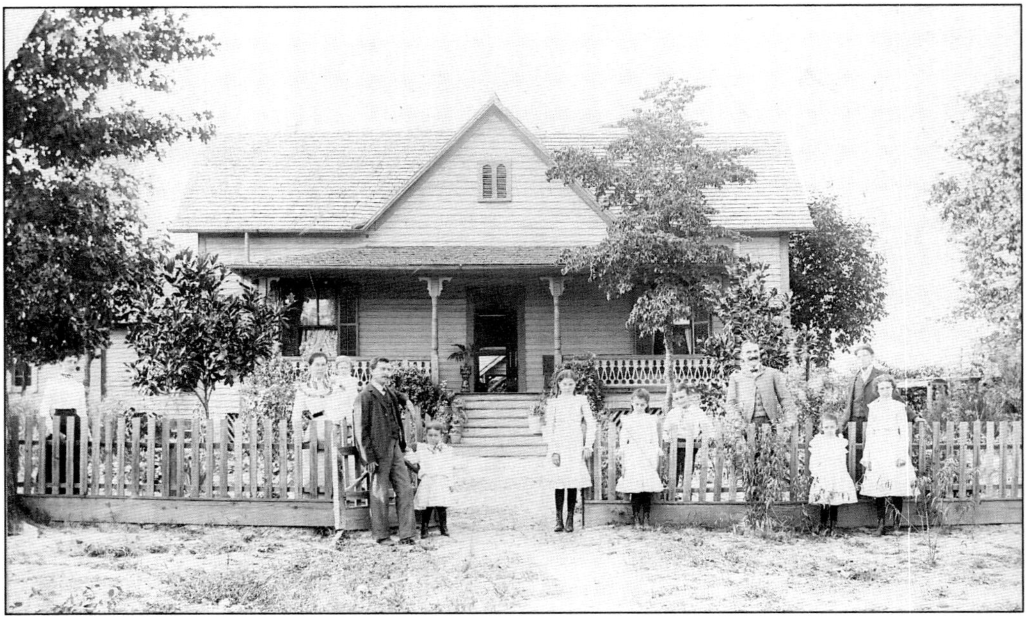

Charles Pleasants' house was built in 1895 on the Old Bethesda Church Road. Pictured are members of the Pleasants family and some early Aberdeen residents.

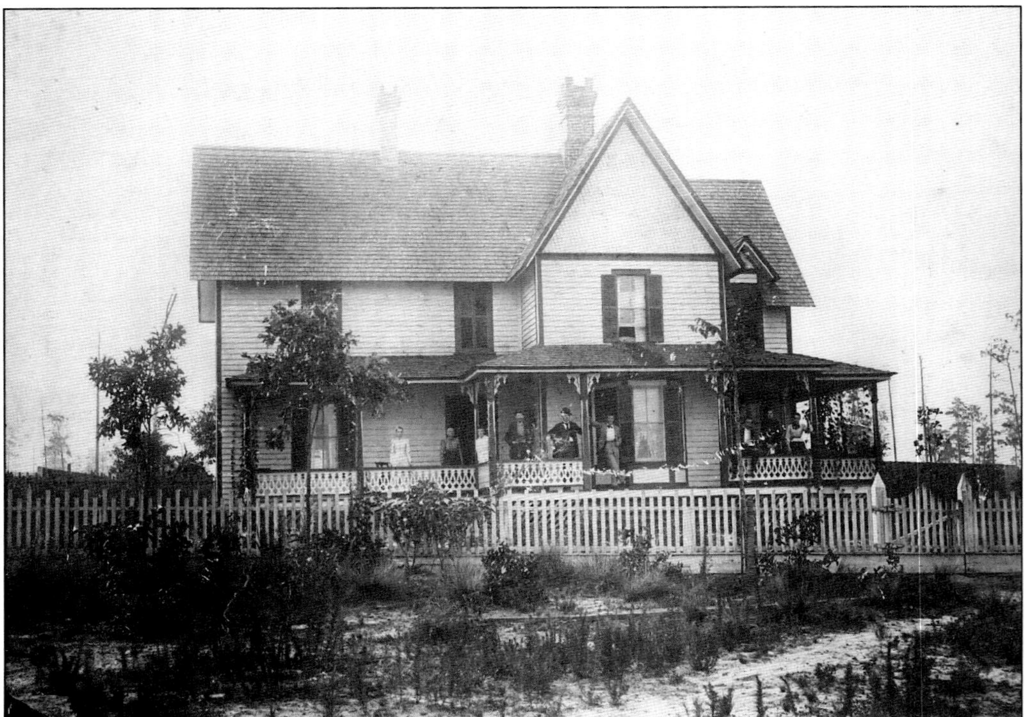

The Molly McKeithen House stood on the corner of East Main and Blue Streets and was designed and built by A.C. Campbell in 1896. Campbell was an early Aberdeen building contractor who constructed most of the buildings in nearby Pinehurst between 1895 and 1897.

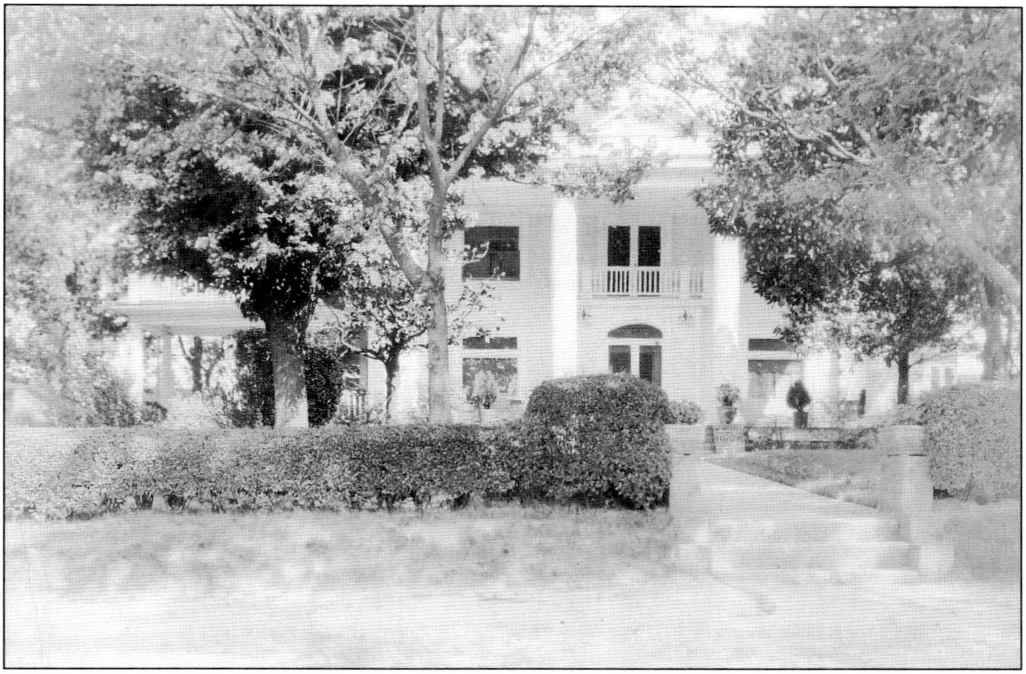

The John Blue House was built in 1888 and extensively remodeled in 1903 by Charlotte architect C.C. Hook. Blue was founder and president of the Aberdeen and Rockfish Railroad and one of the region's largest landowners.

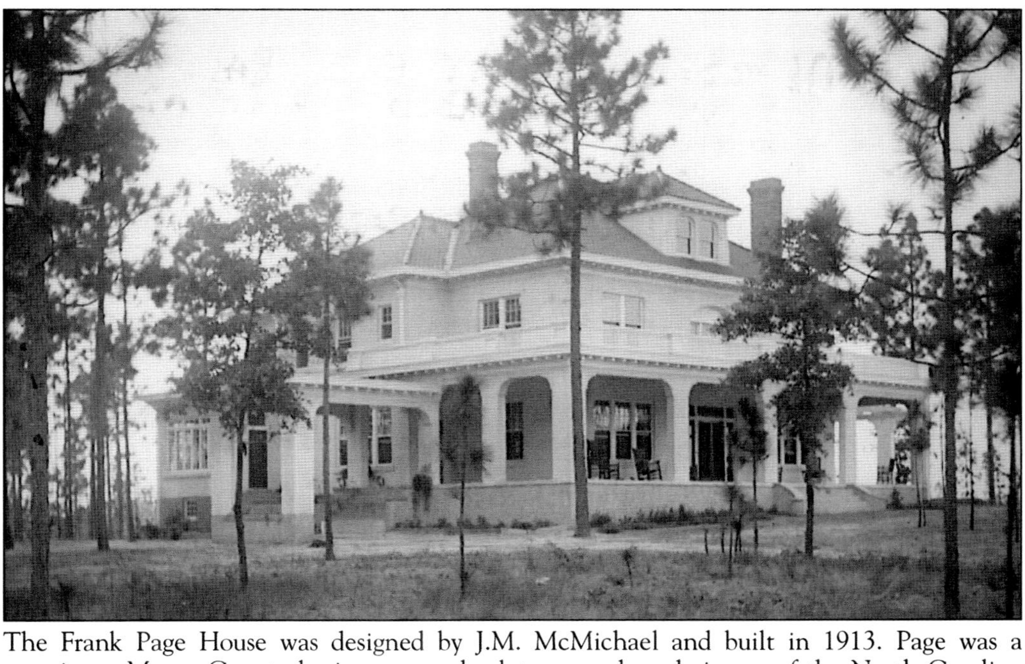

The Frank Page House was designed by J.M. McMichael and built in 1913. Page was a prominent Moore County businessman who later served as chairman of the North Carolina Highway Commission.

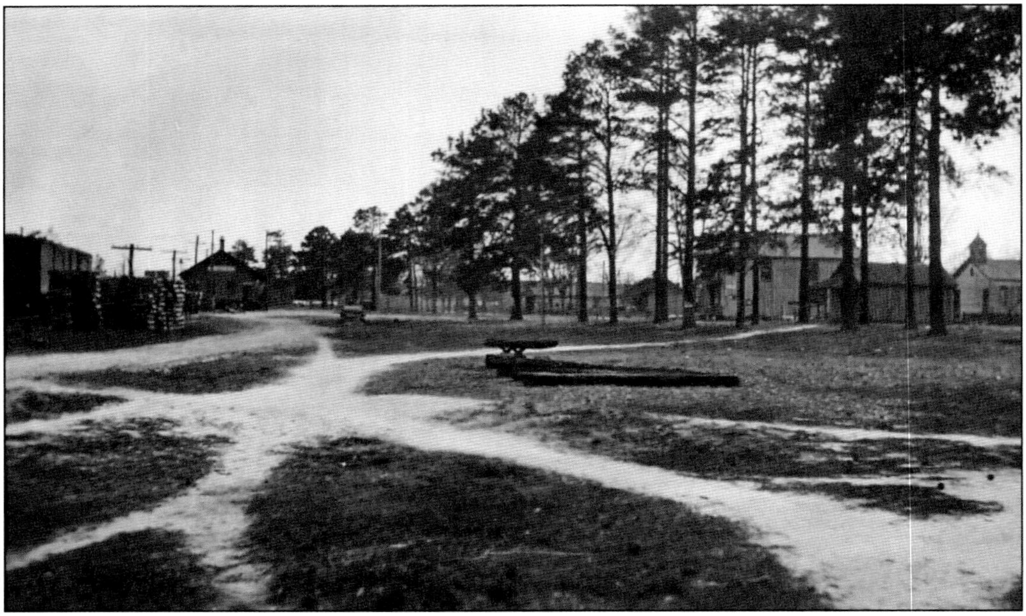

The town of Keyser was a bustling community along the route of the Raleigh and Augusta Railroad in the late 1870s and early 1880s. Pictured are the railroad depot, several stores, a church, and the town hall.

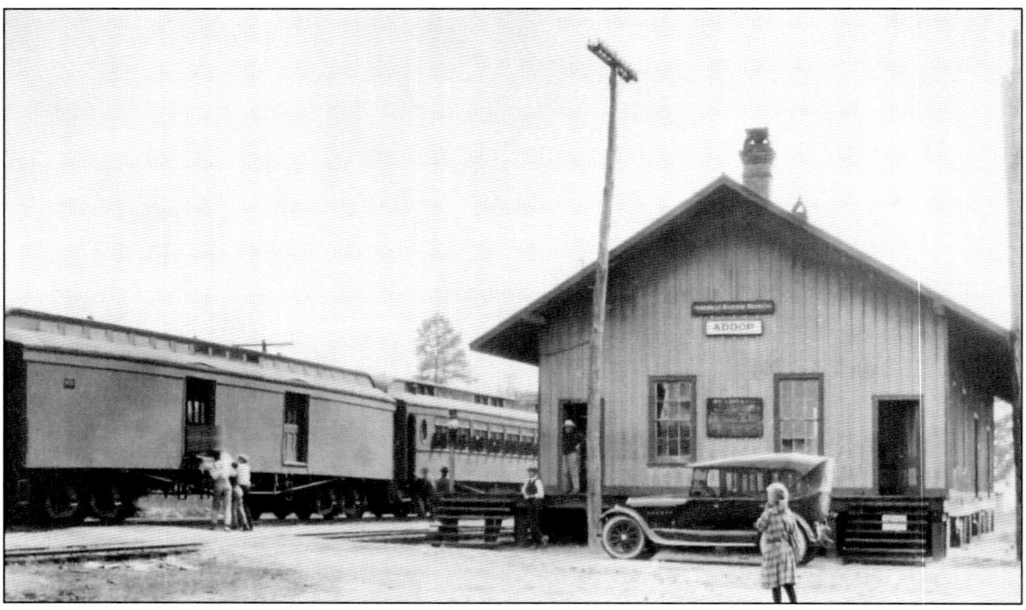

The name of the town was changed to Addor in 1918 in honor of Felix Eugene Addor, one of Moore County's first casualties during World War I.

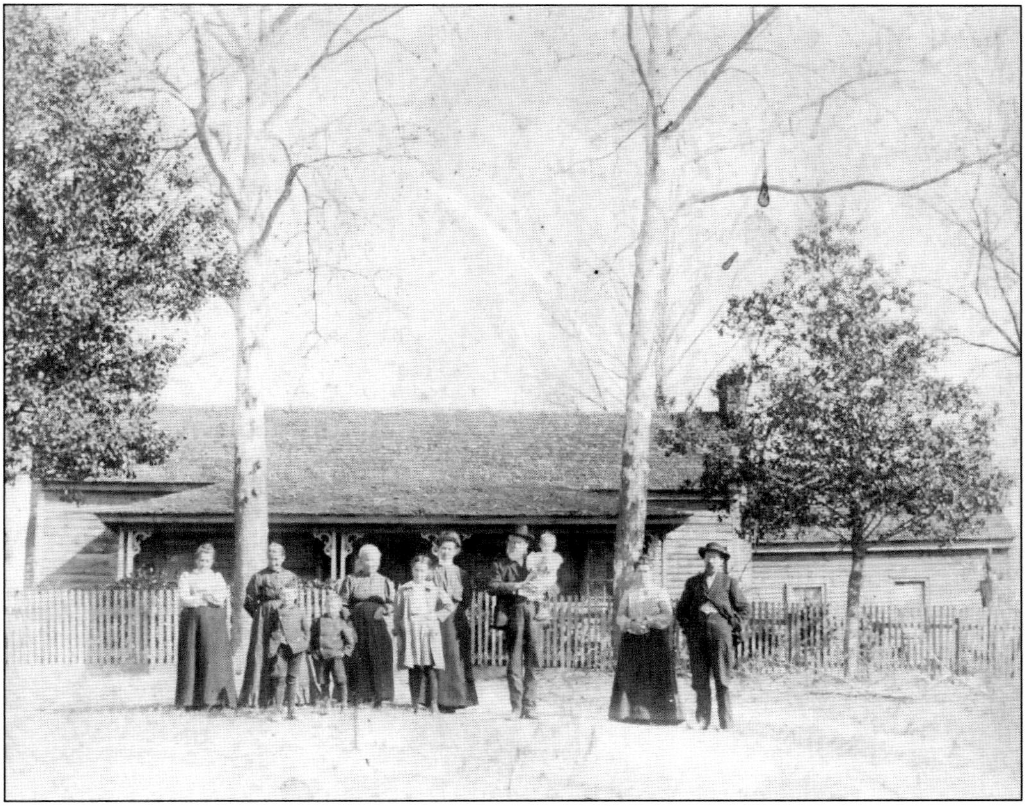

This is a late nineteenth-century photograph of the Addor family.

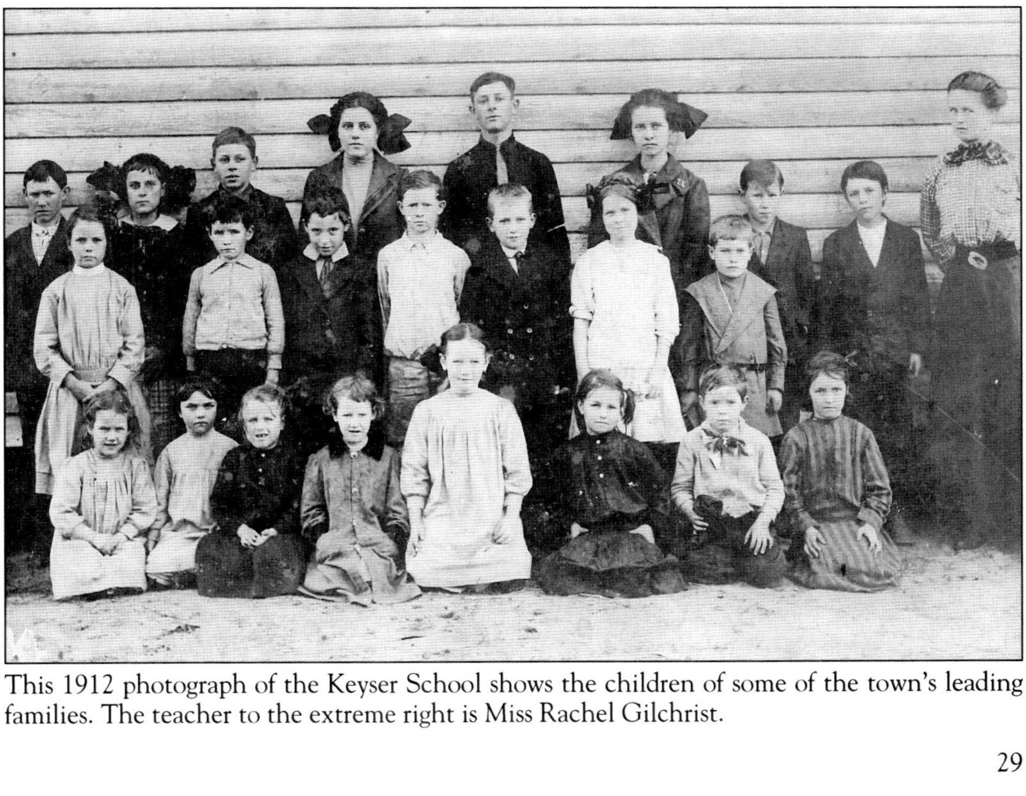

This 1912 photograph of the Keyser School shows the children of some of the town's leading families. The teacher to the extreme right is Miss Rachel Gilchrist.

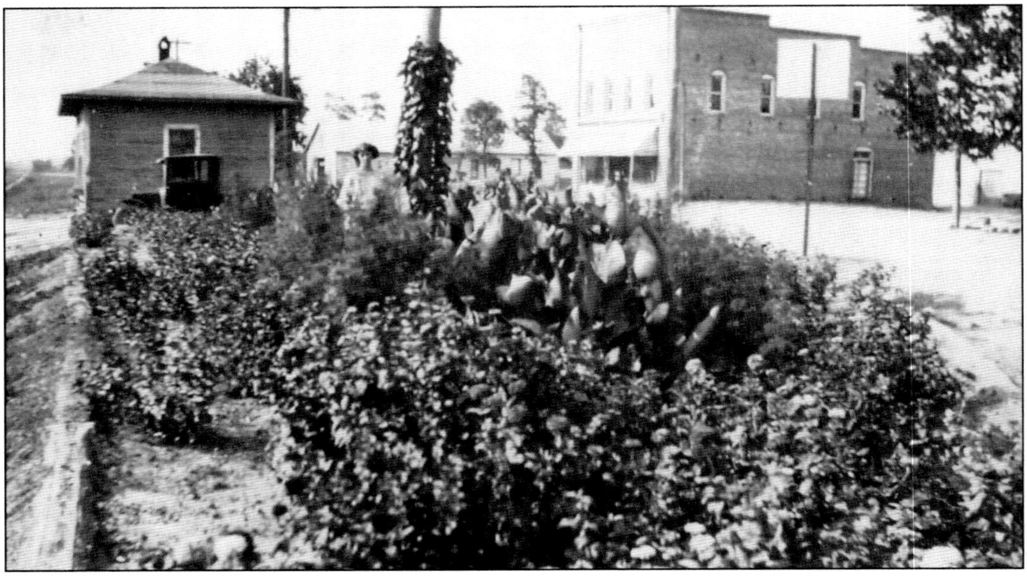

This view of the town of West End shows the Aberdeen and Asheboro Railroad Depot to the left, with Mrs. Irma Cheek, agent/operator, barely visible in the foreground. The town sprang up in 1890 as the railhead for the Aberdeen and West End Railroad.

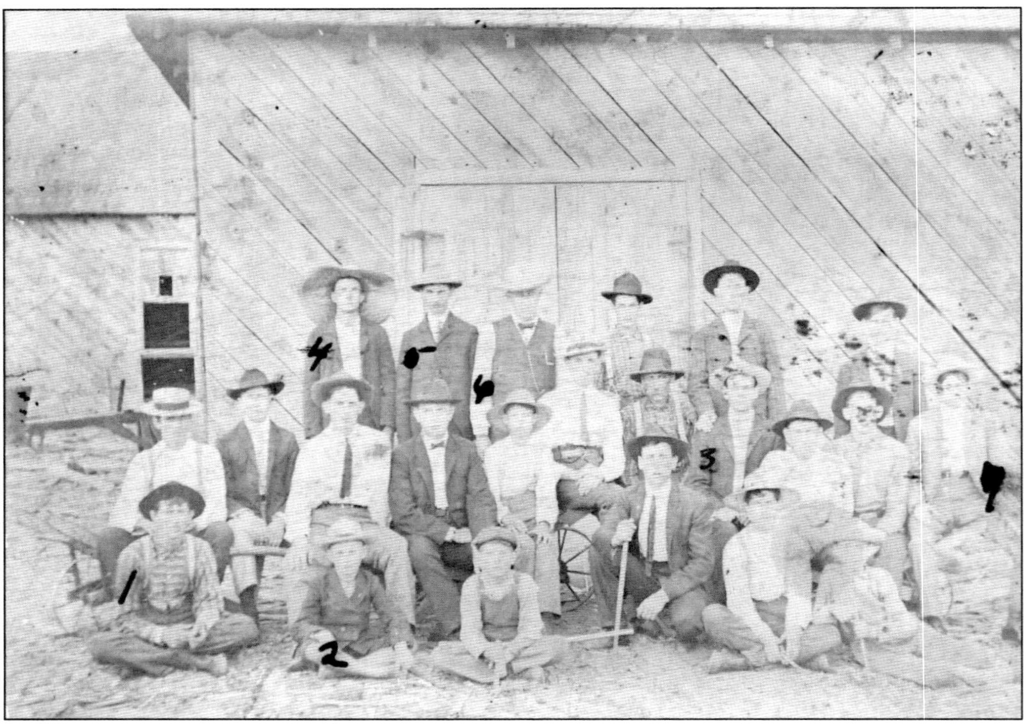

Pictured are some of West End's early citizens standing in front of a warehouse and facing the Aberdeen and Asheboro Railroad tracks.

Three

CARTHAGE

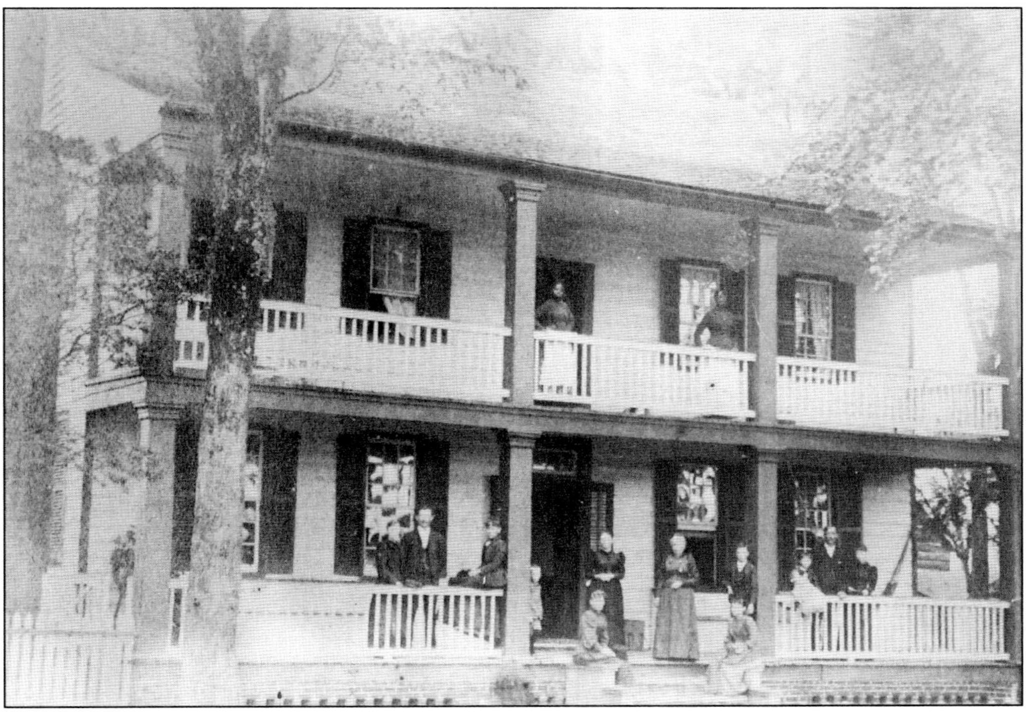

This early Carthage boarding house was built in the late nineteenth century. The town was made the county seat in 1786 and was later incorporated in 1796.

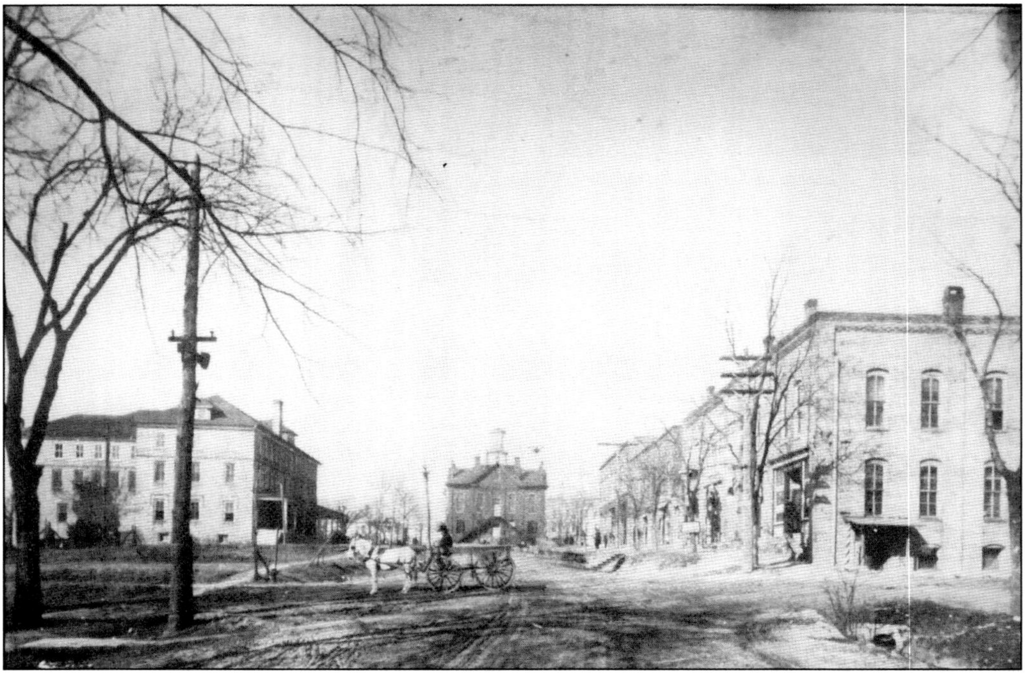

This is an early-twentieth-century view of the town of Carthage showing some of the newly constructed brick or masonry buildings along Monroe Street. The town was laid out in a grid pattern around the courthouse square in 1796 and comprised 60 acres.

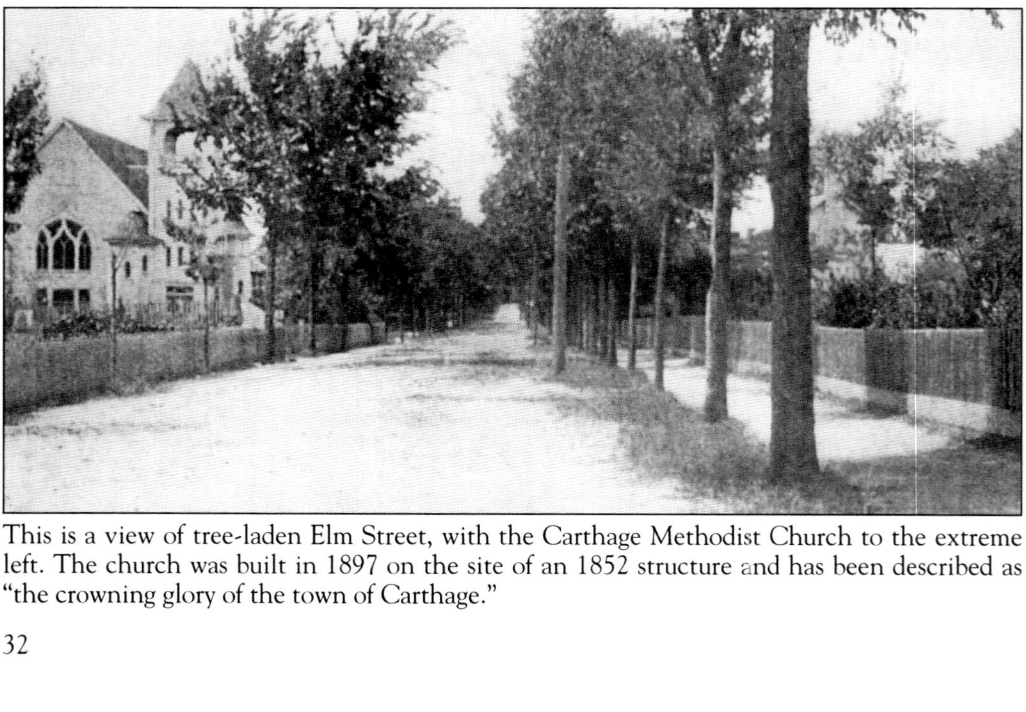

This is a view of tree-laden Elm Street, with the Carthage Methodist Church to the extreme left. The church was built in 1897 on the site of an 1852 structure and has been described as "the crowning glory of the town of Carthage."

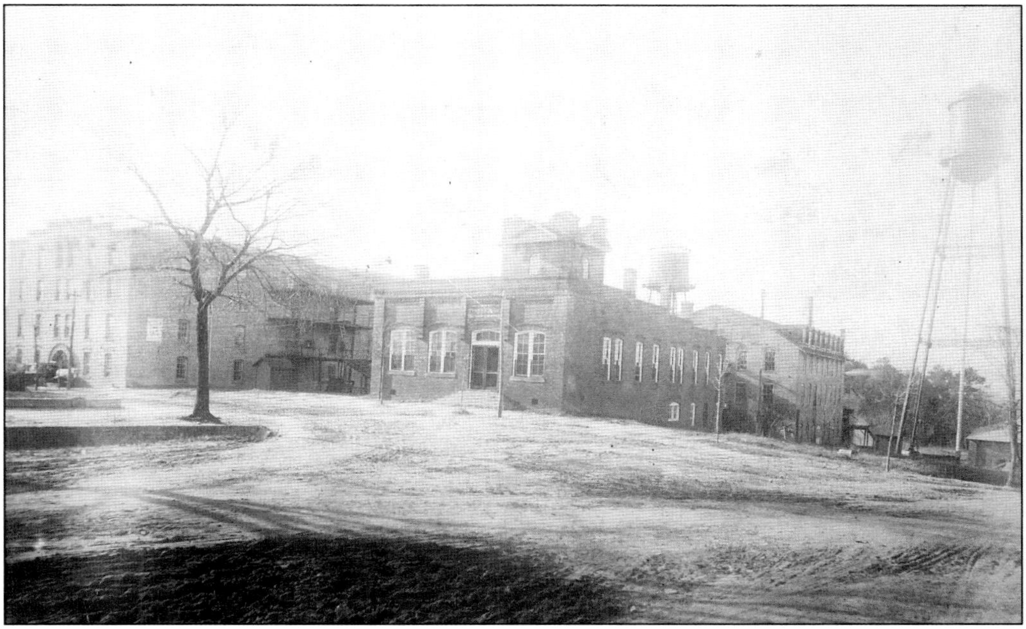

The Tyson and Jones Buggy Company was founded in the mid-1850s and was for over half a century Moore County's largest manufacturing concern. It included two smaller wagon-making shops and employed forty-six highly skilled workers.

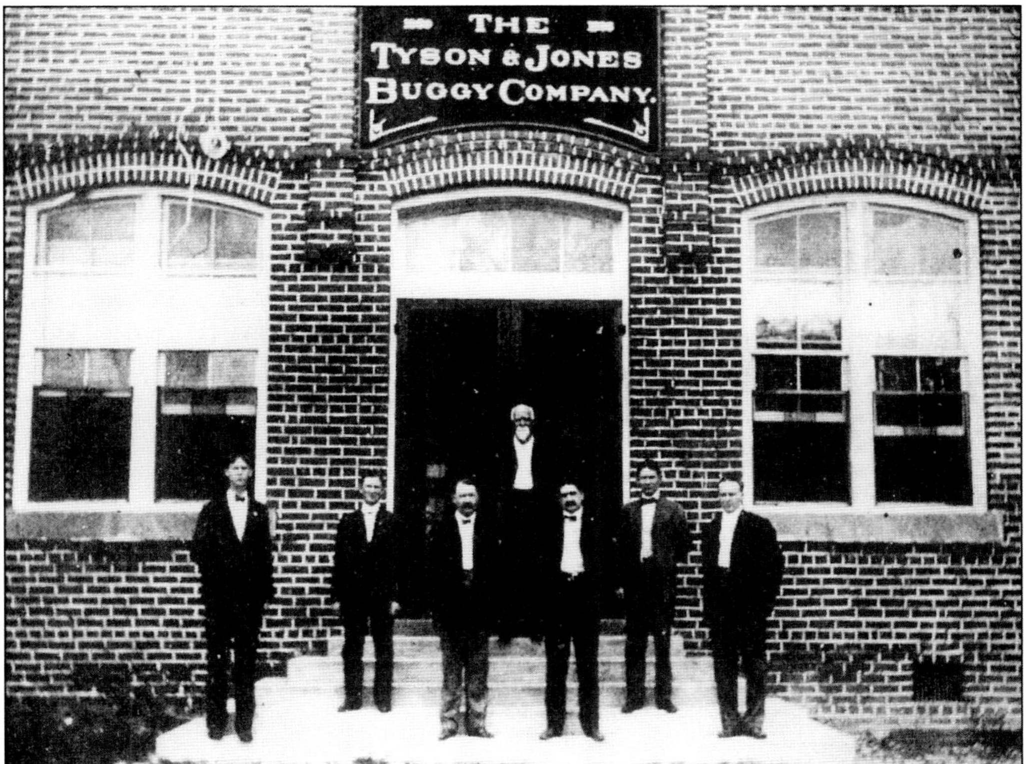

The Office Building of the Tyson and Jones Buggy Company was built in 1906. Pictured in the center foreground (from left to right) are partners Thomas B. Tyson II and W.T. Jones.

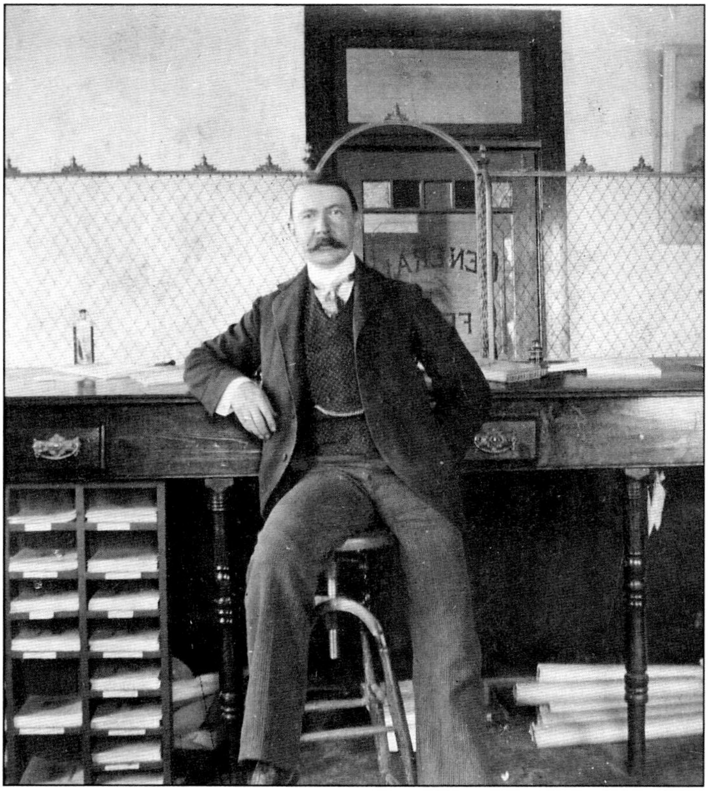

Thomas B. Tyson II is pictured in the office of the Tyson and Jones Buggy Company. He was a grandson of Thomas Bethune Tyson (1813–1893), co-founder of what was originally called the Tyson and Kelley Buggy Company.

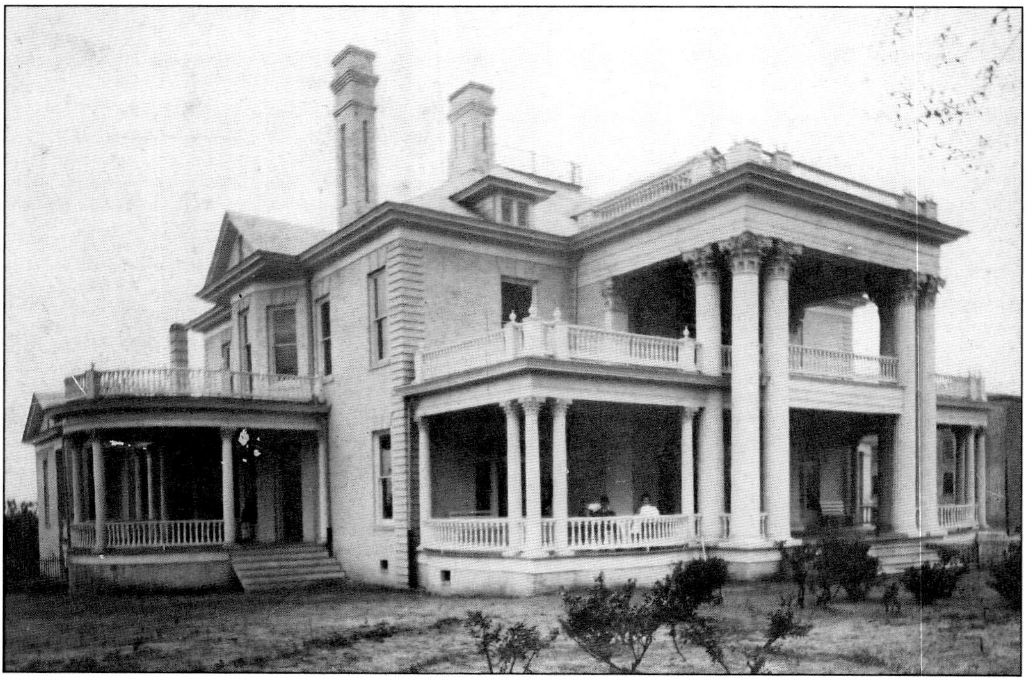

The magnificent residence of Thomas B. Tyson II was constructed on the site of an earlier Tyson home built in the mid-nineteenth century. It fronted McReynolds Street, with the side elevation facing the courthouse square.

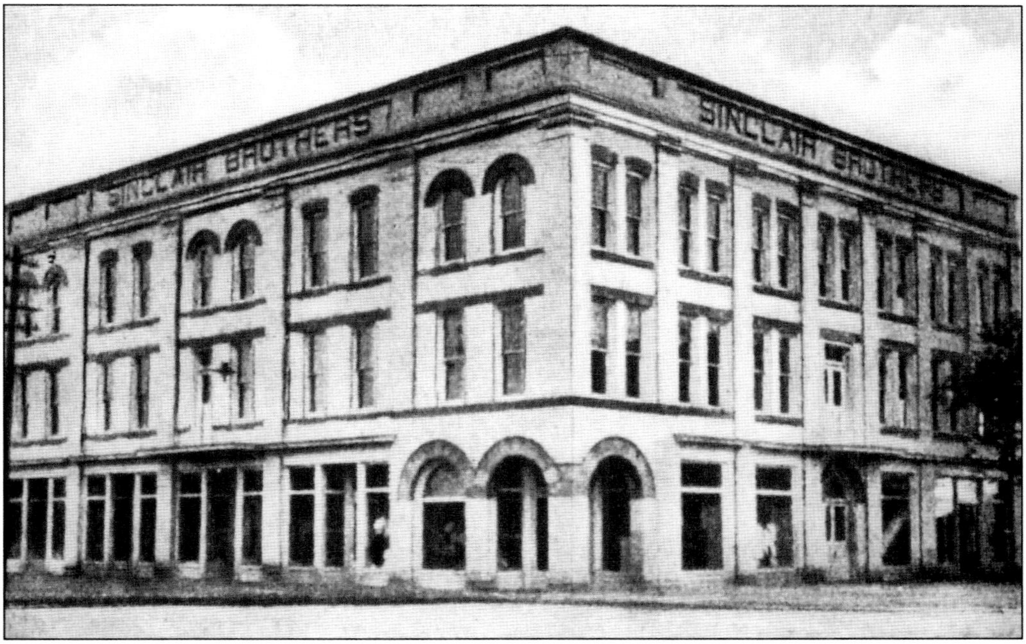

The Sinclair Brothers Building was constructed in 1907 across from the courthouse square and was once described as "one of the most impressive buildings west of Fayetteville and south of Raleigh." The ground floor housed the Sinclair Brothers Department Store, and the upper floors were used for office space.

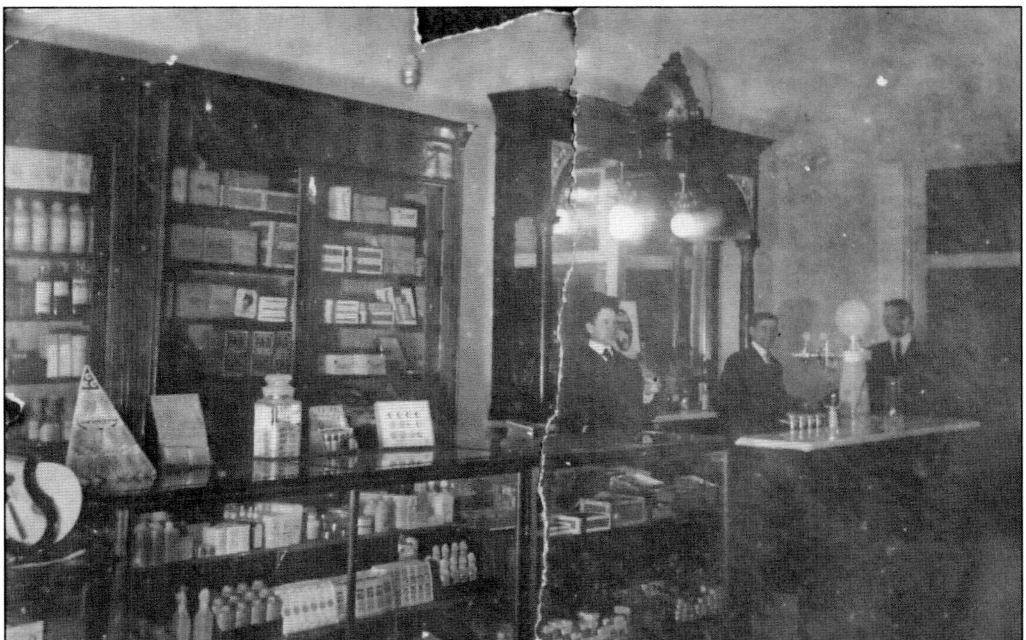

This is a 1910 photograph of an early Carthage drugstore, with owners Dr. Frederick Watson (on the left) and Reid Pleasants (on the right) in the foreground. It was in the Vann Larkin building on Elm Street.

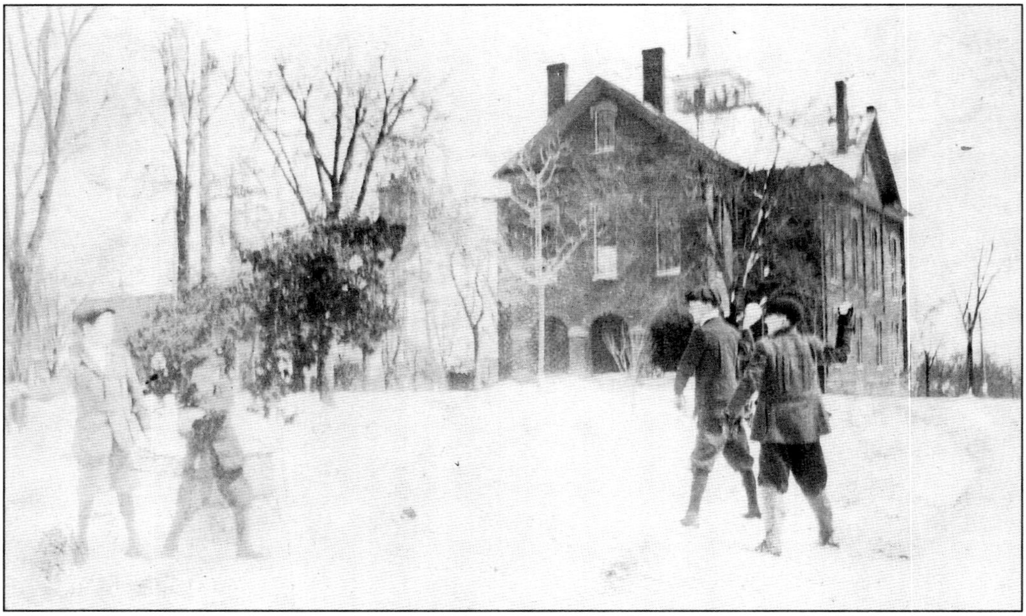

Here, children play in the snow near the courthouse, *c.* 1910. The courthouse square is the highest point in the town of Carthage.

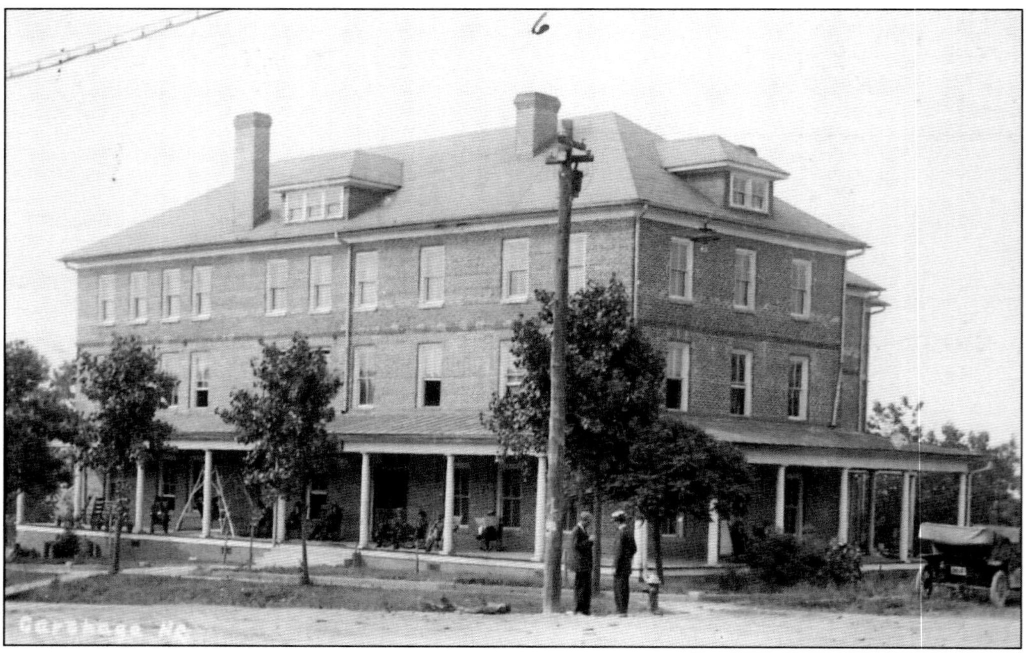

The Tyson House, a hotel, was built in 1901 on the site of a two-story frame hotel building owned and operated by Mr. and Mrs. L.P. Tyson Sr. In 1917, the third story was added after the structure was damaged by fire. The building became known as the Carthage Hotel after 1929.

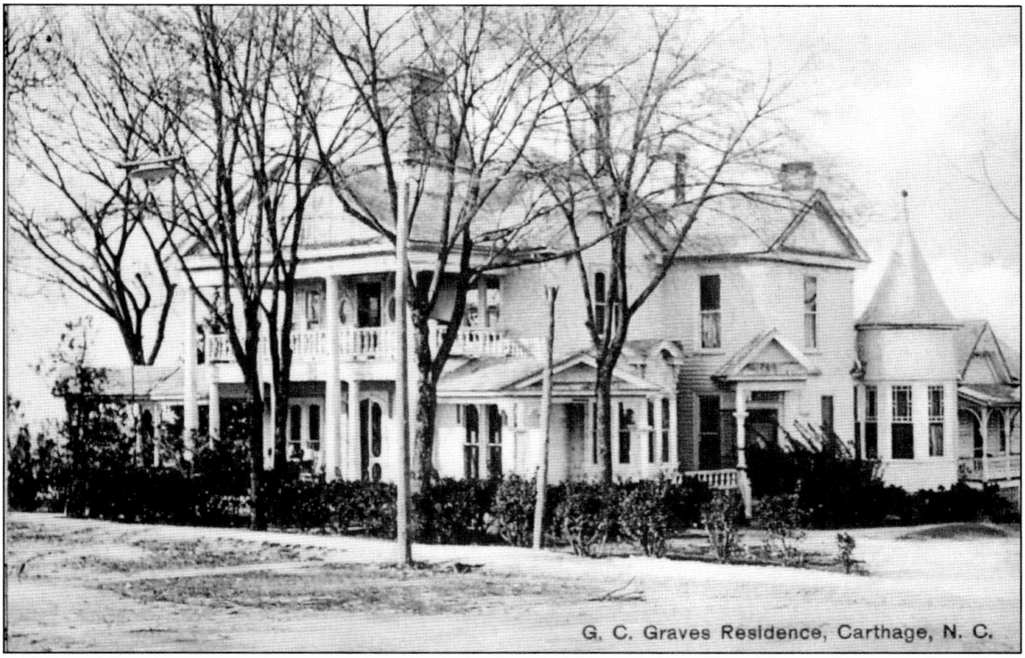

The George Calvin Graves House was built in 1882 and extensively remodeled in 1897. Graves was the town's first druggist, a prominent merchant, and businessman.

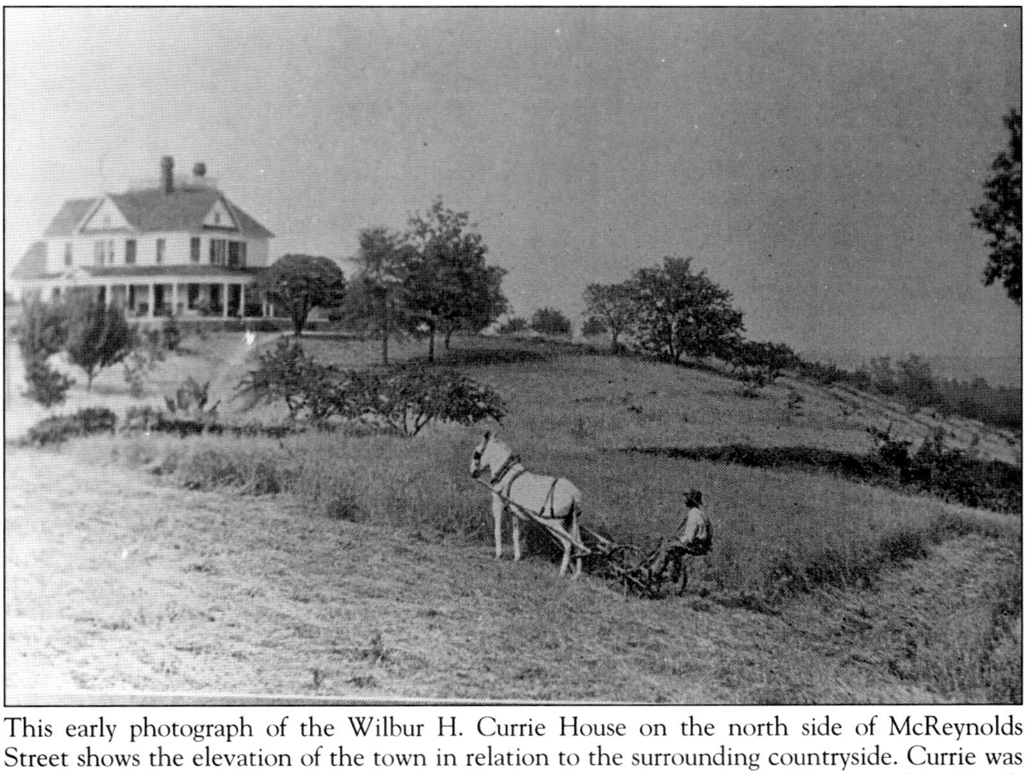

This early photograph of the Wilbur H. Currie House on the north side of McReynolds Street shows the elevation of the town in relation to the surrounding countryside. Currie was president of Currie Mills and the Carolina Bank and served terms in both houses of the North Carolina legislature.

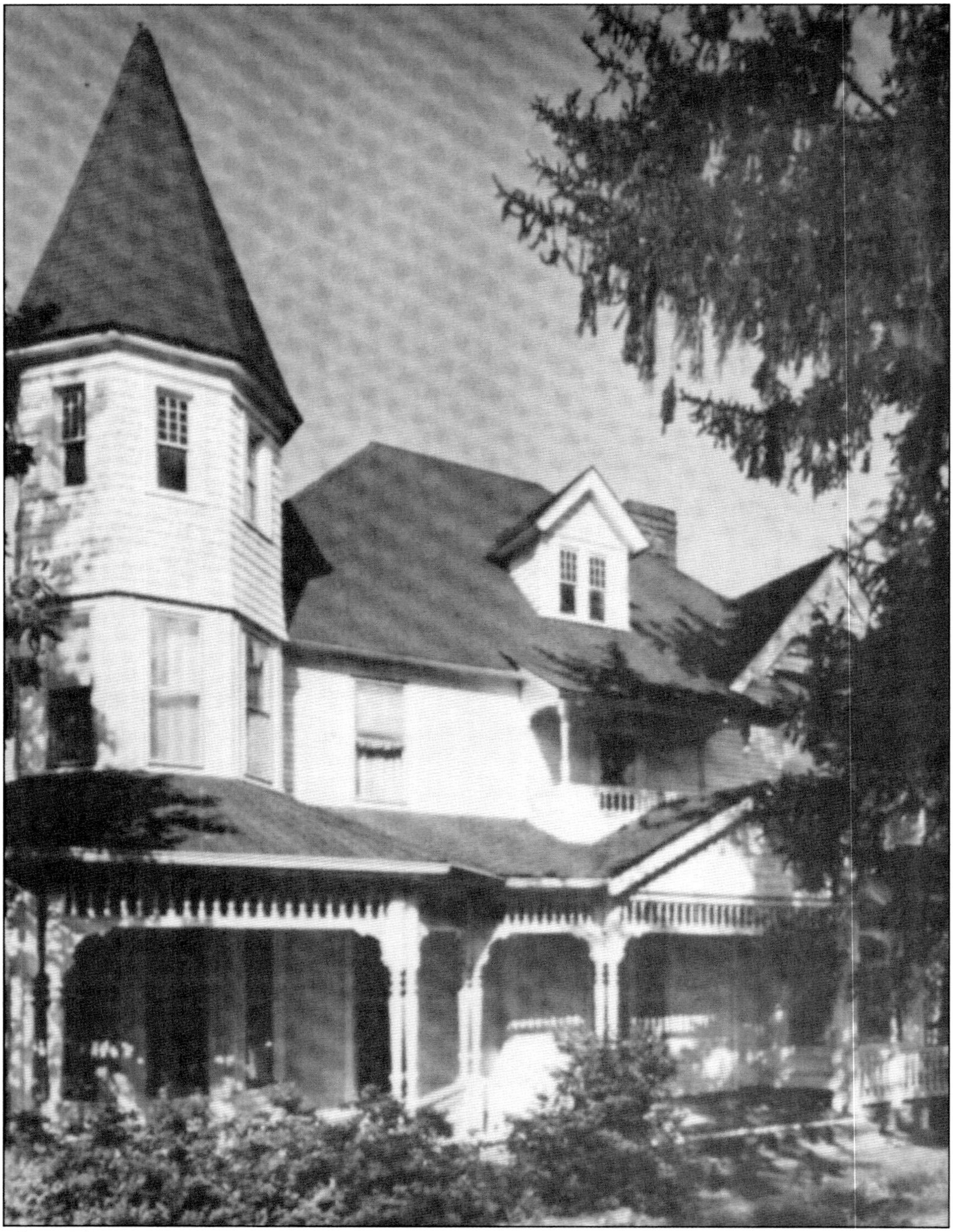

This elaborately embellished Queen Anne-styled house reflects the opulence of many of the homes built in Carthage between 1890 and the early years of the twentieth century. It was constructed in 1897 for W.T. Jones, president of the Tyson and Jones Buggy Company and the Carriage Builders Association.

Four

Upper Moore/ The County

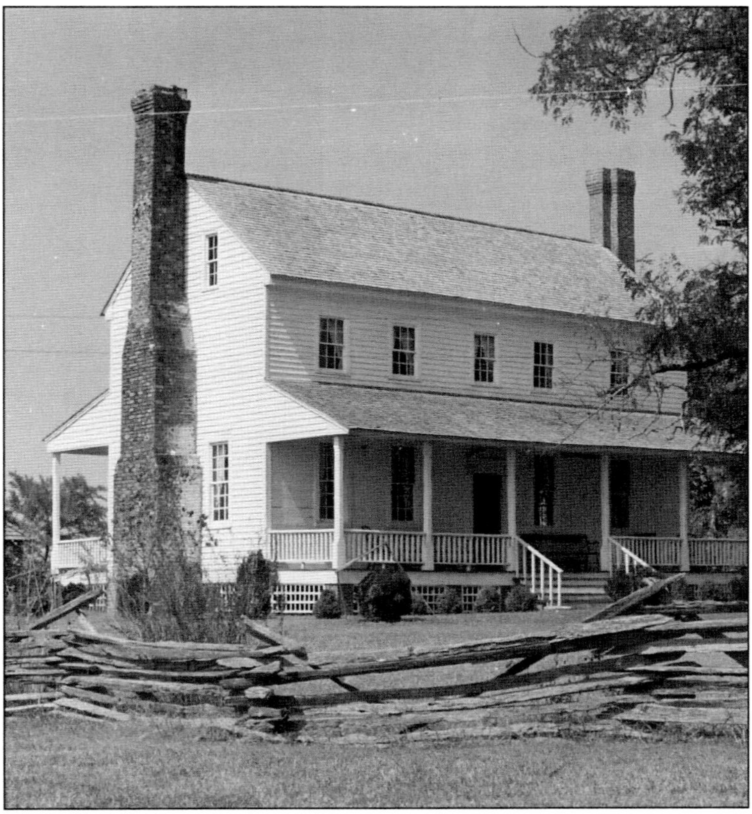

The House in the Horseshoe was built in 1772 by Phillip Alston as the center of his 4,000-acre plantation on Deep River. Alston served as a colonel in the Whig militia during the Revolutionary War, and a small skirmish took place at the homestead between Whig and Loyalist troops on August 5, 1781. Alston was implicated in a murder in 1790 and fled the state.

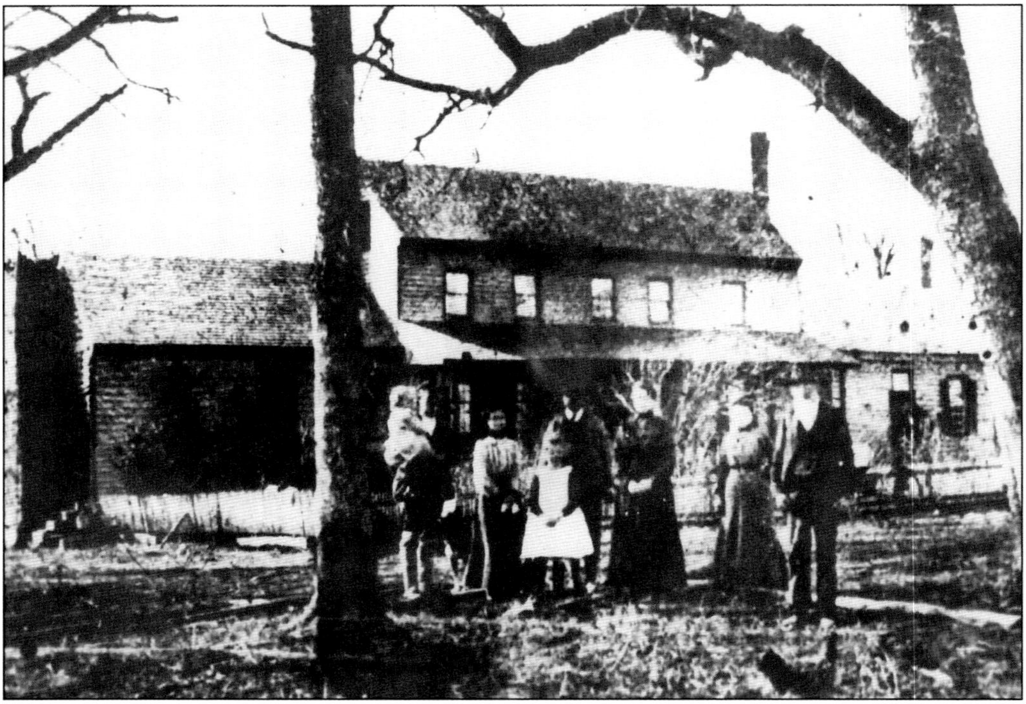

This is the House in the Horseshoe as it appeared in 1899. The two wings were added by Governor Benjamin Williams between 1800 and 1805.

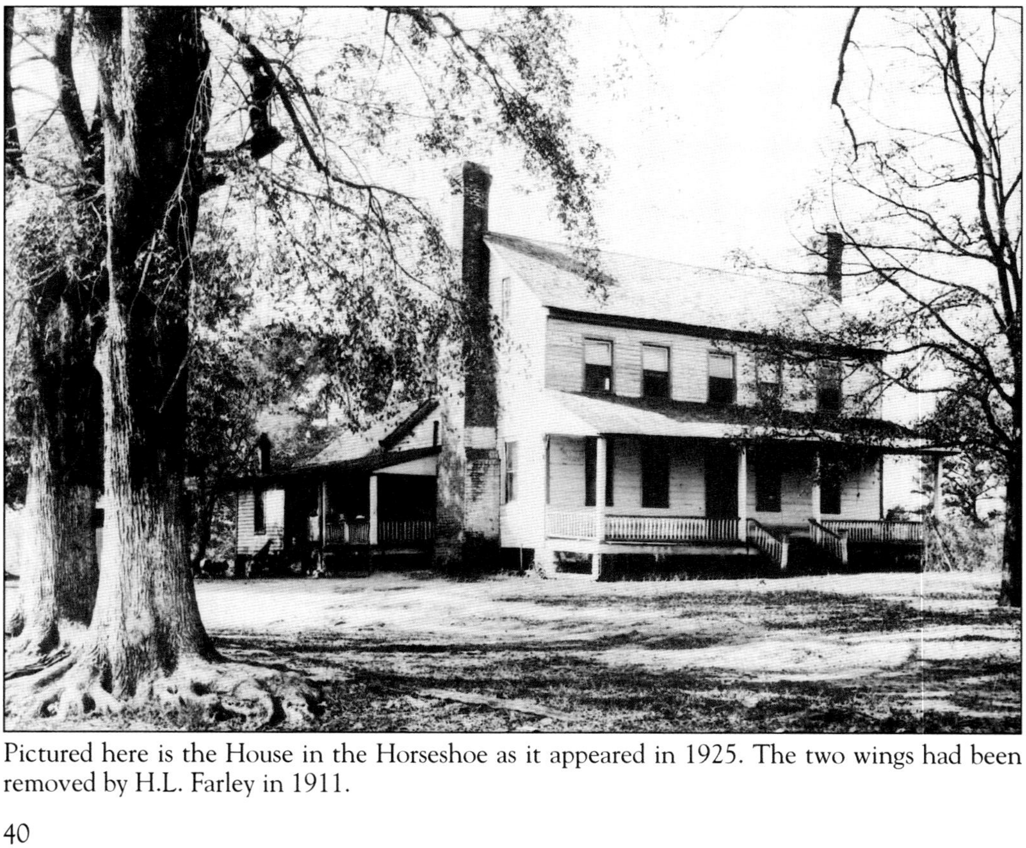

Pictured here is the House in the Horseshoe as it appeared in 1925. The two wings had been removed by H.L. Farley in 1911.

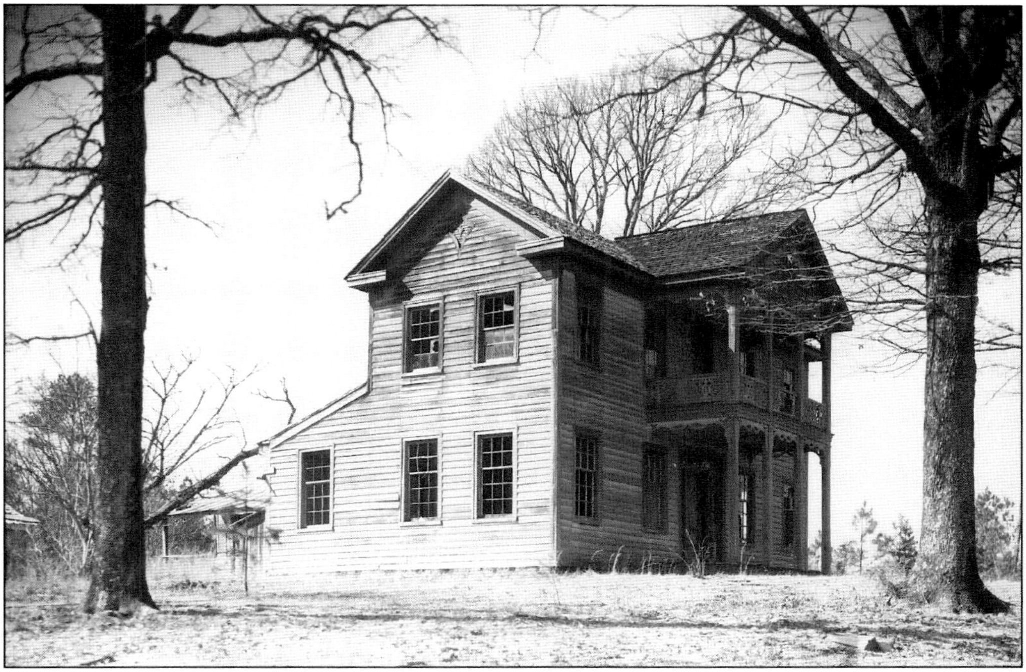

This was the summer home of Governor Benjamin Williams on his Deep River plantation. Governor Williams purchased the House in the Horseshoe and 2,500 acres of land for a cotton plantation in 1798. He died there on July 20, 1814.

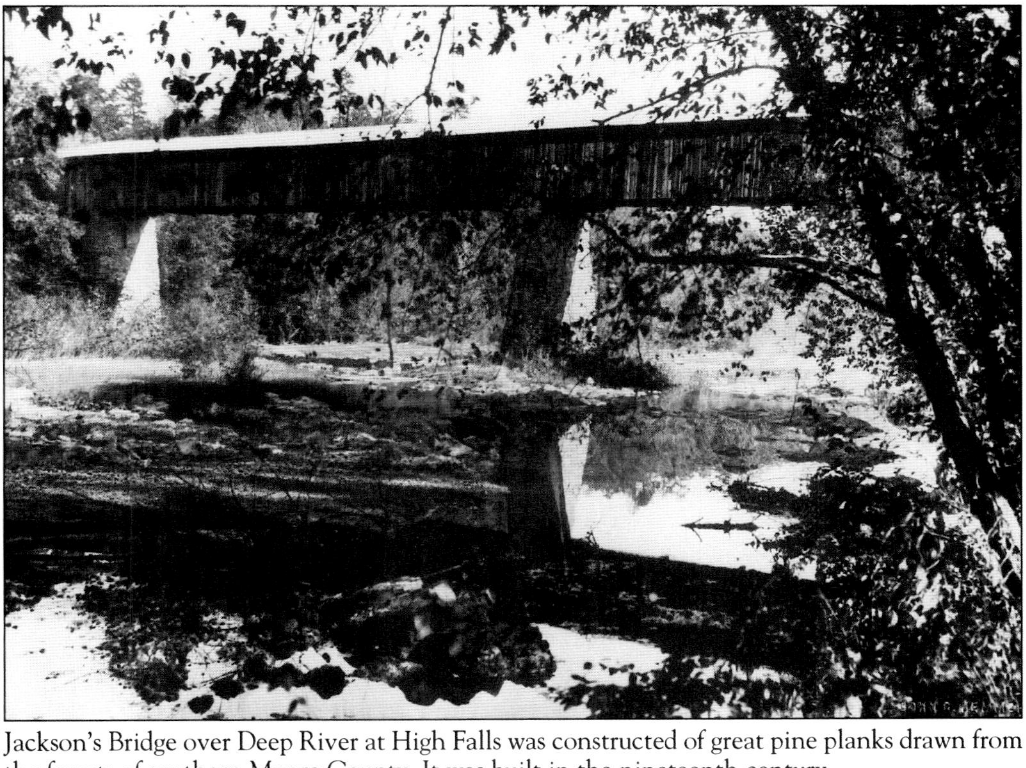

Jackson's Bridge over Deep River at High Falls was constructed of great pine planks drawn from the forests of southern Moore County. It was built in the nineteenth century.

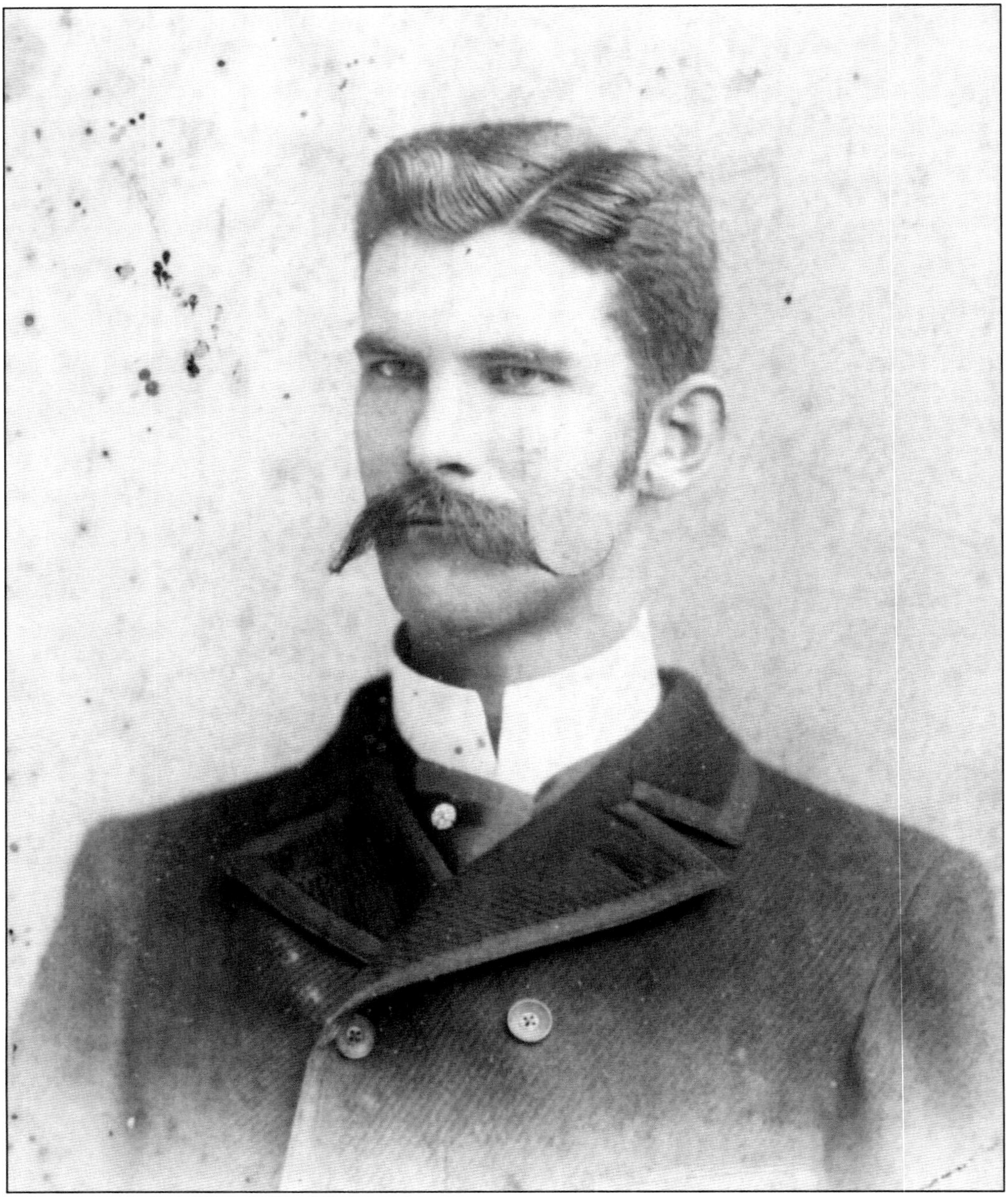

Dr. Murdo Eugene Street (1866–1944) was a son of Dr. Richard Street III (1822–1899) and a great grandson of Richard Street I (1799–1804) who moved to Moore County from Virginia in 1787. Dr. Murdo Street was head of the state sanatorium and practiced medicine from his 1500-acre Deep River farm until his death in 1944.

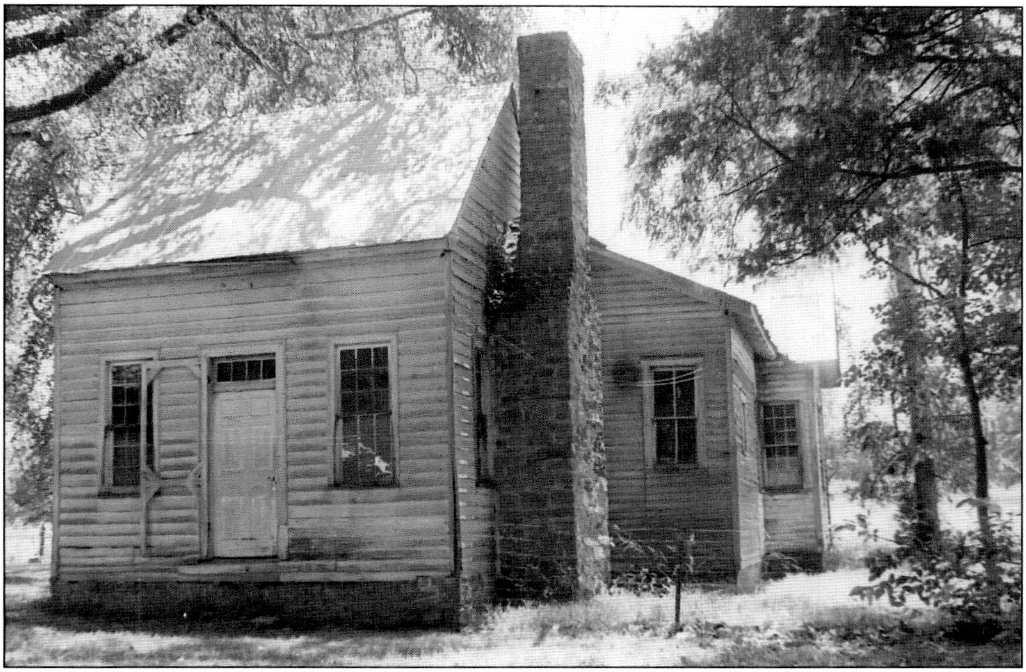

The Street Medical Building was built on the Street farmstead in 1820 as a law office and was subsequently used by three generations of doctors to practice medicine.

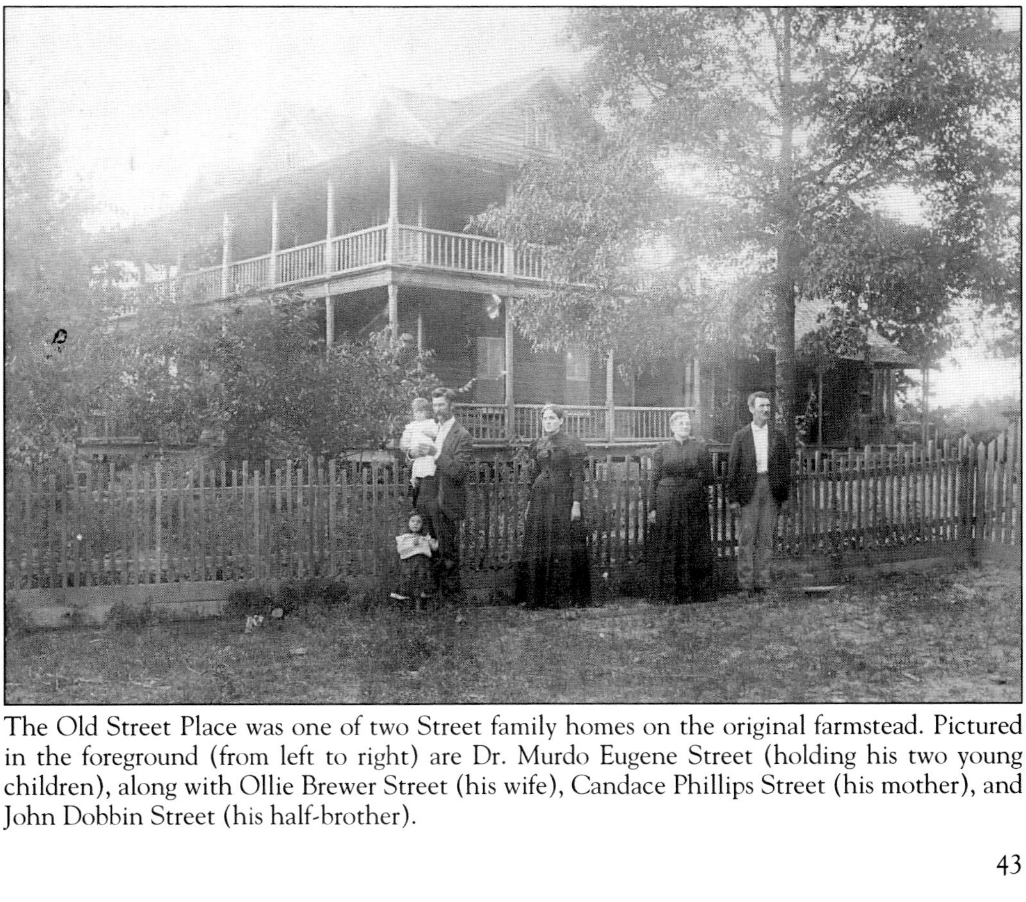

The Old Street Place was one of two Street family homes on the original farmstead. Pictured in the foreground (from left to right) are Dr. Murdo Eugene Street (holding his two young children), along with Ollie Brewer Street (his wife), Candace Phillips Street (his mother), and John Dobbin Street (his half-brother).

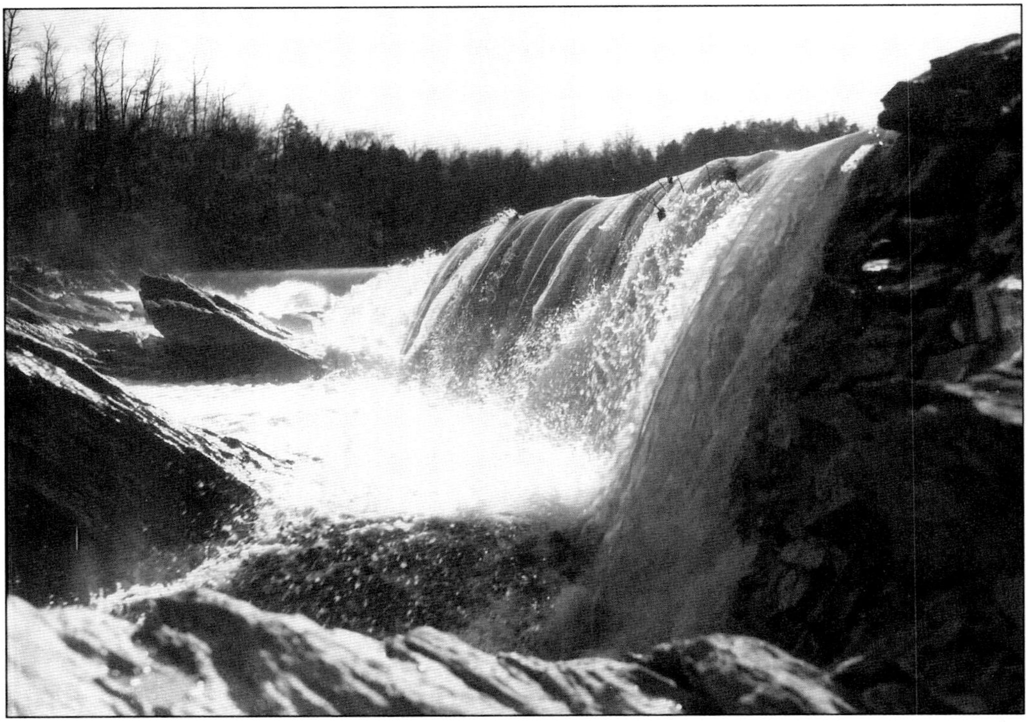

The falls over Deep River gave the town of High Falls its name. The town was at one time the site of one of Moore Country's largest cotton mills.

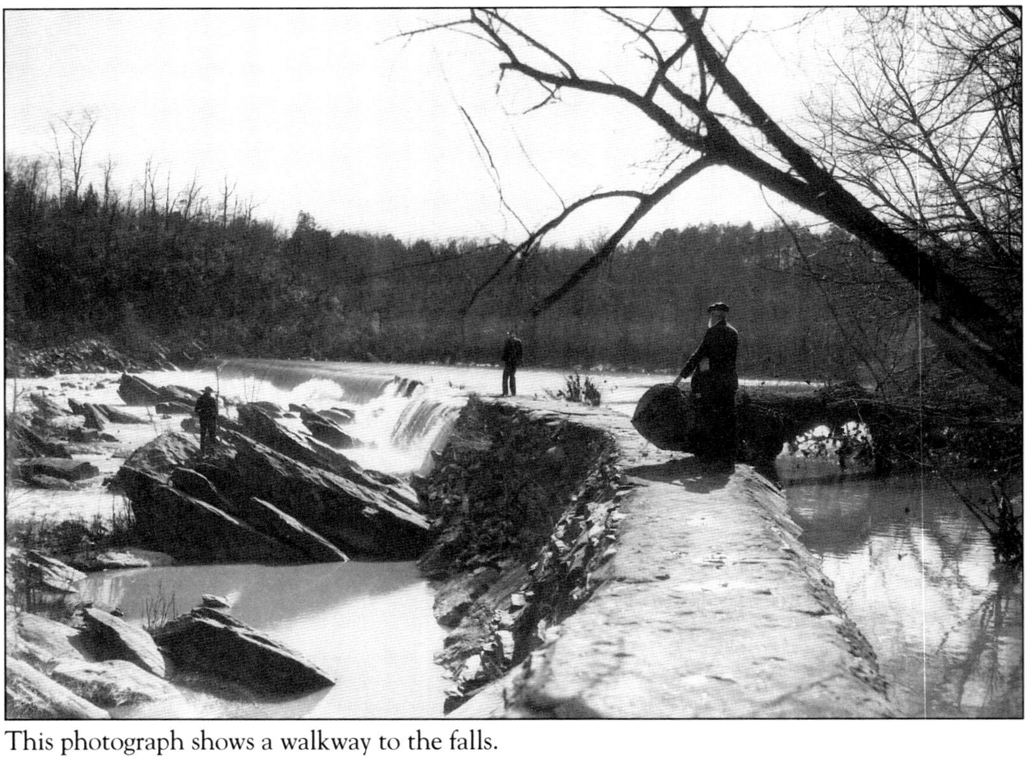

This photograph shows a walkway to the falls.

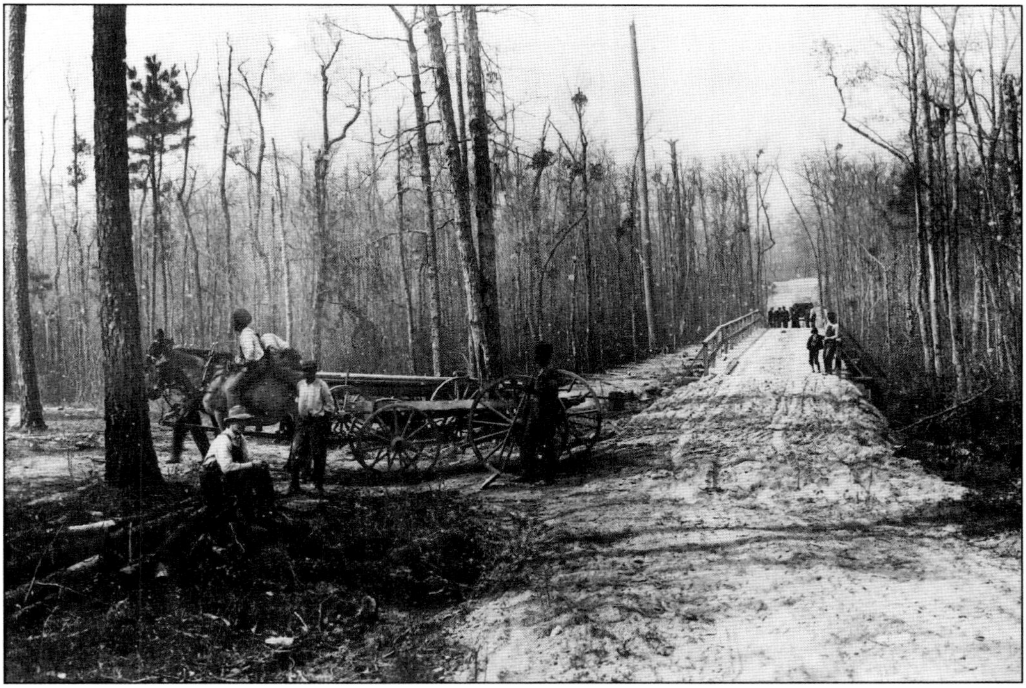

Pictured here is a road scene in upper Moore County between Glendon and Parkwood.

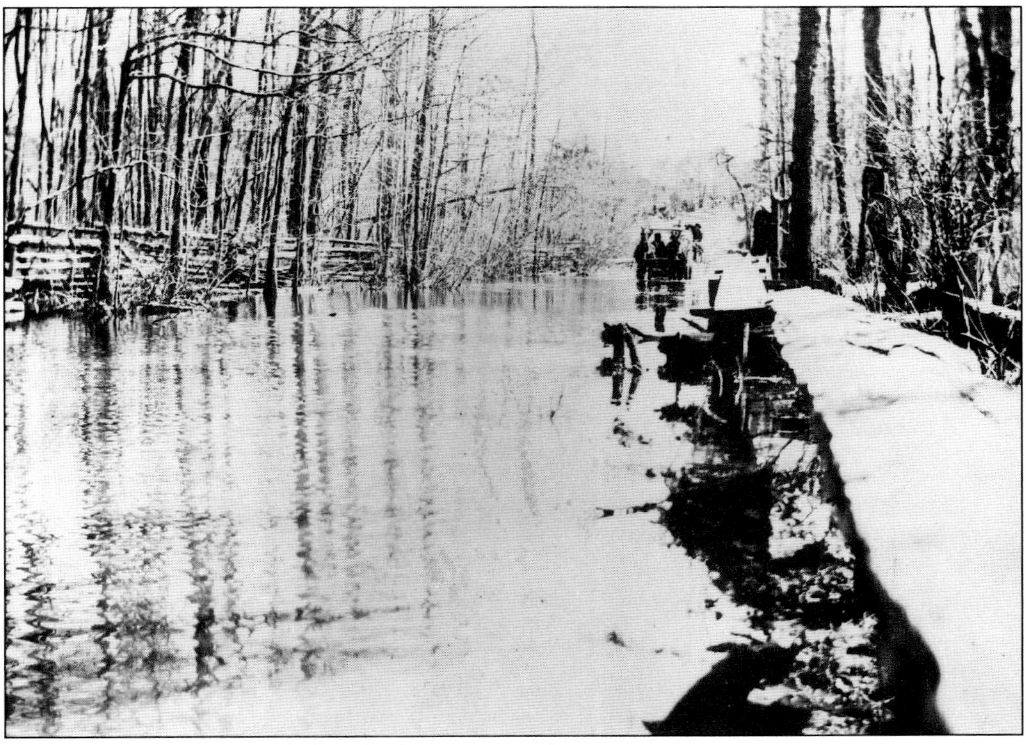

This county road was flooded in the late nineteenth century.

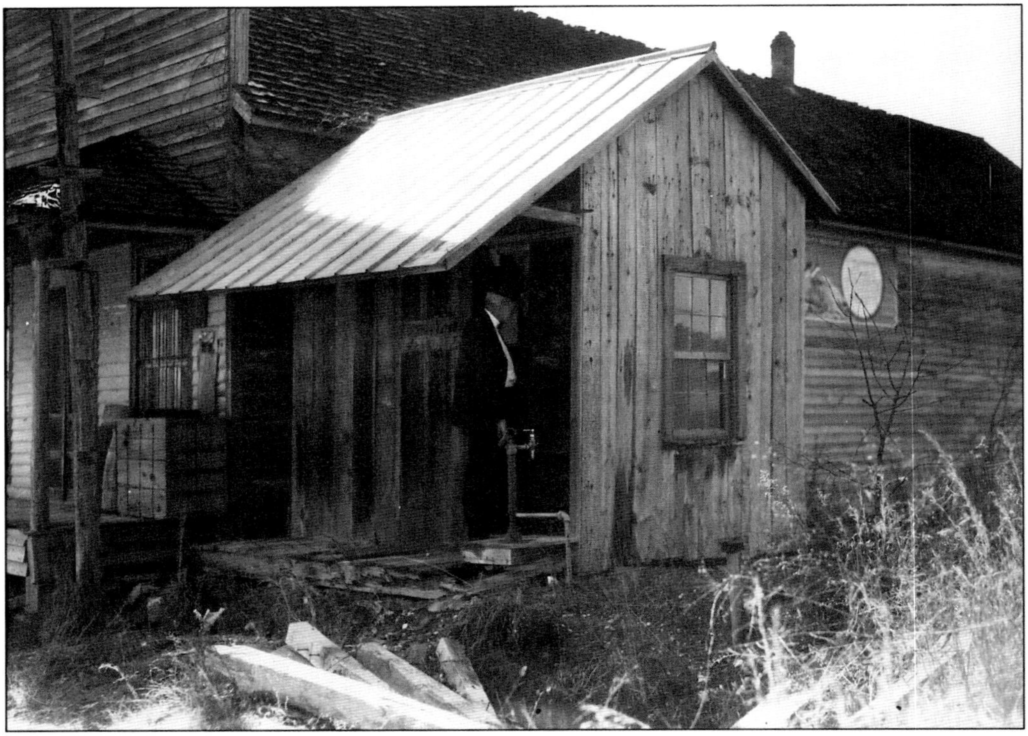

The old post office and country store at Prosperity served upper Moore County from the first half of the nineteenth century until April 30, 1931.

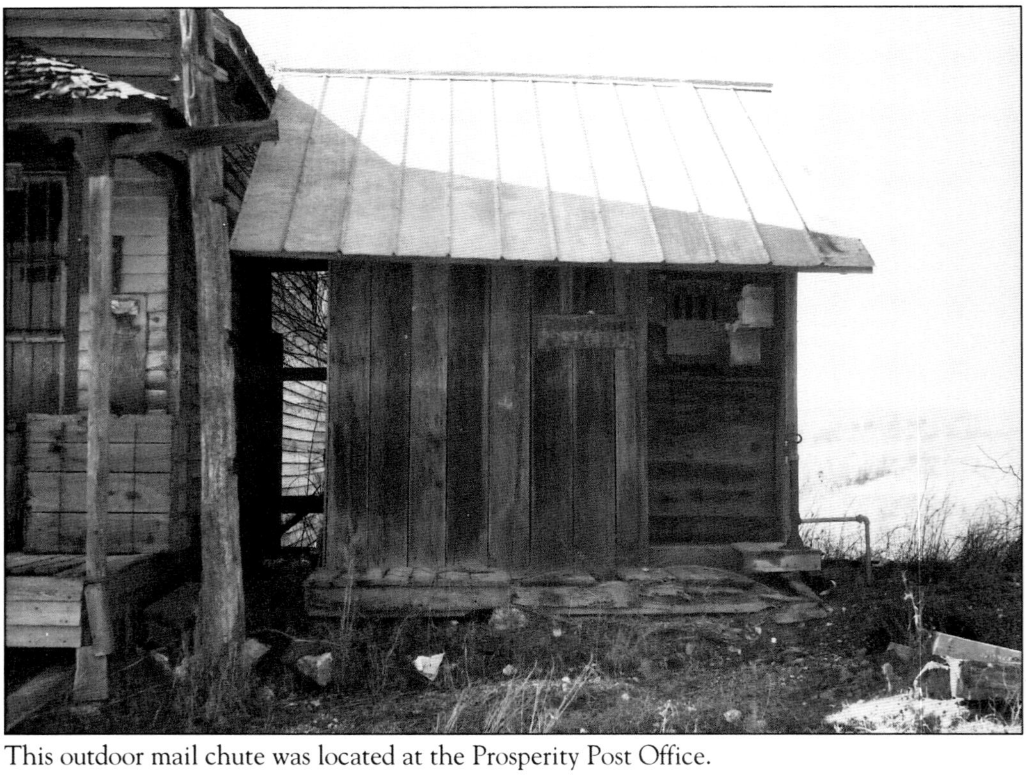

This outdoor mail chute was located at the Prosperity Post Office.

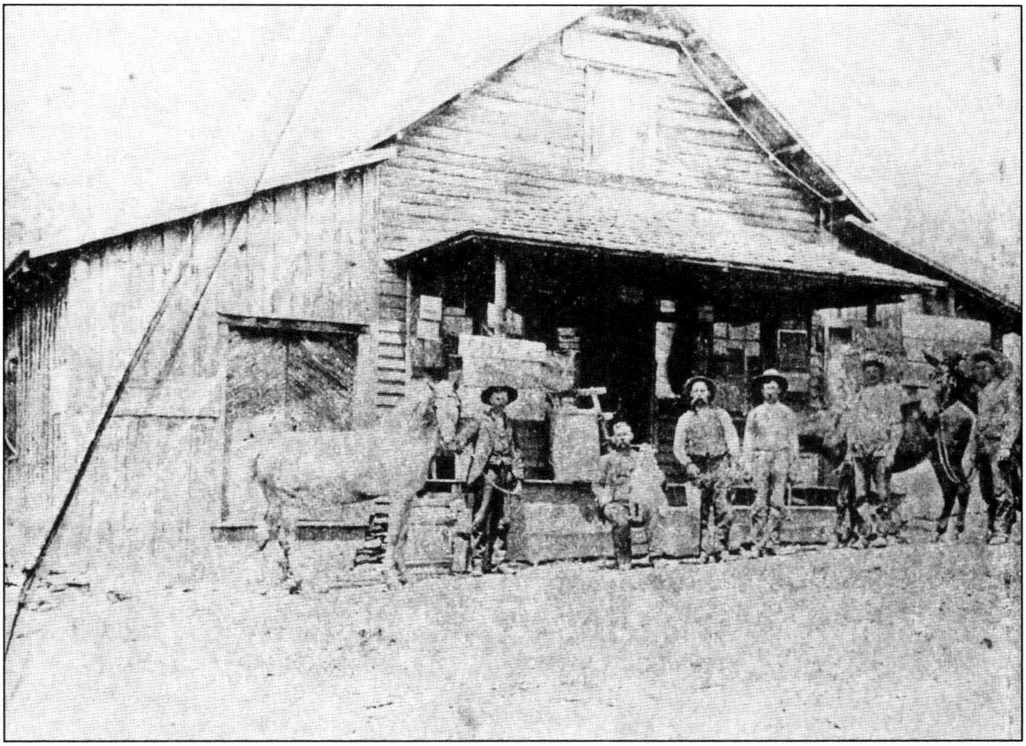

Sol Howard's store in Noise, a small town, was established in the early 1800s and remained open until the early twentieth century. The town of Noise was also known as "Howard's Mill."

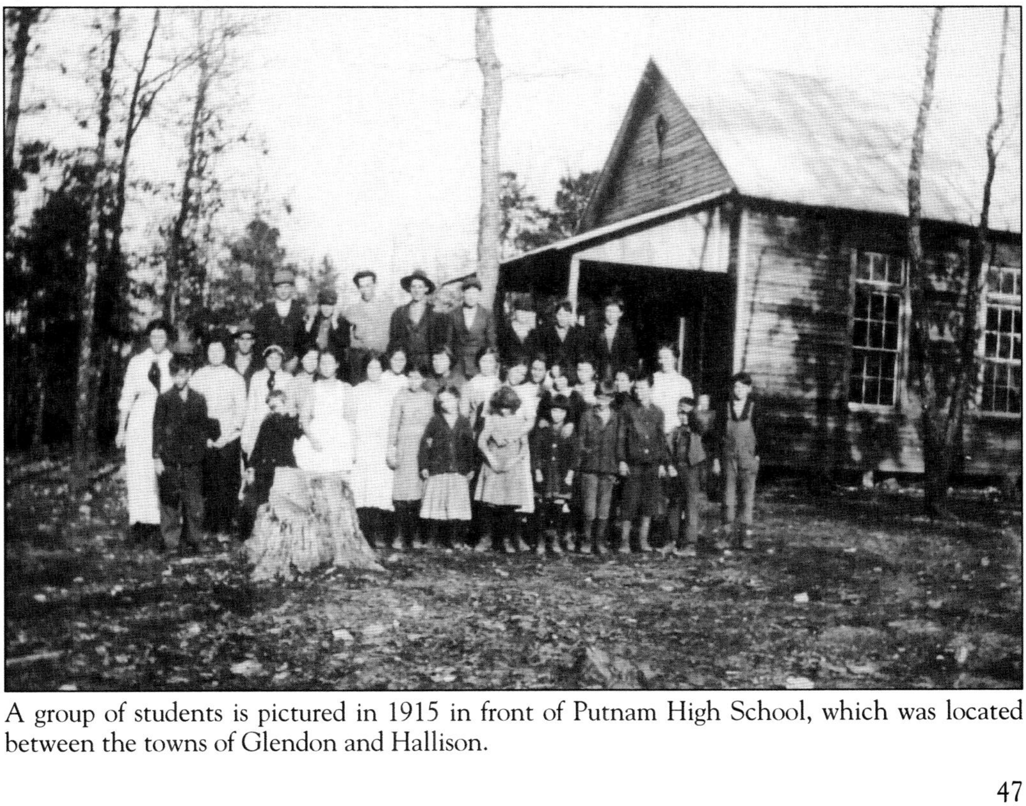

A group of students is pictured in 1915 in front of Putnam High School, which was located between the towns of Glendon and Hallison.

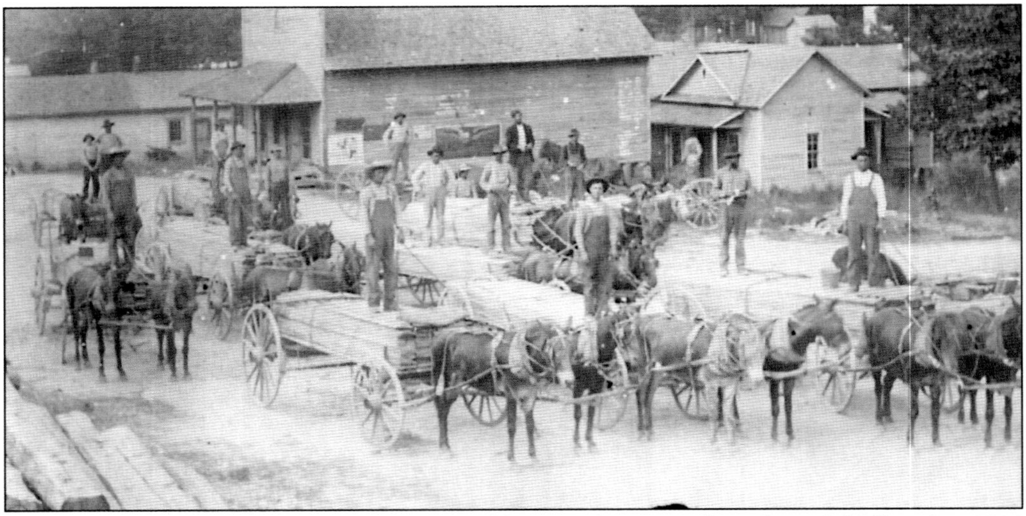

C.C. Frye's store and lumber yard are pictured here in the town of Mechanic's Hill in this 1896 photograph. The name of the town was changed to Elise in 1899 and later renamed Hemp.

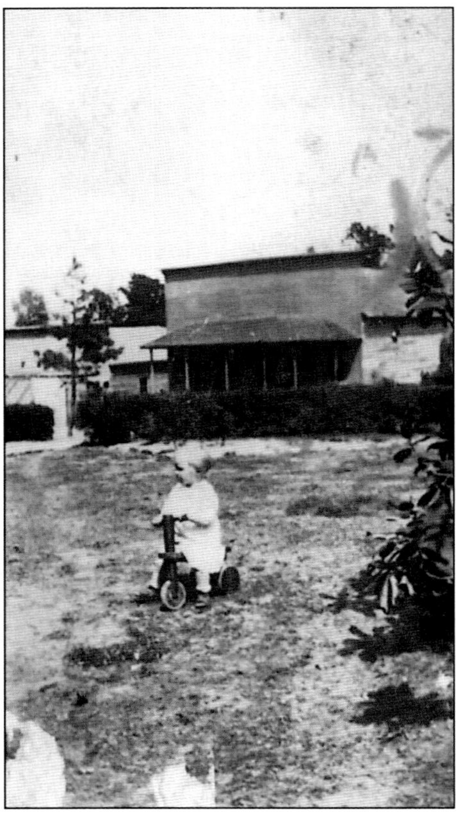

This is a picture of C.C. Frye's store after an addition was made for a millinery shop. Pictured in the foreground is C.C. Frye's son, John L. Frye, at age one.

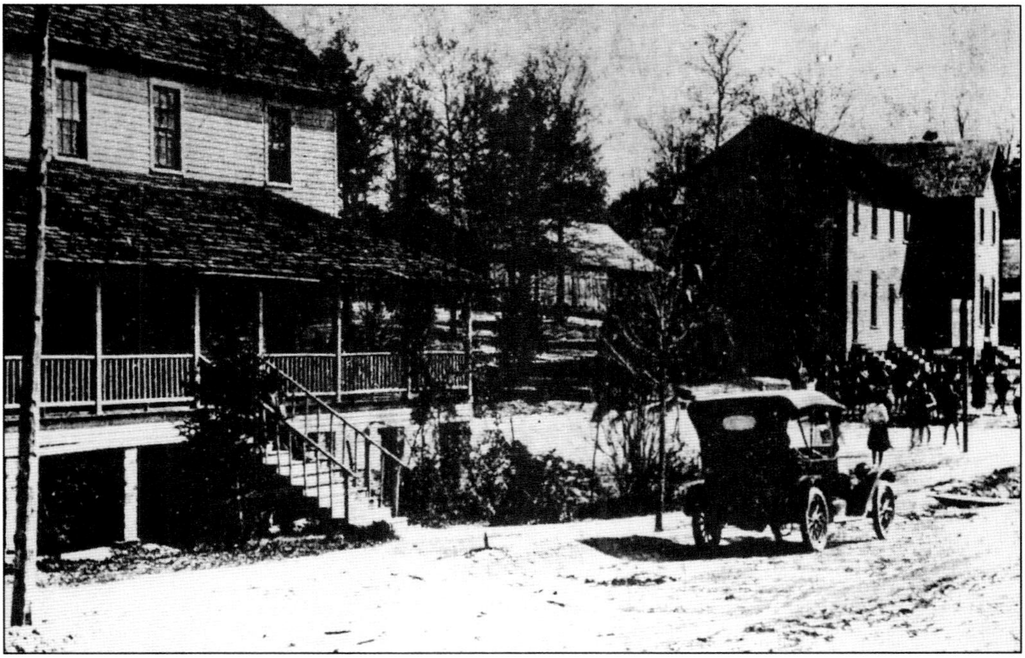

This street scene shows some early homes in the Hemp community around 1916.

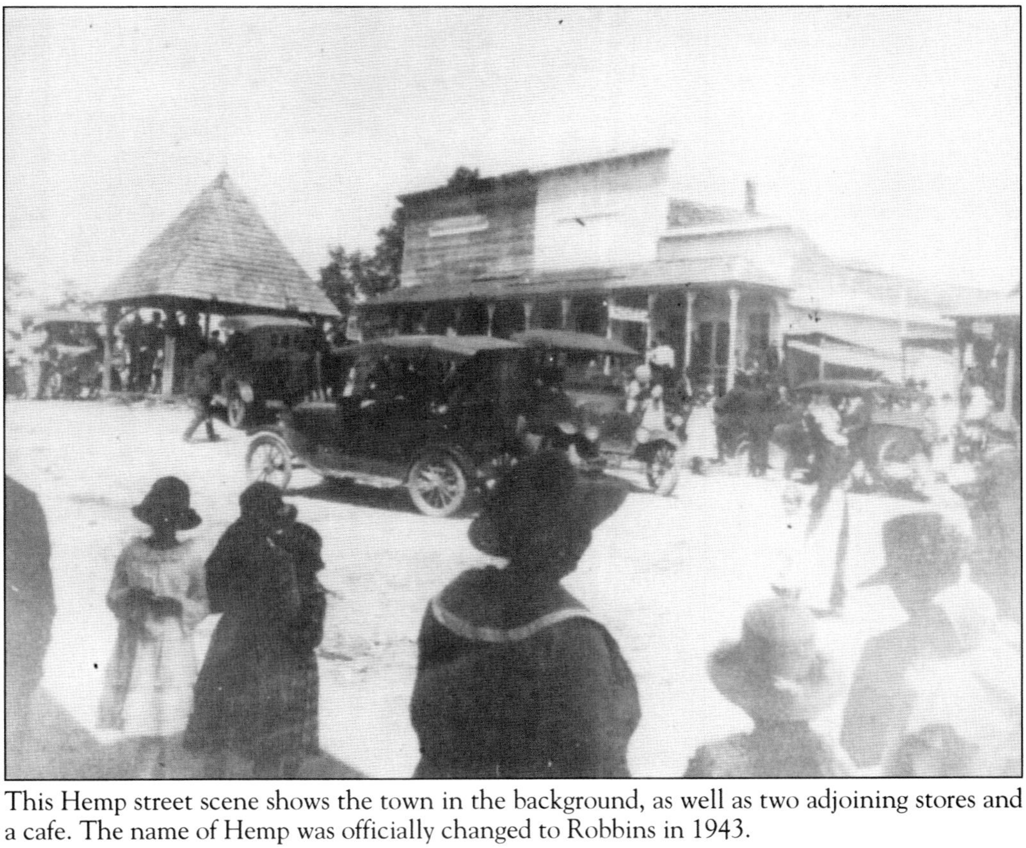

This Hemp street scene shows the town in the background, as well as two adjoining stores and a cafe. The name of Hemp was officially changed to Robbins in 1943.

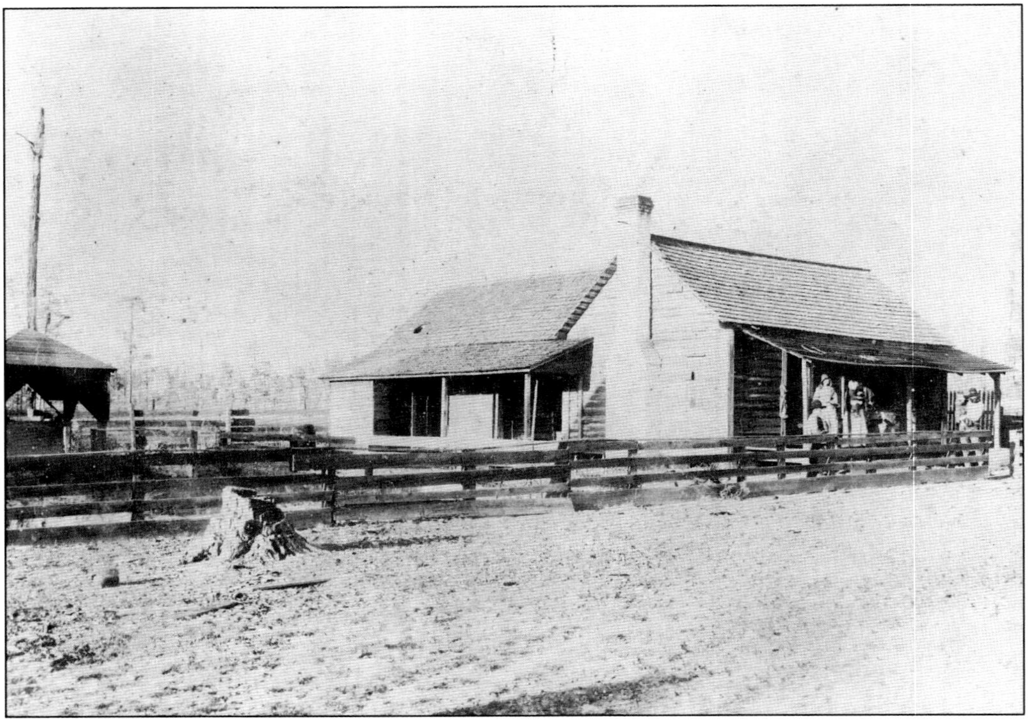

This late nineteenth-century photograph of an early Moore County farmhouse shows the typical rear ell or "bedroom wing." Most of the houses had detached kitchens.

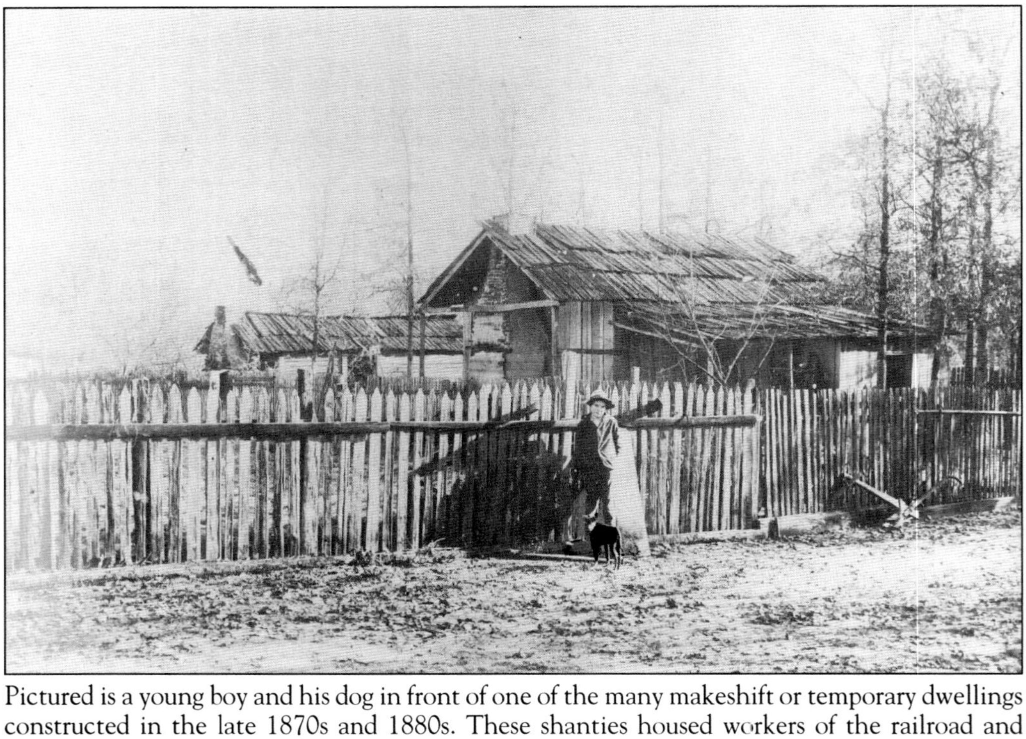

Pictured is a young boy and his dog in front of one of the many makeshift or temporary dwellings constructed in the late 1870s and 1880s. These shanties housed workers of the railroad and lumber industries and usually comprised only one room.

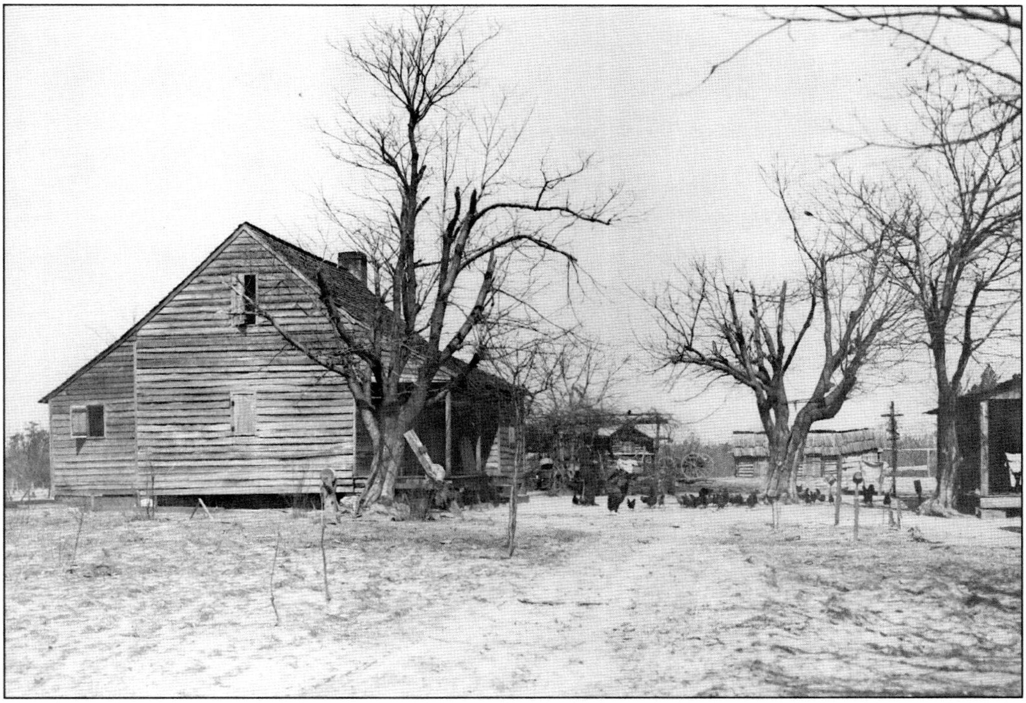

This is a 1909 photograph of a late eighteenth-century farmstead located between Carthage and West End.

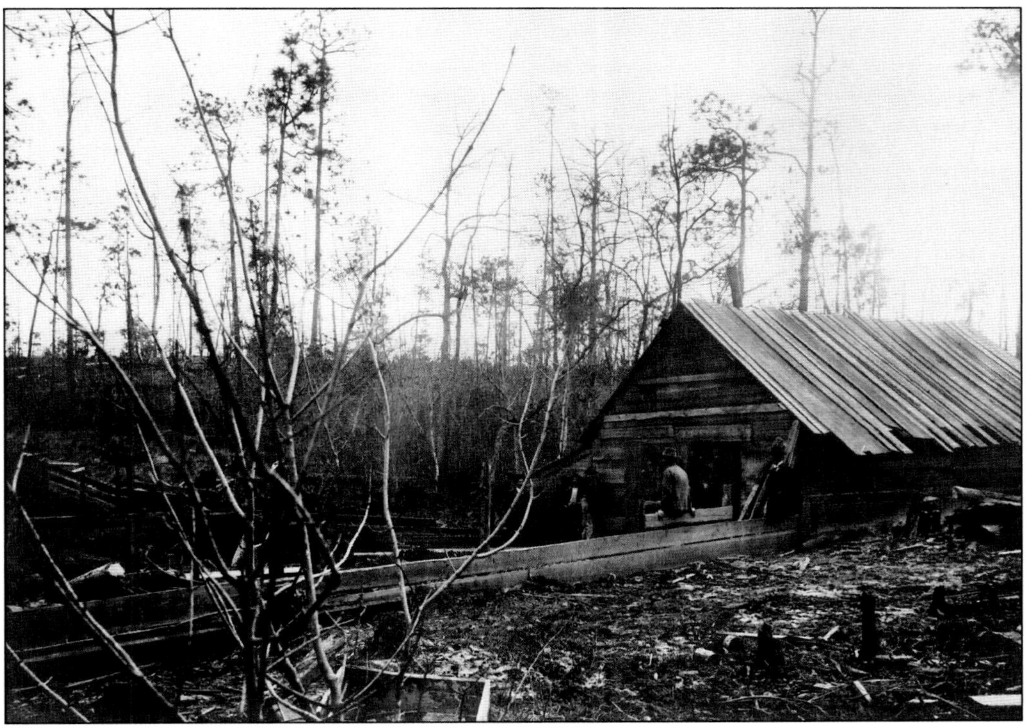

This is a group of workers in front of a barn in upper Moore County.

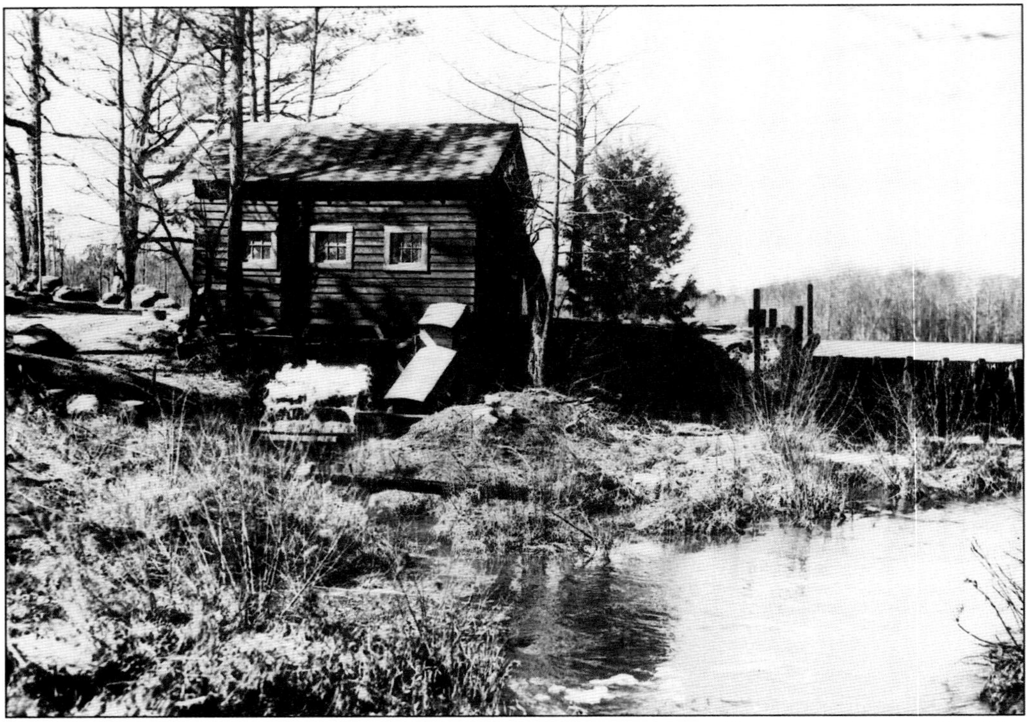

The original dam and mill at Old Black's Mill were constructed *c.* 1792 to grind corn. The lake was operated as a fishing preserve by Owner Claude Leavitt in the early twentieth century.

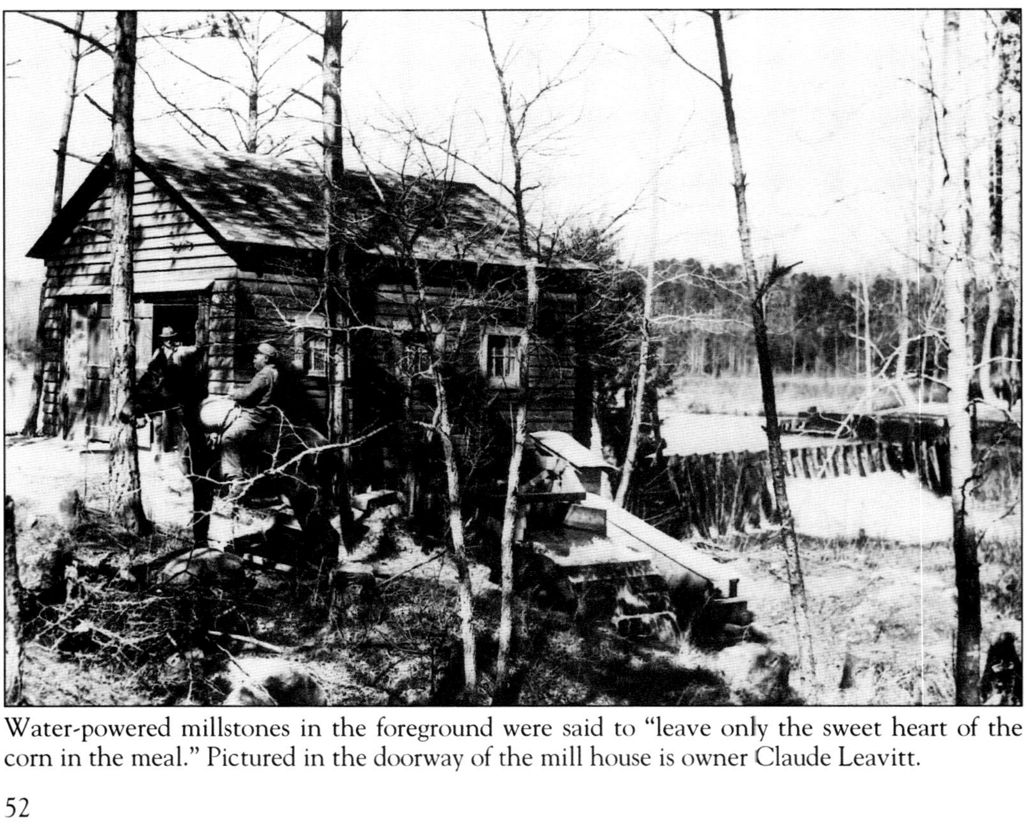

Water-powered millstones in the foreground were said to "leave only the sweet heart of the corn in the meal." Pictured in the doorway of the mill house is owner Claude Leavitt.

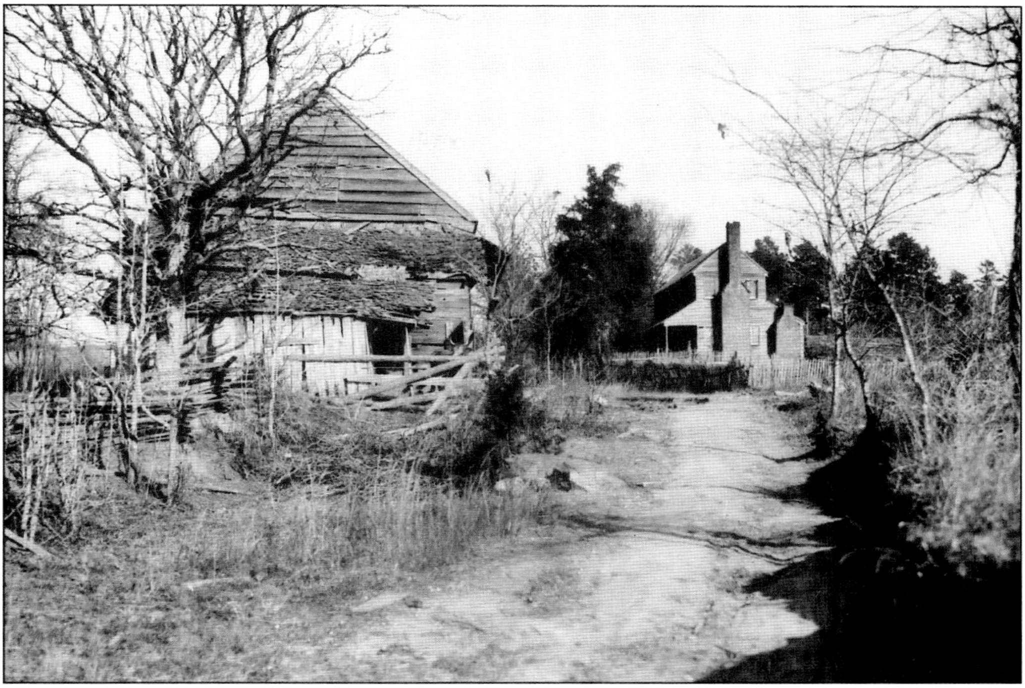

This farm scene shows the Bryant-Davis farmstead, with the Bryant-Davis House in the background. The home was built in 1820 by James Bryant.

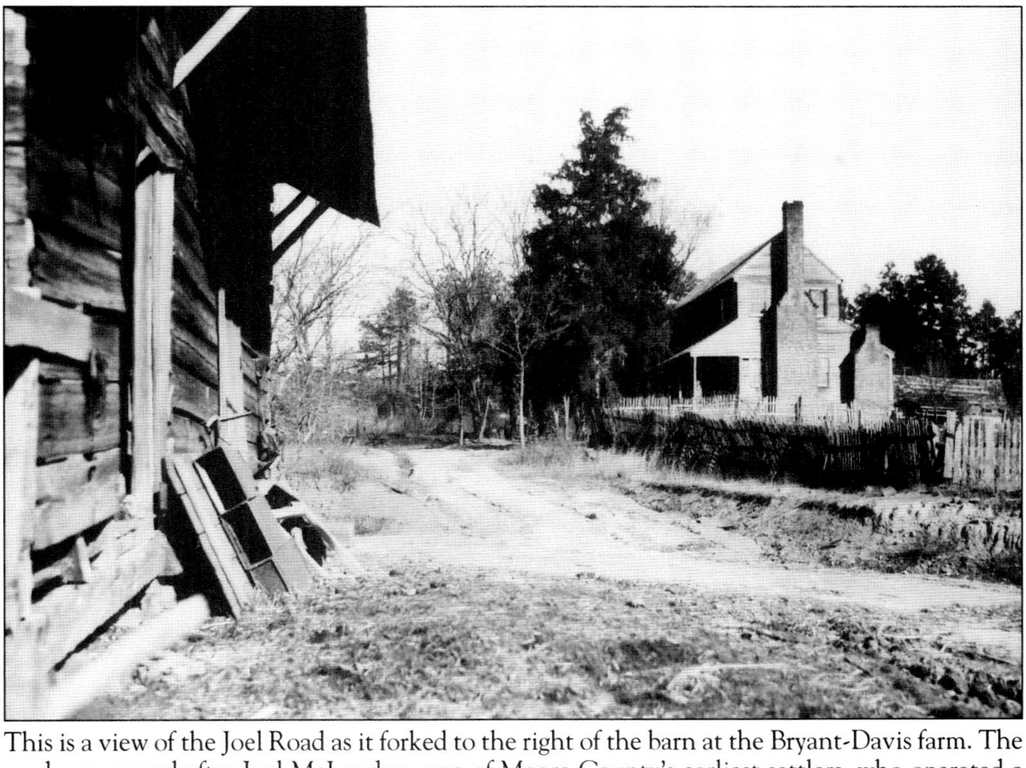

This is a view of the Joel Road as it forked to the right of the barn at the Bryant-Davis farm. The road was named after Joel McLendon, one of Moore County's earliest settlers, who operated a gristmill on nearby McLendon's Creek.

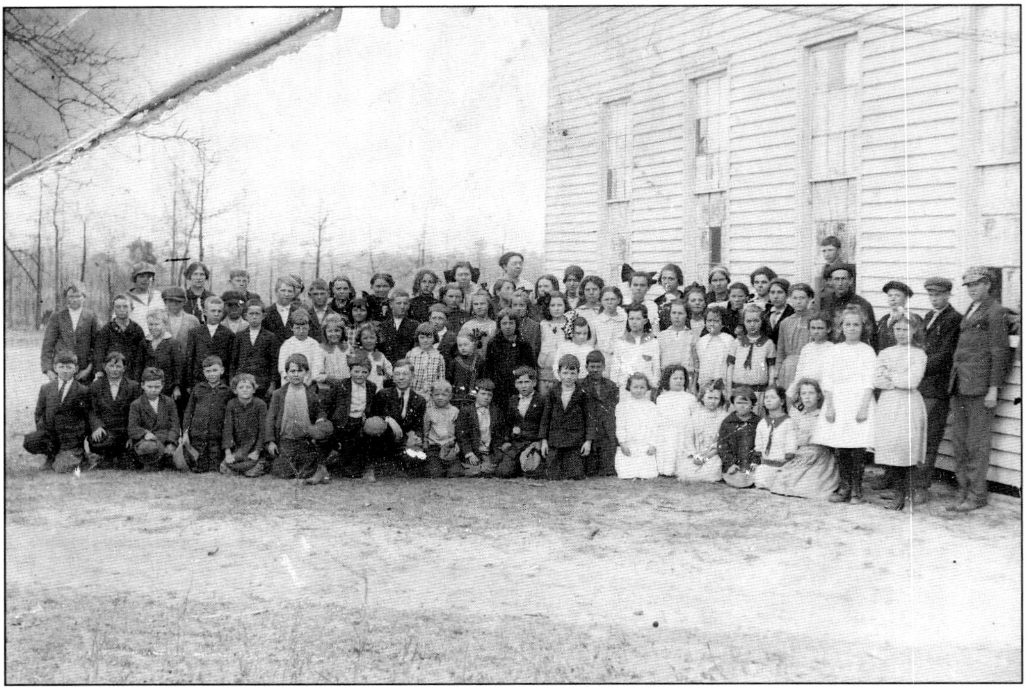

These unidentified school children were photographed at a church in northern Moore County.

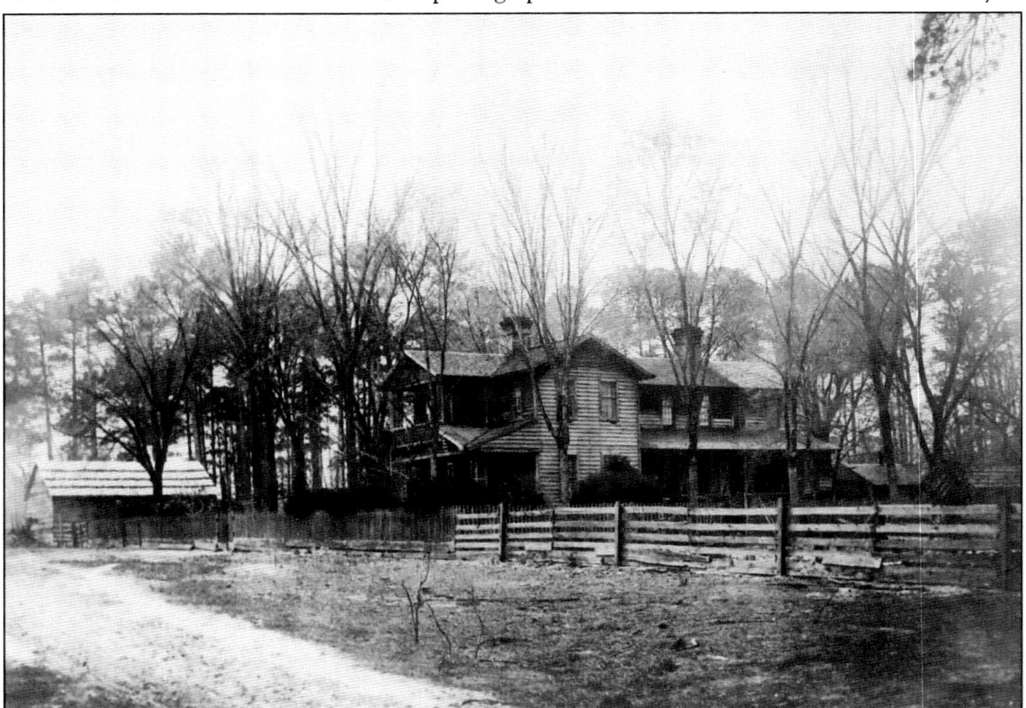

This large two-story frame house was constructed in 1850 by William Calvin Thagard on what was formerly the Dowd Plantation. Thagard was a prosperous farmer who also operated a gristmill and sawmill at nearby Thagard's Pond, formerly the Smith-Ray-Dowd mill pond, on Lower Little River.

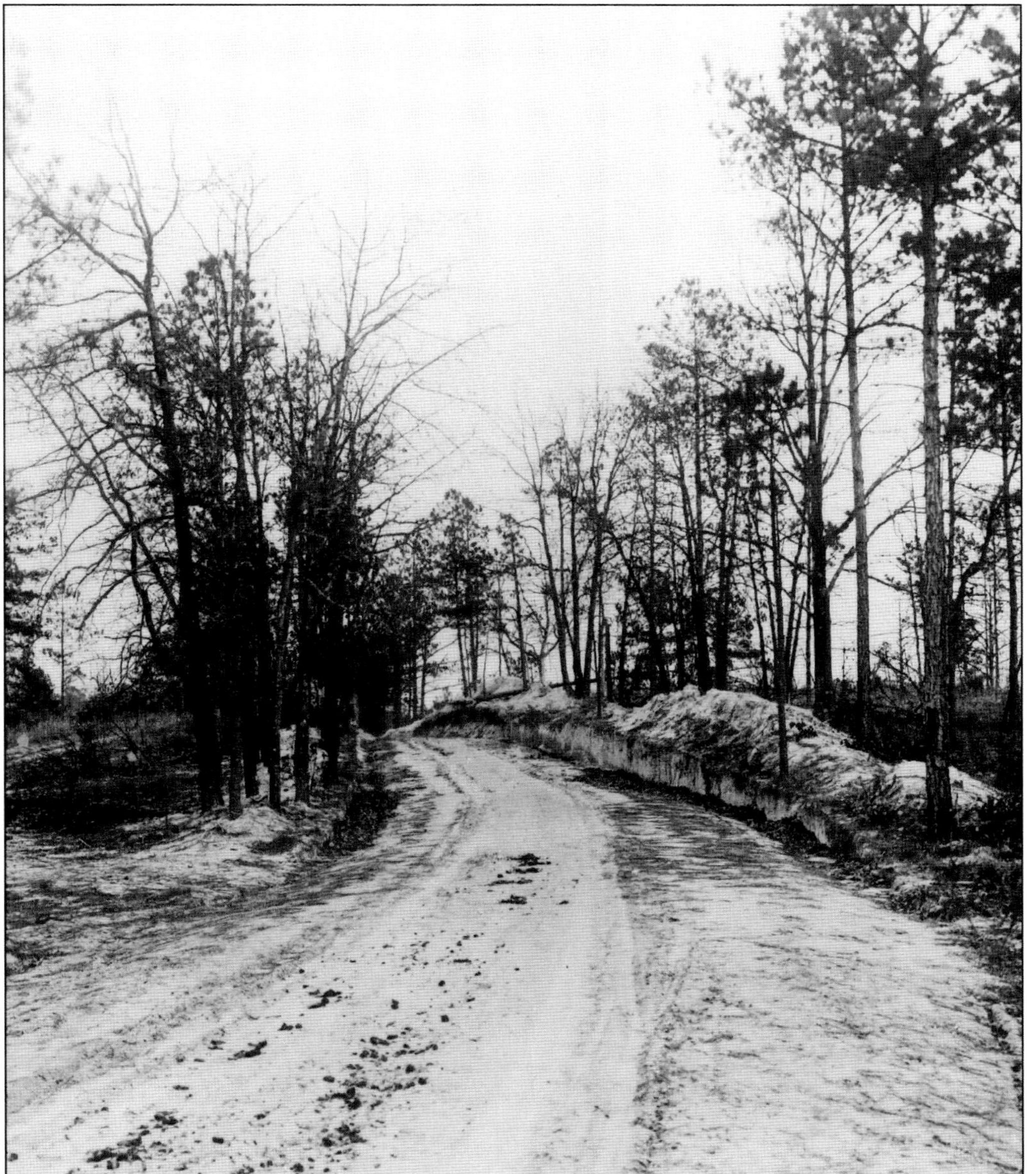

This photograph shows one of Moore County's early roads.

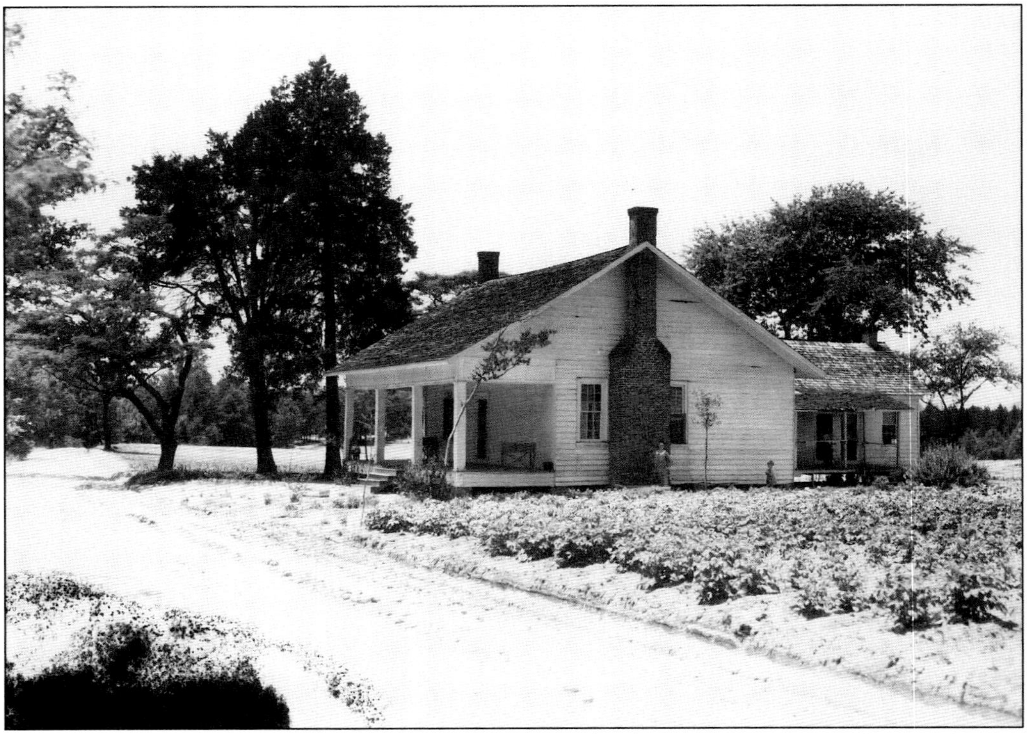

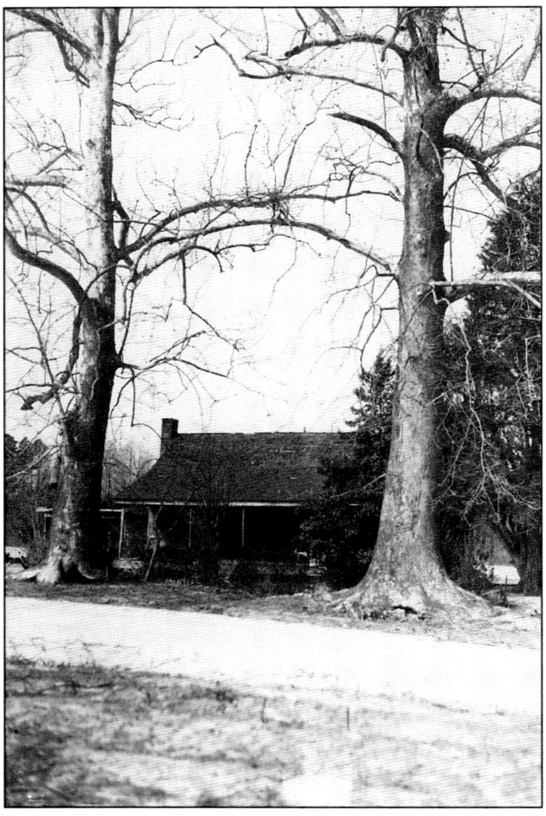

This house was constructed *c.* 1825 near Bethesda Presbyterian Church and Cemetery by Malcolm M. Blue, one of southern Moore County's largest landowners. Blue donated the land on which the third church structure was erected in 1860.

This house was built in 1772 near the Old Mill Creek and Pee Dee Road on a farmstead owned by James Ray, one of Moore County's earliest settlers. Ray died in 1794, and the property has been continuously owned and occupied by his descendants.

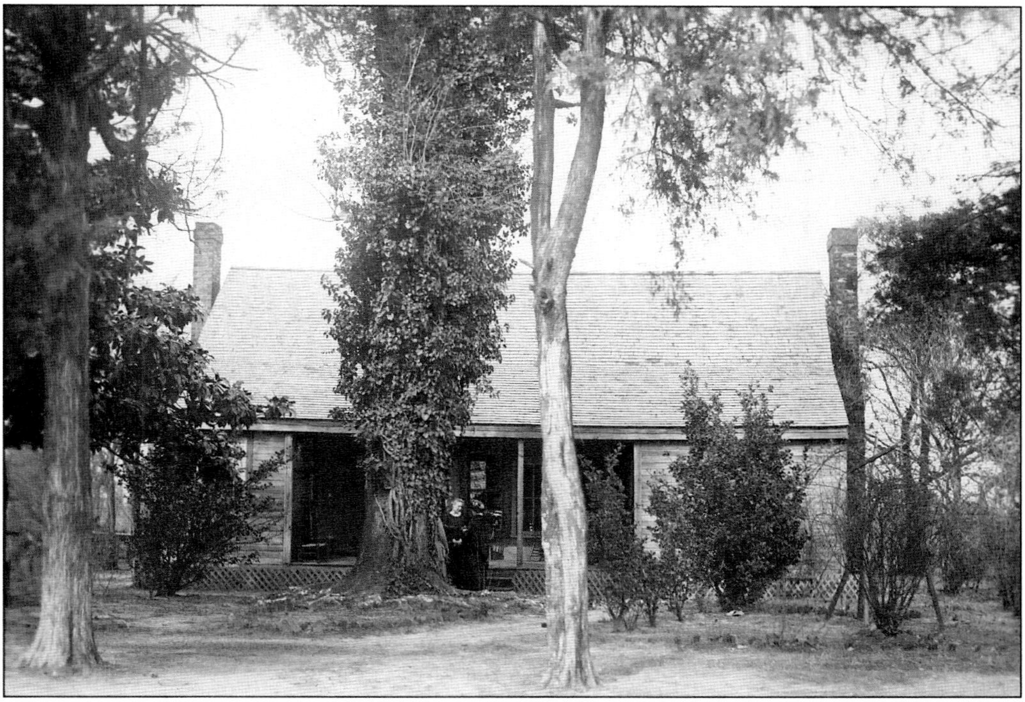

The Shaw House was built in 1821 and remodeled in 1842 as the center of a 2,500-acre plantation owned by Charles Cornelius Shaw. Shaw's son, Charles Washington Shaw, acquired the property in 1874 and became the first mayor of Southern Pines in 1887.

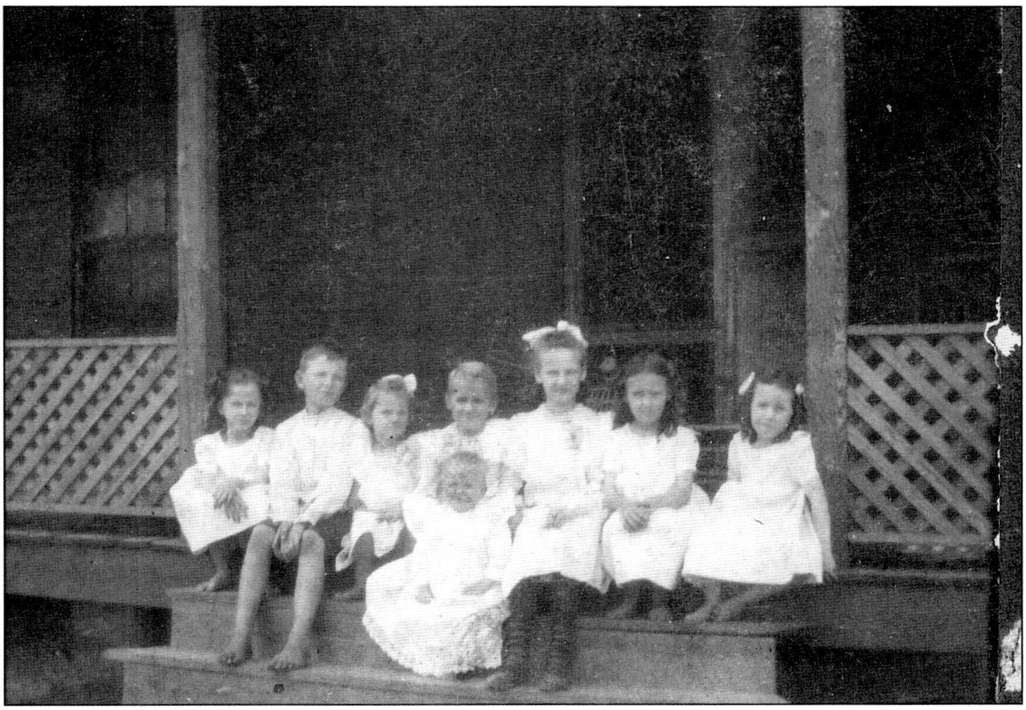

This photograph shows an unidentified group of young children sitting on the porch steps of a home in southern Moore County.

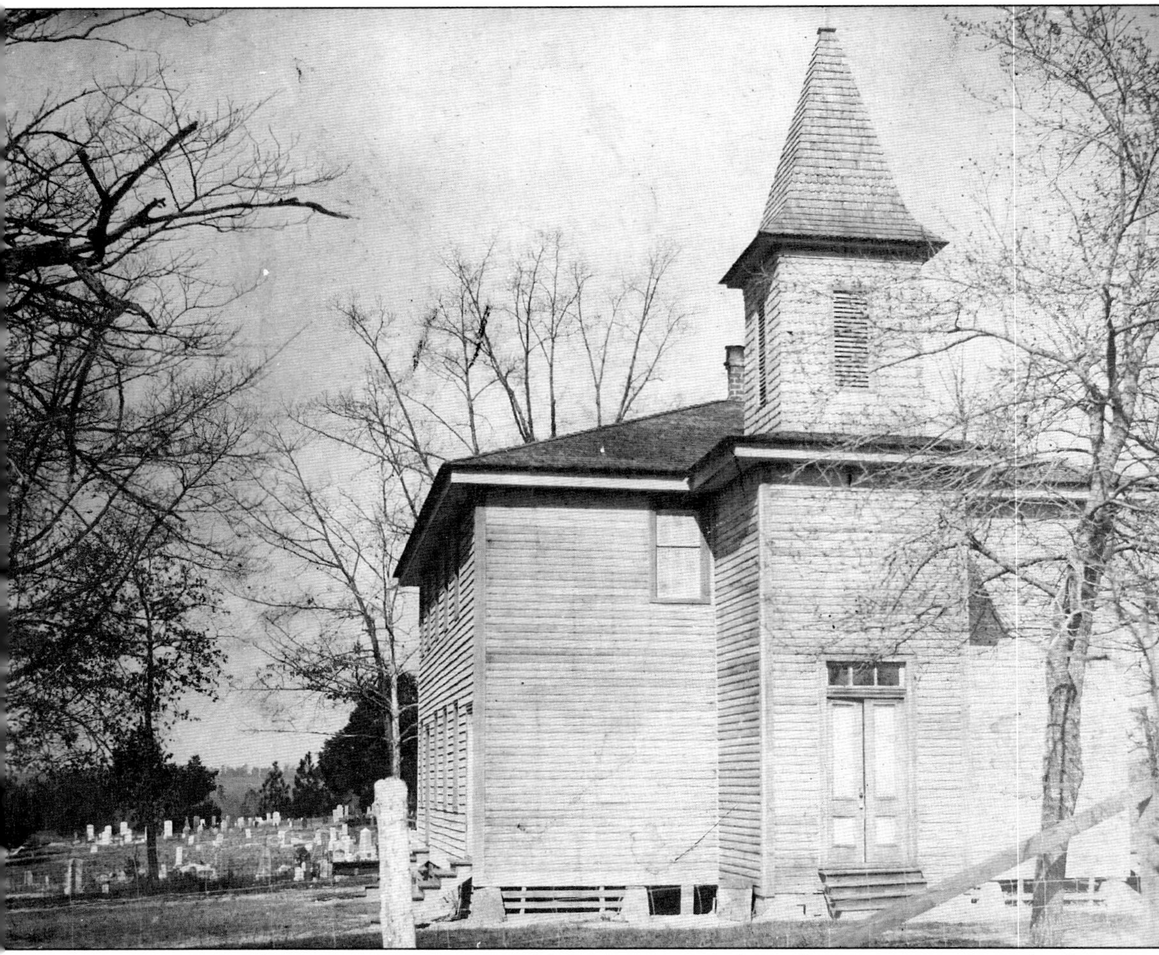

Bethesda Presbyterian Church was established in 1788 and was for many years the only church in southern Moore County. The structure shown was built in 1860 and was the site of a Union encampment during the Civil War. The adjoining cemetery contains the graves of some of Moore County's earliest settlers.

Five

JACKSON SPRINGS

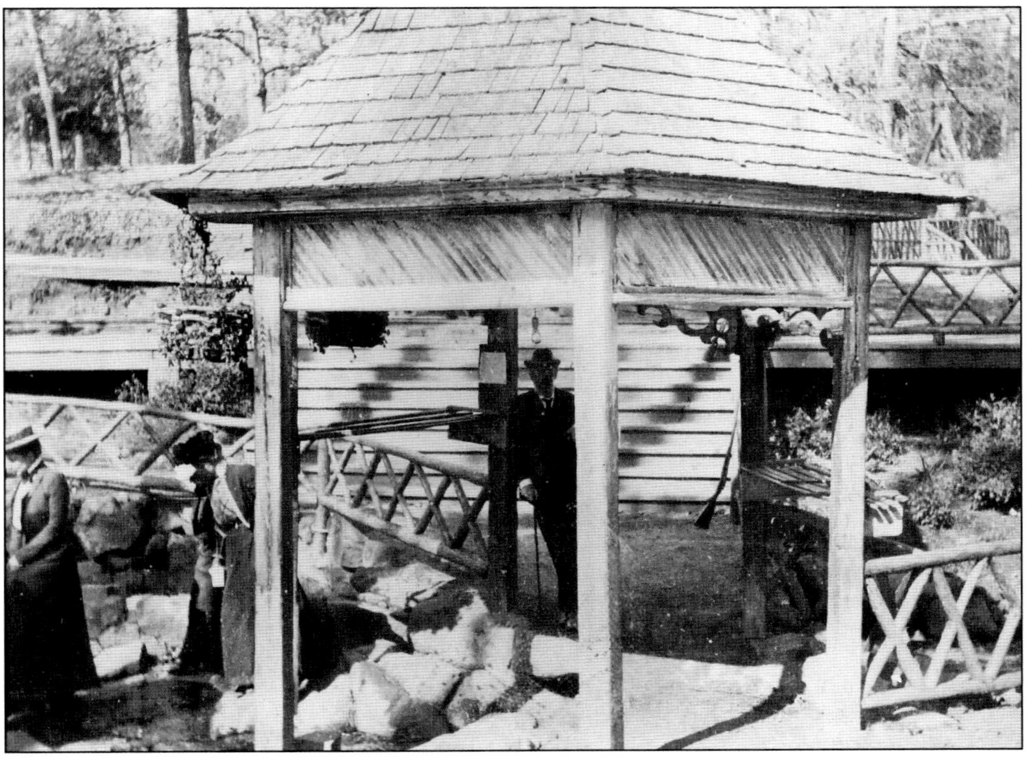

The mineral springs at Jackson Springs were known to Colonial settlers as early as 1747. The town was established as a resort area in the early 1870s.

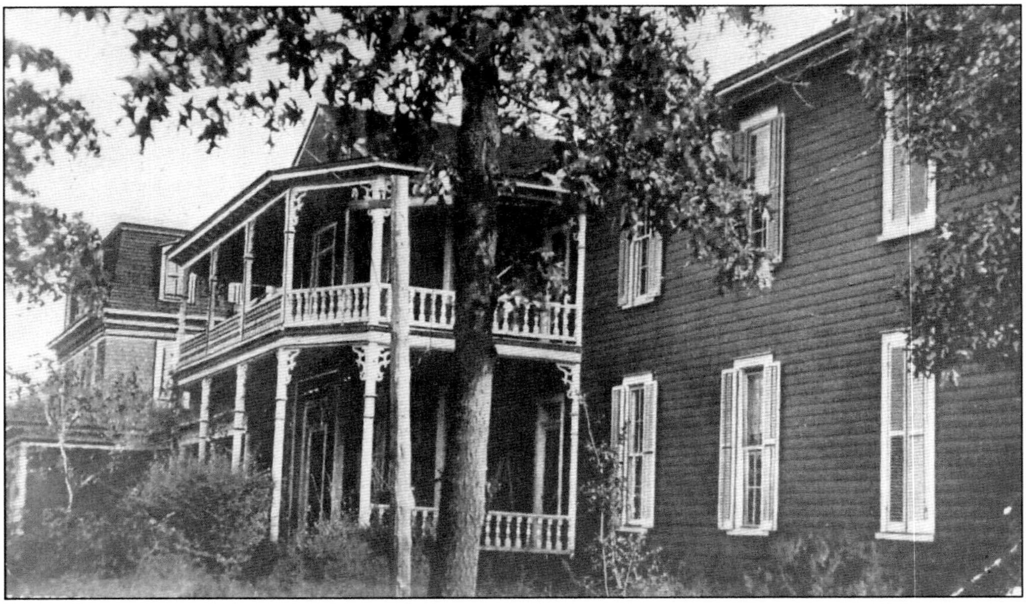

The Jackson Springs Hotel was built in 1890 on a high bluff overlooking the springs. It was initially a fashionable summer resort frequented by such notable men as James Buchanan Duke, John Angier, Robert N. Page, and John Blue.

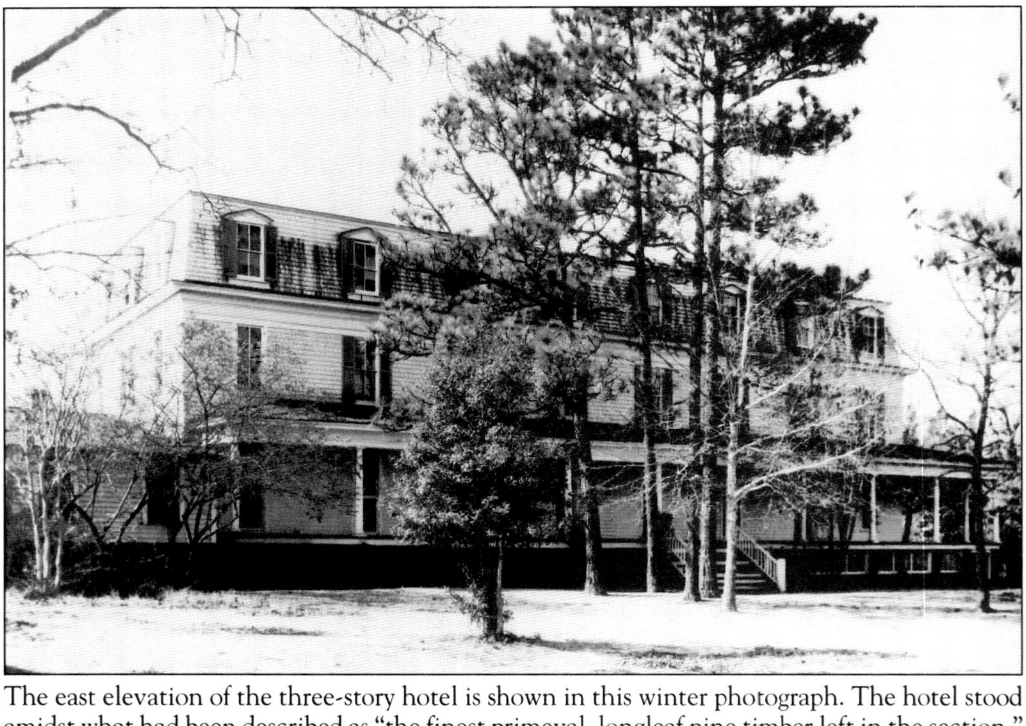

The east elevation of the three-story hotel is shown in this winter photograph. The hotel stood amidst what had been described as "the finest primeval, longleaf pine timber left in the section," and the hotel also had a lake, large swimming pool, tennis courts, baseball field, and several outdoor pavilions.

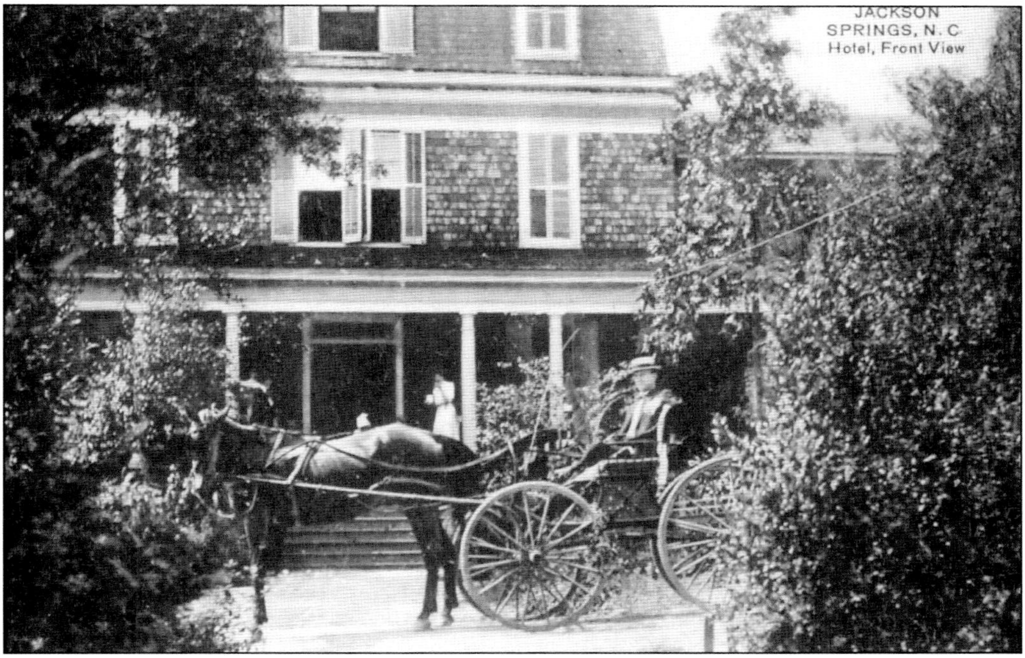

Here, a horse-and-buggy are pictured in front of the main entrance to the hotel. The building had two rear wings and nine family cottages on the grounds.

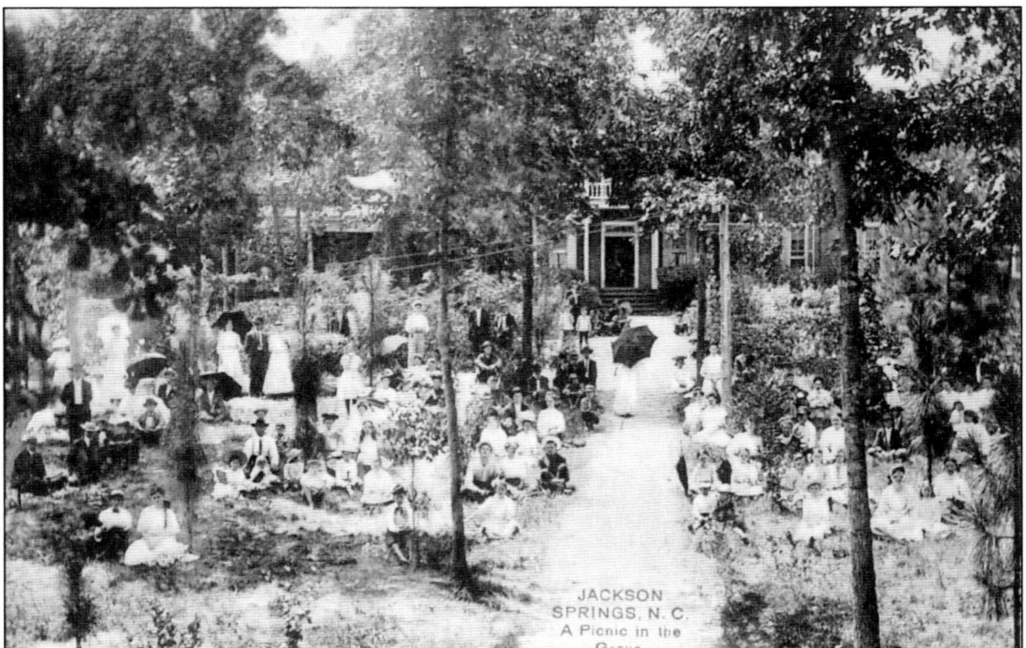

The grove in front of the hotel was a popular gathering spot for hotel guests and nearby residents. The sandy path in the center foreground led to the site of the mineral springs.

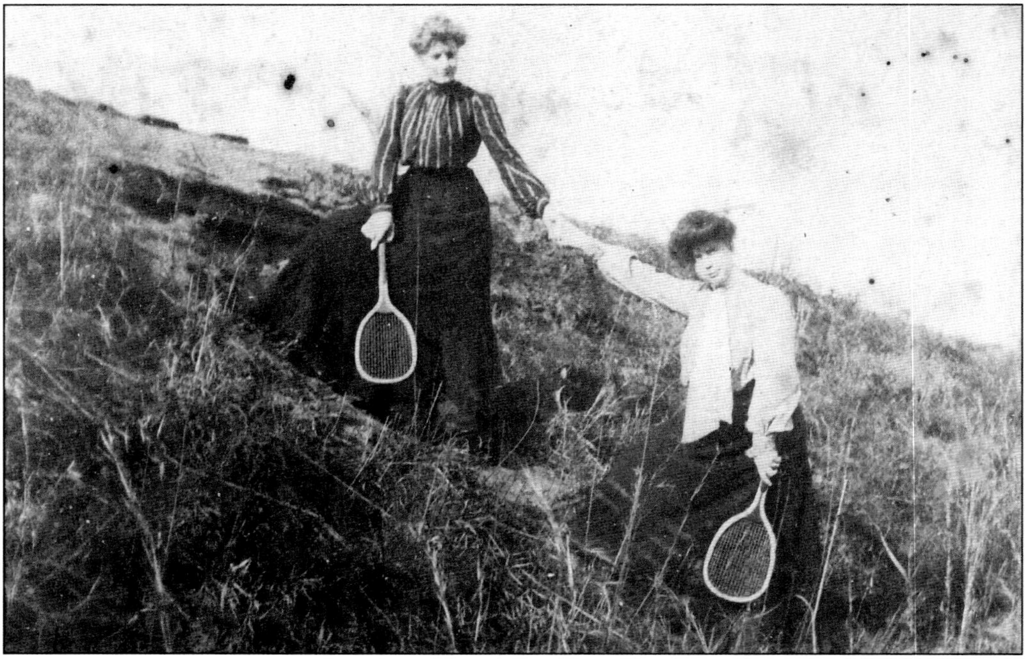

Two young women frolic in the countryside near the Jackson Springs Hotel after a game of tennis. Pictured in the lower right is Ila Blue, of Aberdeen.

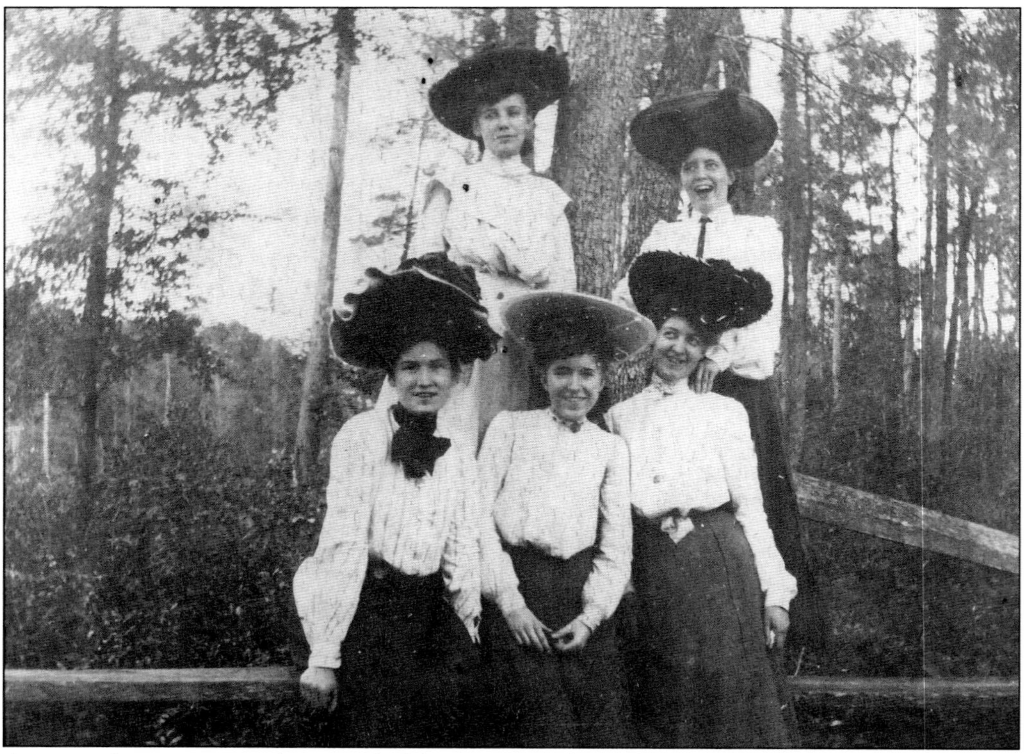

A group of women await the arrival of the train near the Jackson Springs Hotel. The completion of a spur line for the Aberdeen and Asheboro Railroad in 1900 spawned the construction of both summer and winter homes at the popular resort.

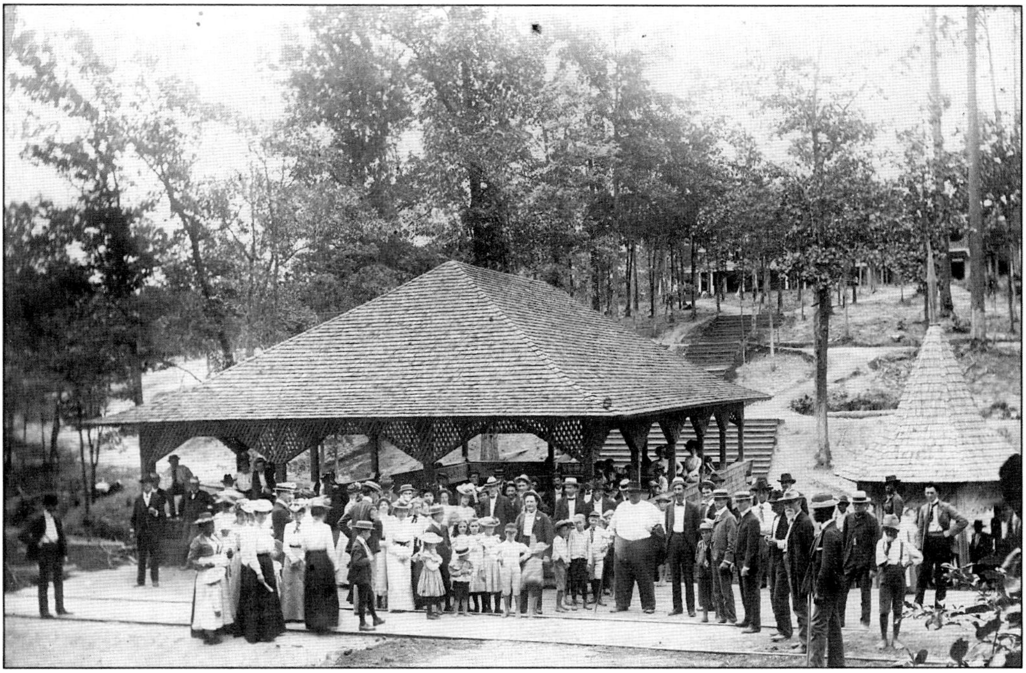

This 1901 photograph shows the main pavilion and train tracks in front of the Jackson Springs Hotel. Pictured are some of the hotel guests and staff, including Maude Angier, granddaughter of Washington B. Duke, and her future husband, William Alexander Blue, son of John Blue and later president of the Aberdeen and Rockfish Railroad, both standing on the train tracks behind the boy in the left foreground.

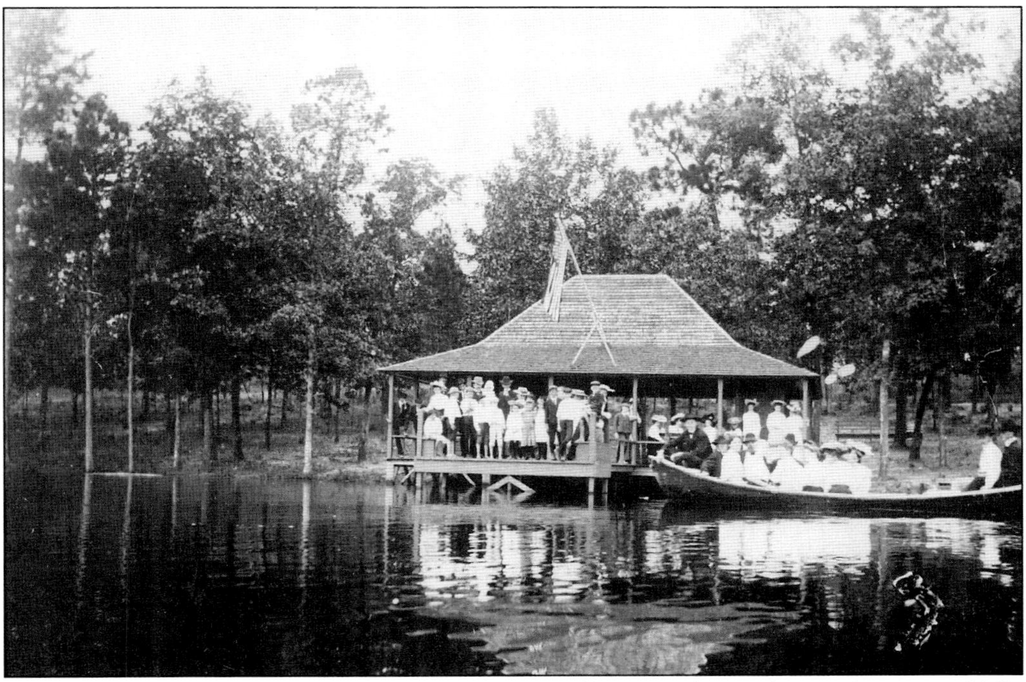

The lake was used for swimming and boating. Pictured here are the pavilion and a group of fully attired hotel guests in a boat during the summer of 1902.

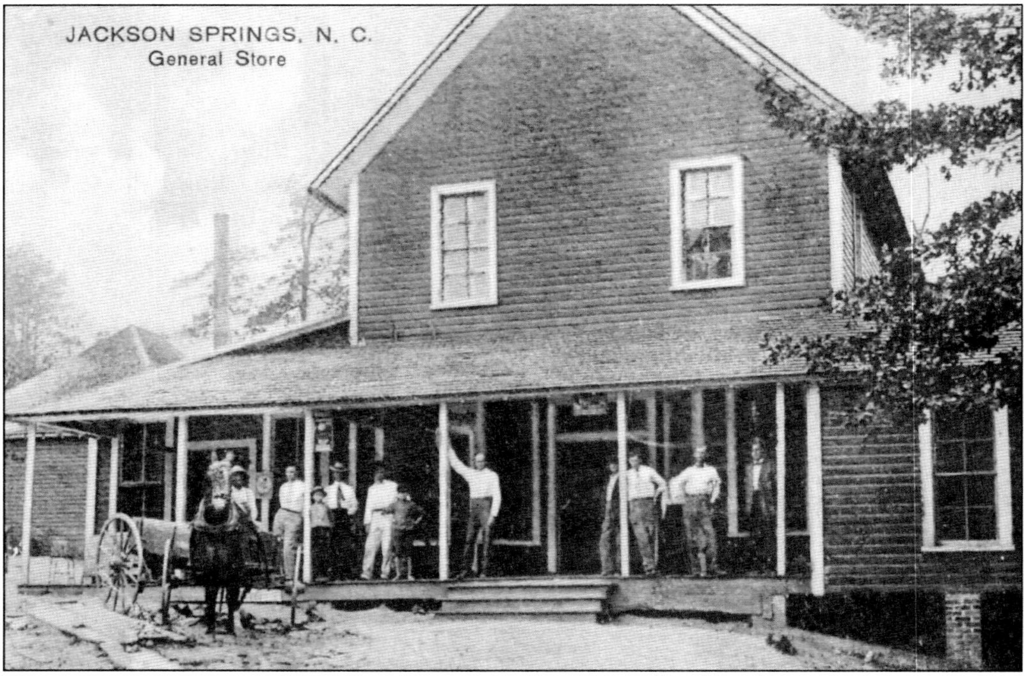

This is a late nineteenth-century photograph of the Jackson Springs General Store. The town of Jackson Springs was established in 1813.

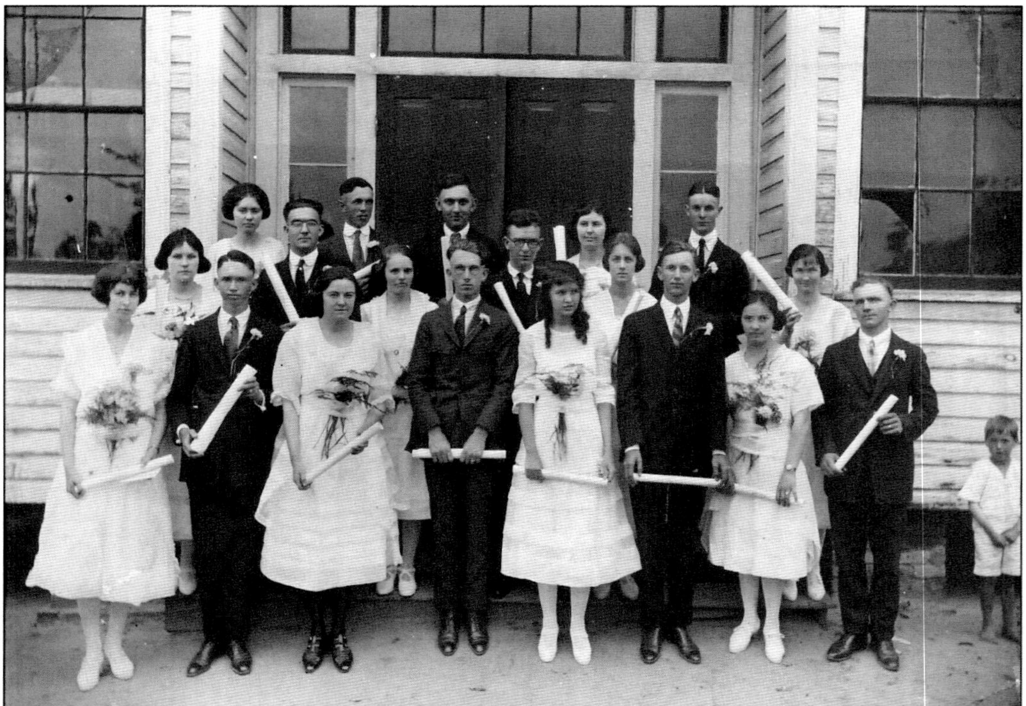

This is the 1922 graduating class of the Jackson Springs High School. The town had four schools in its long history, the most notable of which was the Jackson Springs Academy, founded by instructor Nevin Daniels Josephus Clark in 1858.

Six

SOUTHERN PINES

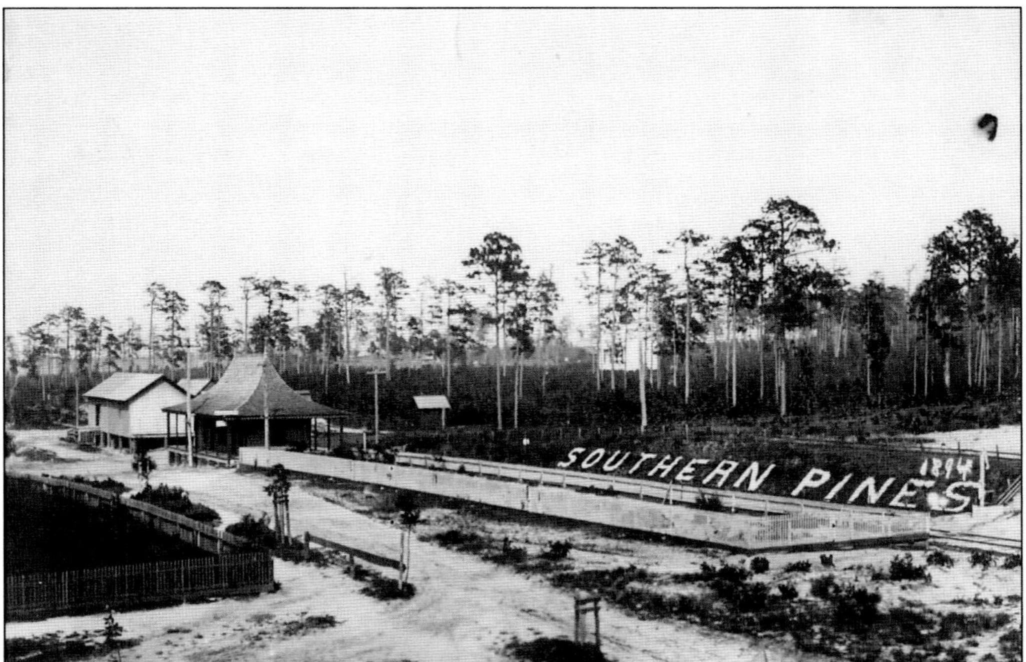

Southern Pines was founded by John T. Patrick in 1883 as a health resort. Pictured is the original Southern Pines Railroad Depot, with the Raleigh and Augusta Railroad (later the Seaboard Air Line Railroad) tracks visible in the center foreground.

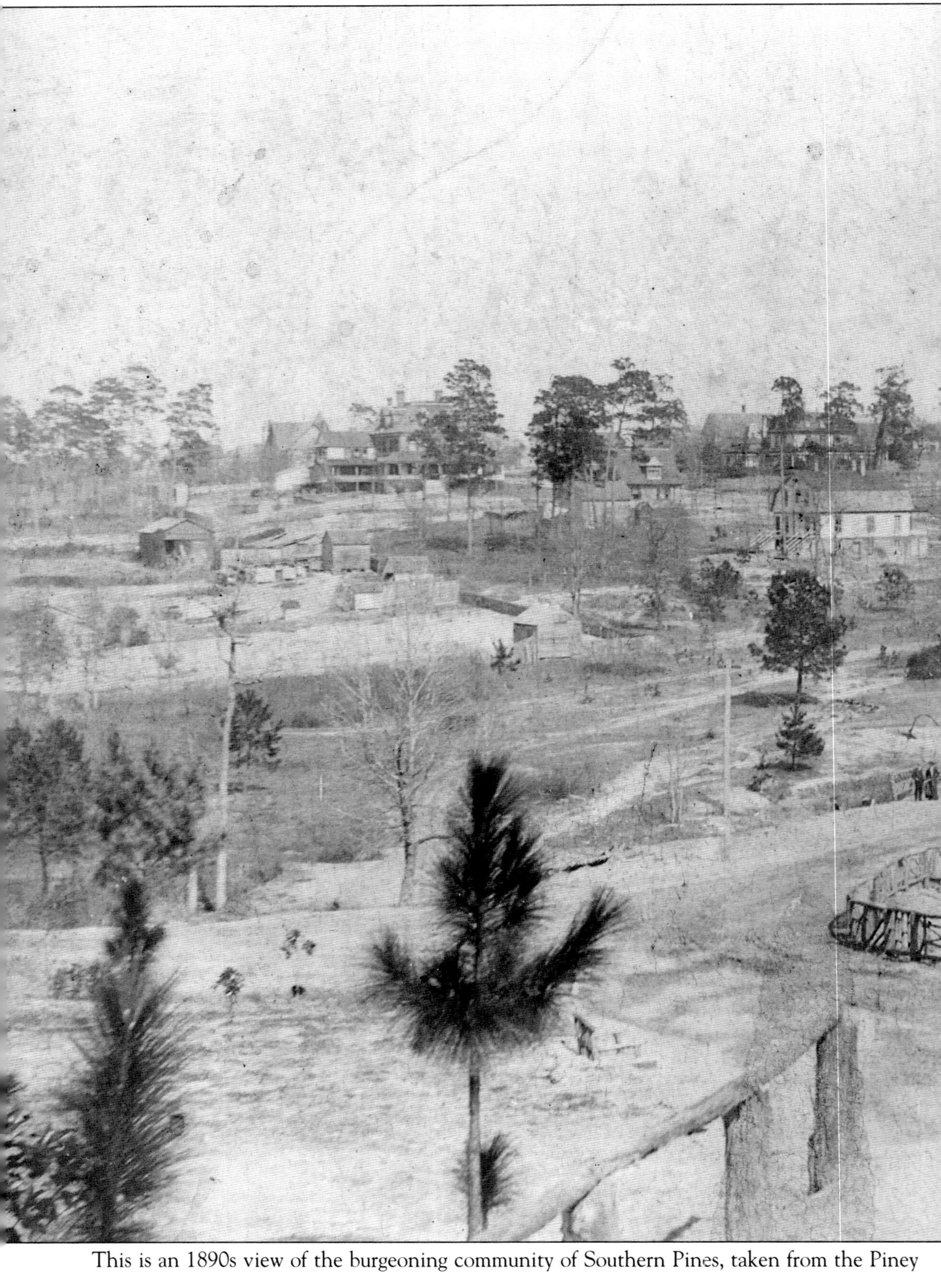

This is an 1890s view of the burgeoning community of Southern Pines, taken from the Piney

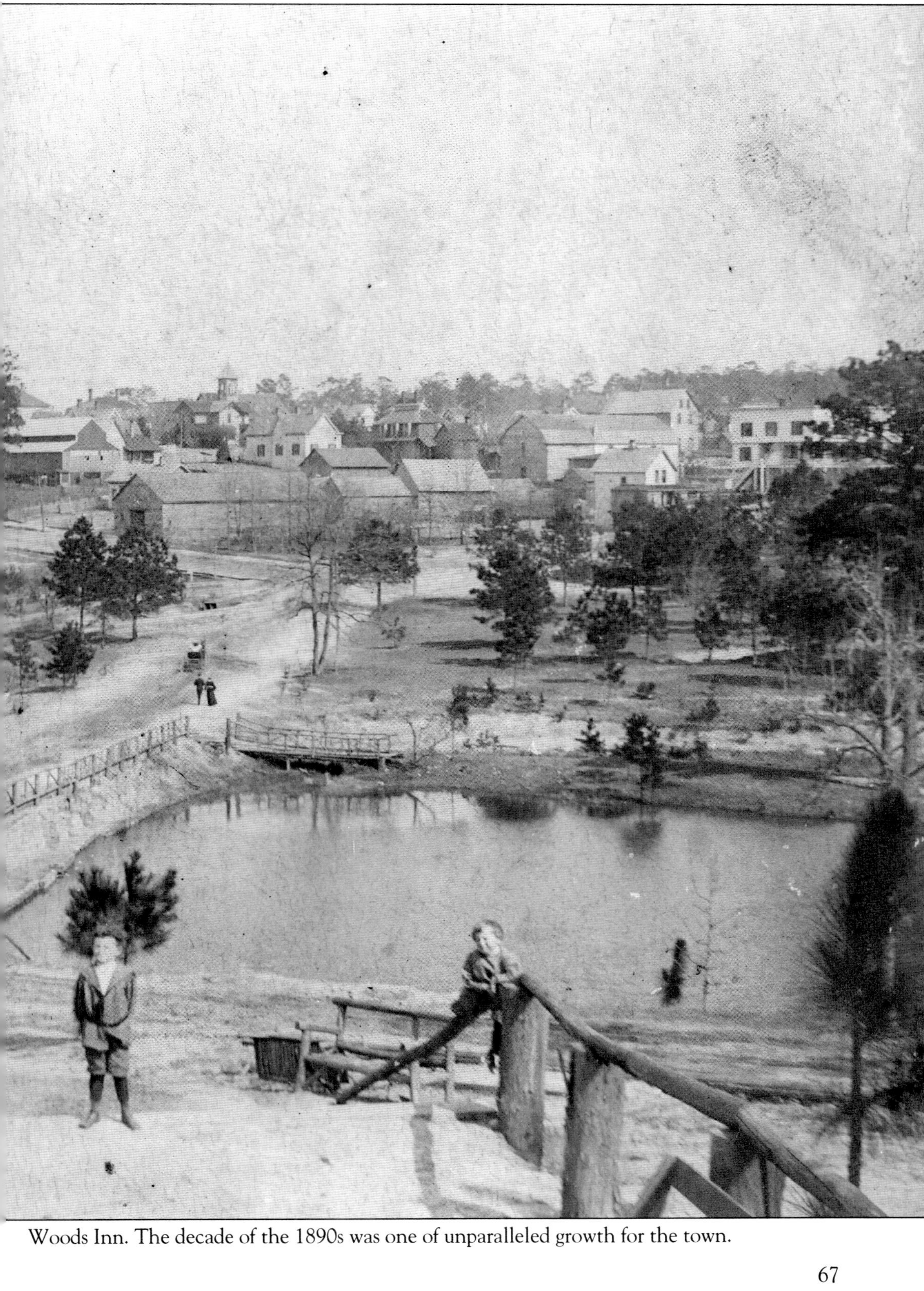

Woods Inn. The decade of the 1890s was one of unparalleled growth for the town.

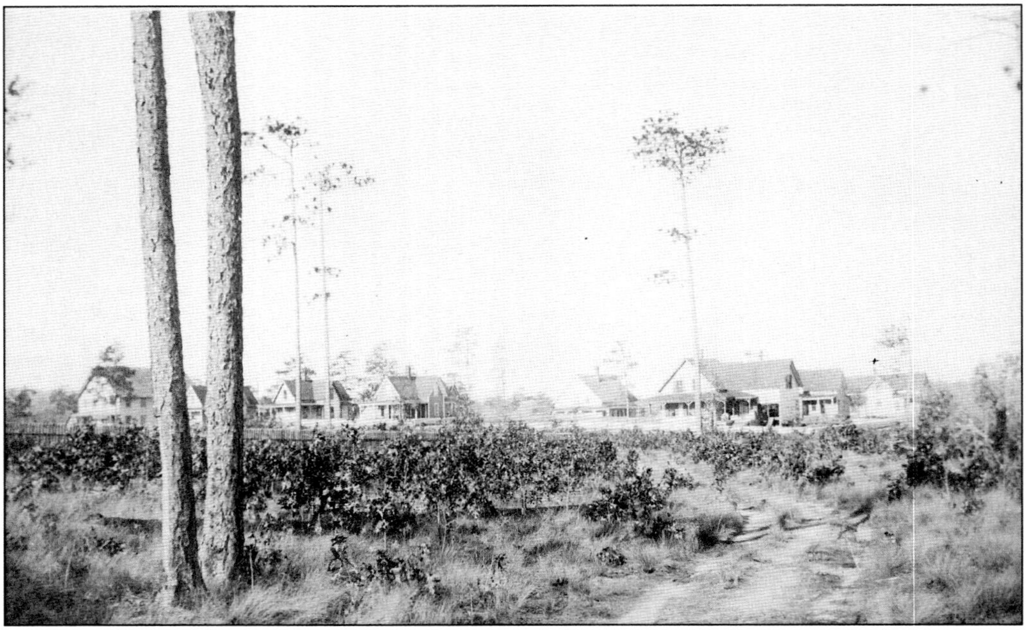

This is an 1880s view of some of Southern Pines' newly constructed residences.

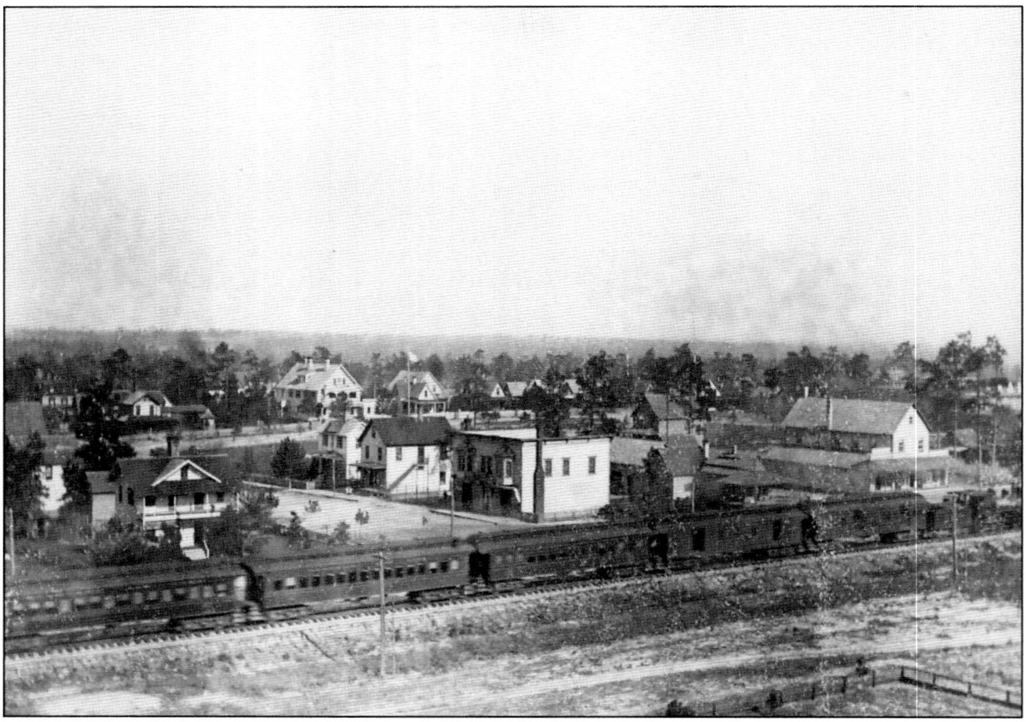

Pictured here are Railroad Street and West Pennsylvania Avenue. In the center foreground is the two-story Lorey Block, *c.* 1890. The gable-roofed, two-and-a-half-story Central Hotel is located a block behind it. Lorey Block, a richly ornamented Queen Anne-style building, was constructed in 1886.

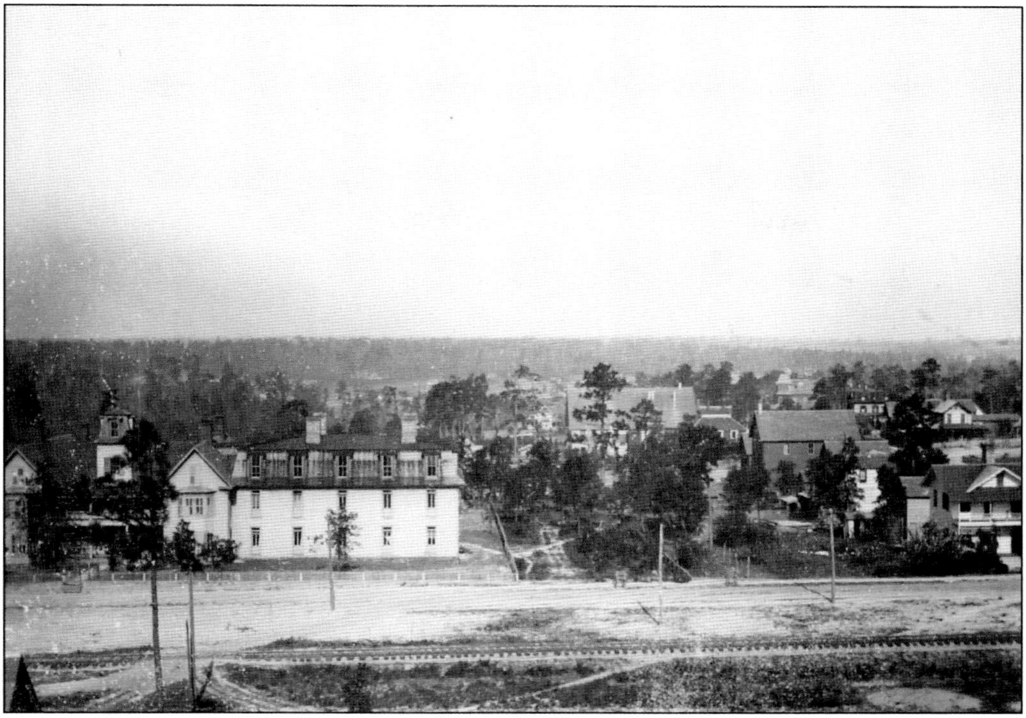

Pictured in the left foreground across Railroad Street is the large Southern Pines Hotel, which was built in 1887 and owned by Allison Page of nearby Aberdeen.

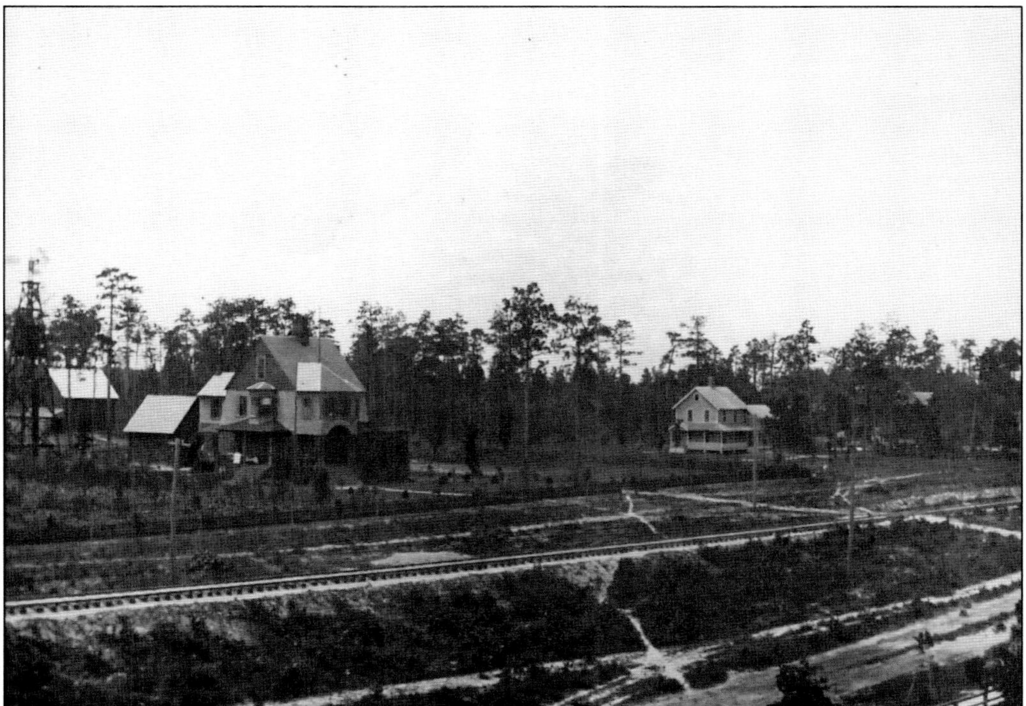

Pictured is the Dr. William P. Swett House, built *c.* 1893, at the corner of New York Avenue and Railroad Street. To the right is the Catlin-Calhoun House, built *c.* 1895.

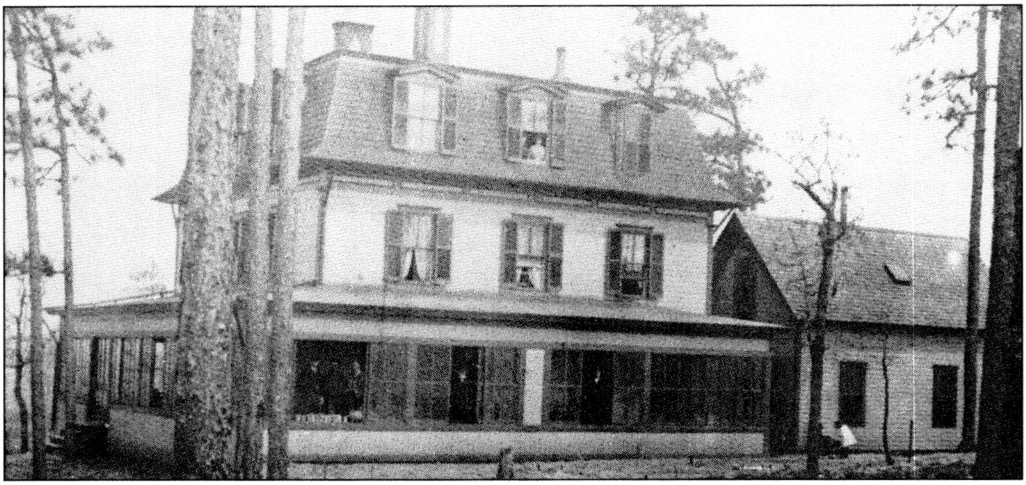

Prospect House was built in 1886 to house prospective settlers to Southern Pines. It was described by one northern newspaper as "one of the most cozy hotels it has been our good fortune to encounter," and a reporter predicted that the region would soon eclipse Florida as a health and winter resort.

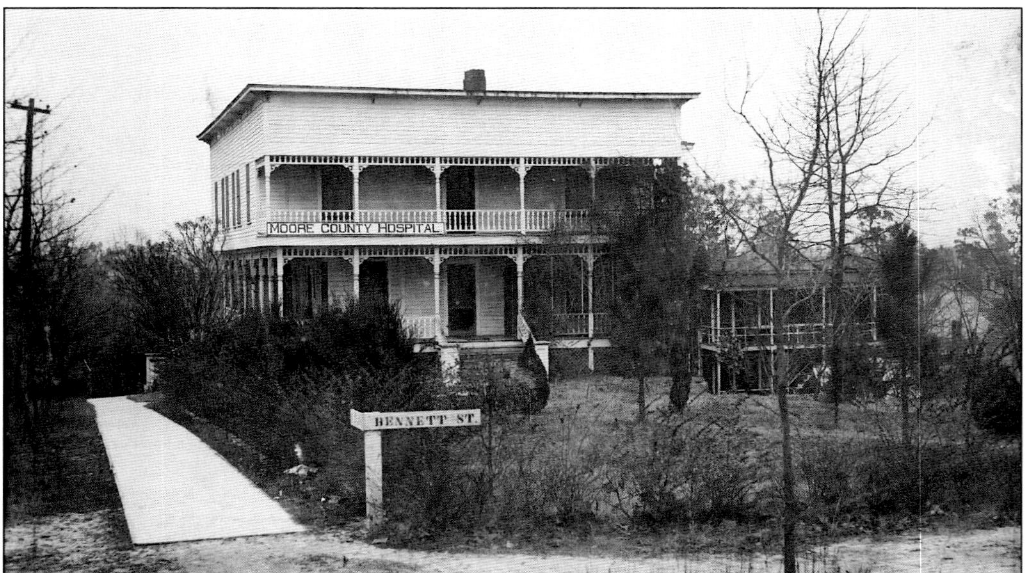

The Vermont House was built in 1897 as a boarding house to accommodate visitors from Vermont. Its name was later changed to New England House, and in 1911, it become the first Moore County Hospital.

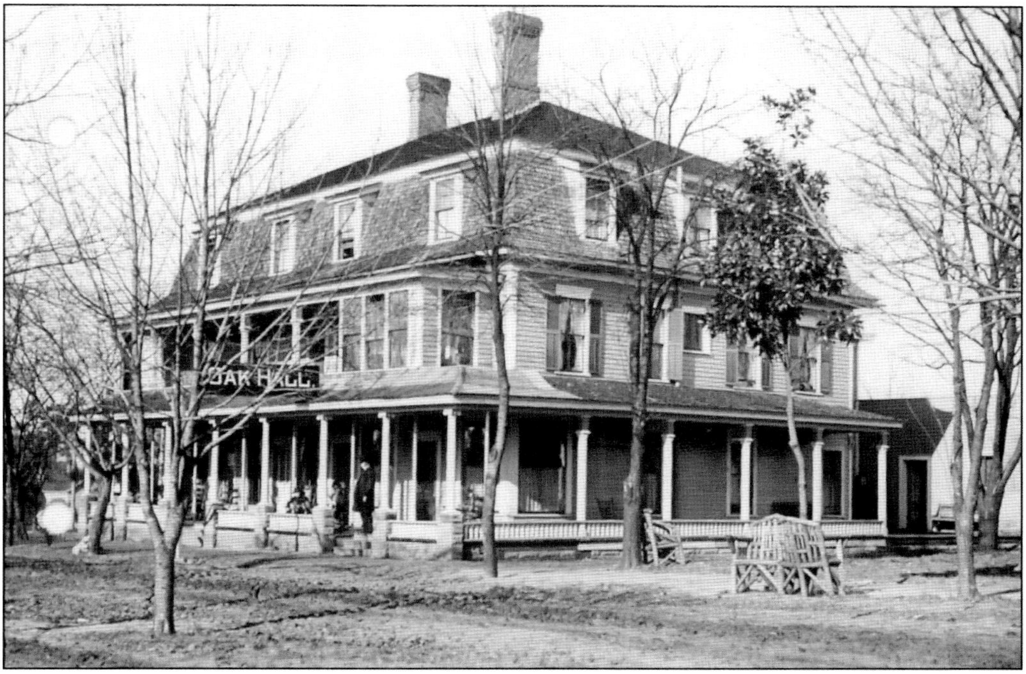

Oak Hall was built in 1890 as the Ozone Hotel and was renamed the Southland after an extensive renovation.

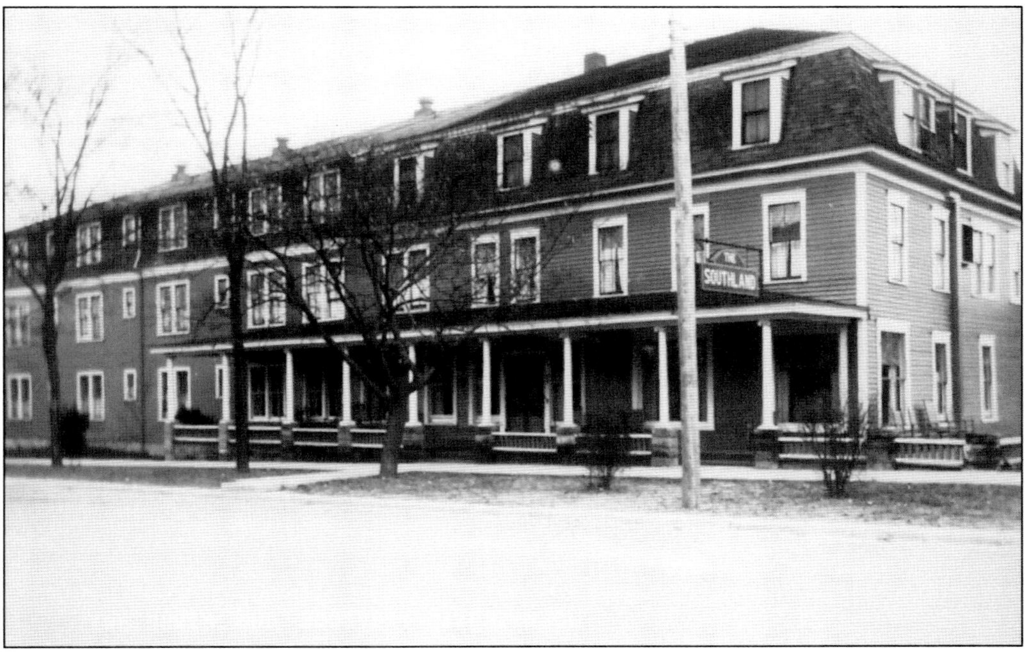

This is a picture of the Southland, taken after the name had changed from the Ozone Hotel.

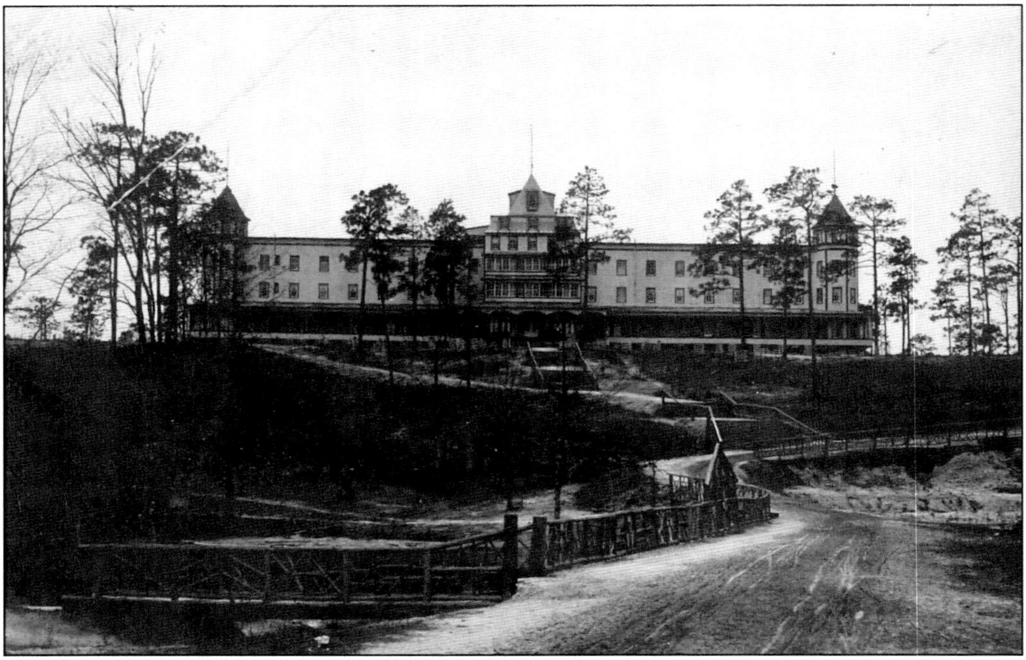

The Piney Woods Inn was built in 1895 on the center of a 50-acre tract that John Patrick had set aside for recreational use. Its large size and imposing facade marked the beginning of a new era for the town.

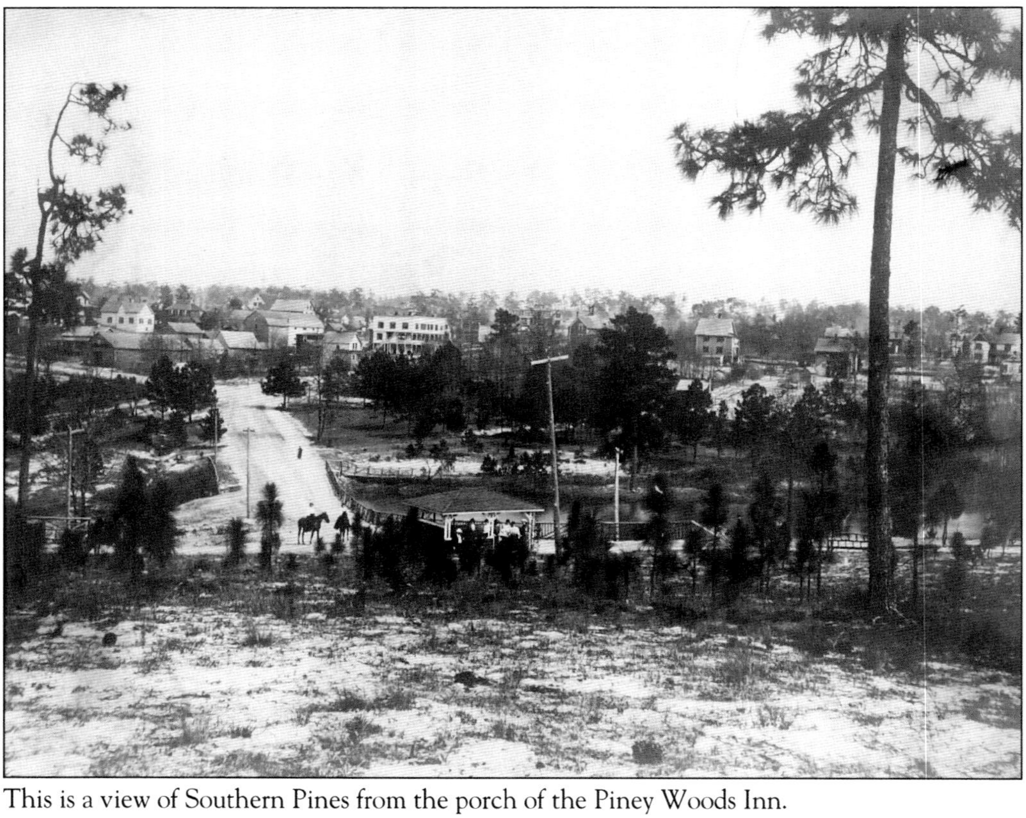

This is a view of Southern Pines from the porch of the Piney Woods Inn.

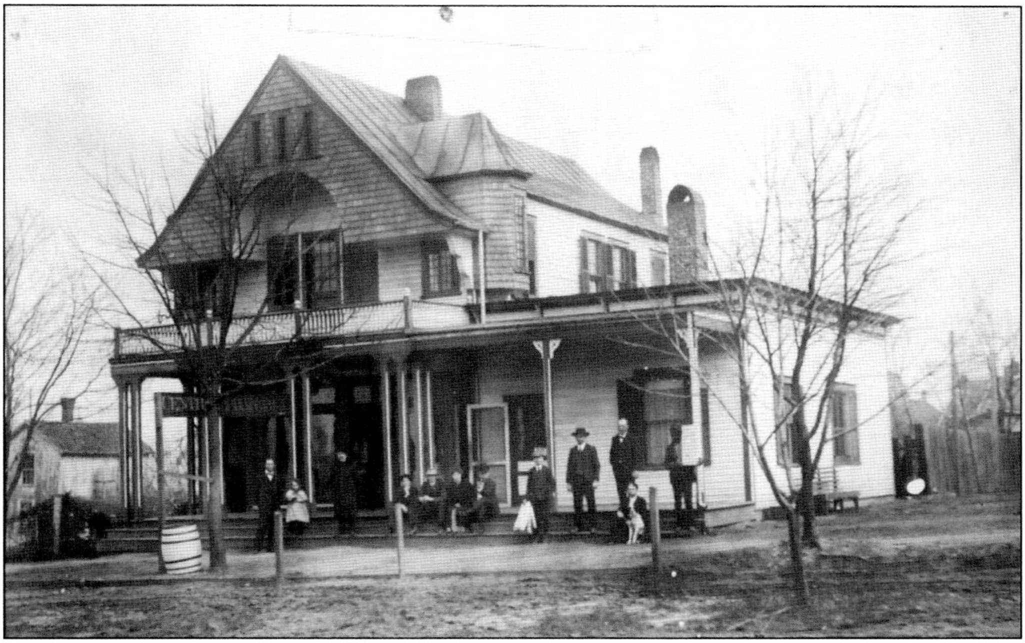

The Johnson Building was constructed in 1898, and it originally served as Ordway's Drygoods Store. After 1896, it housed a pharmacy operated by Dr. Alice Johnson and was for a brief time the Southern Pines Police Station.

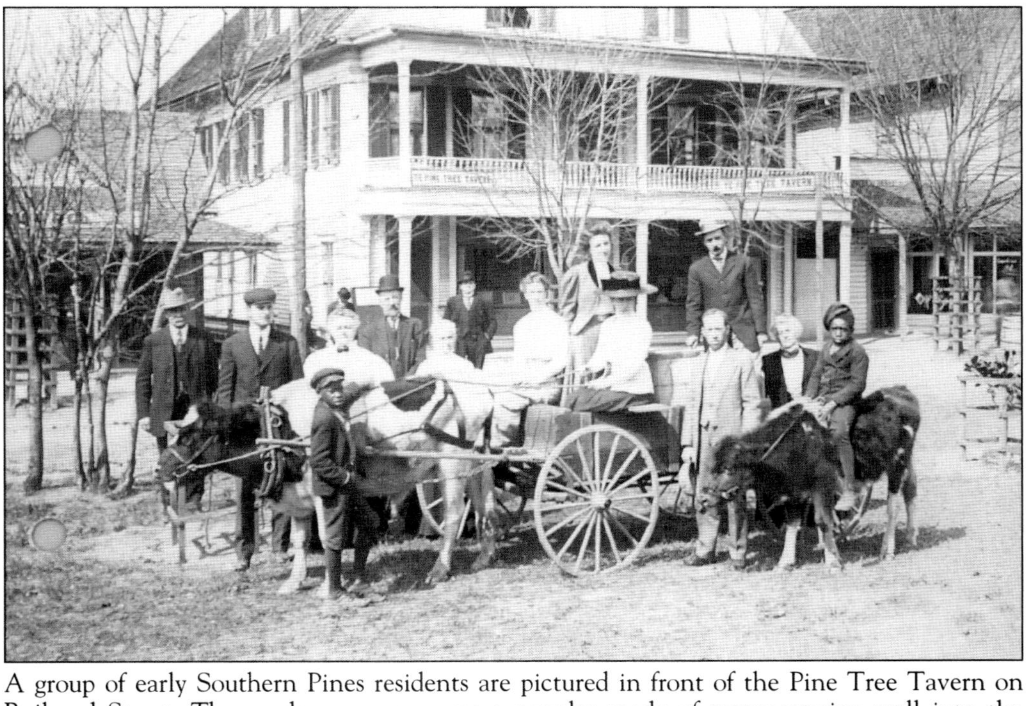

A group of early Southern Pines residents are pictured in front of the Pine Tree Tavern on Railroad Street. The ox-drawn wagon was a popular mode of transportation well into the twentieth century.

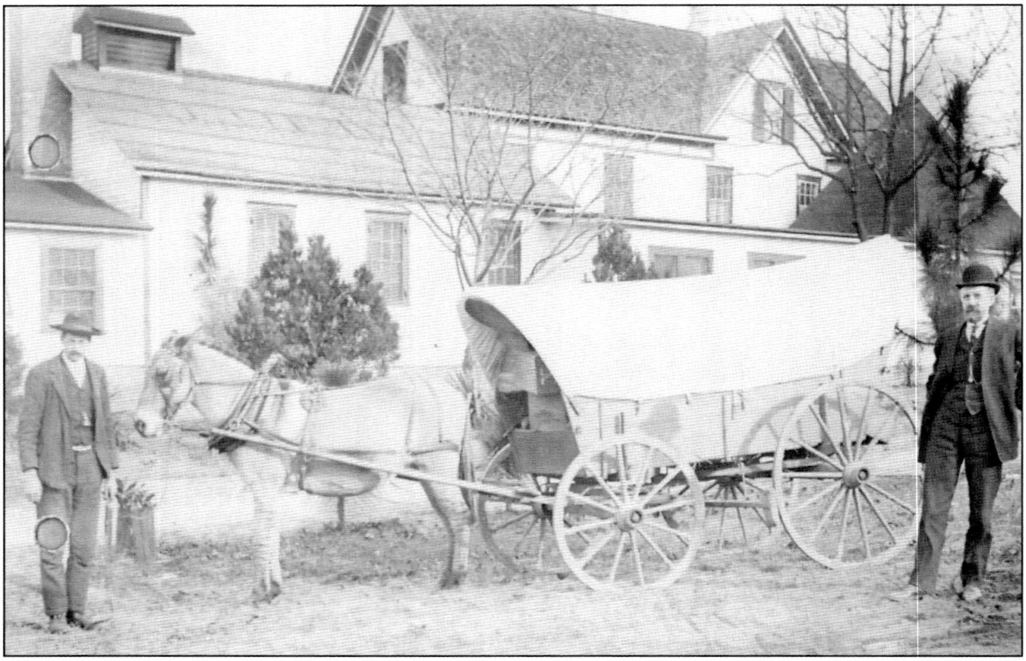

Schooners were used to transport a variety of goods, including farm produce, furniture, and dry goods. Pictured is Bradley Garner in the right foreground with his "pink mule" standing in front of one of Southern Pine's early residences.

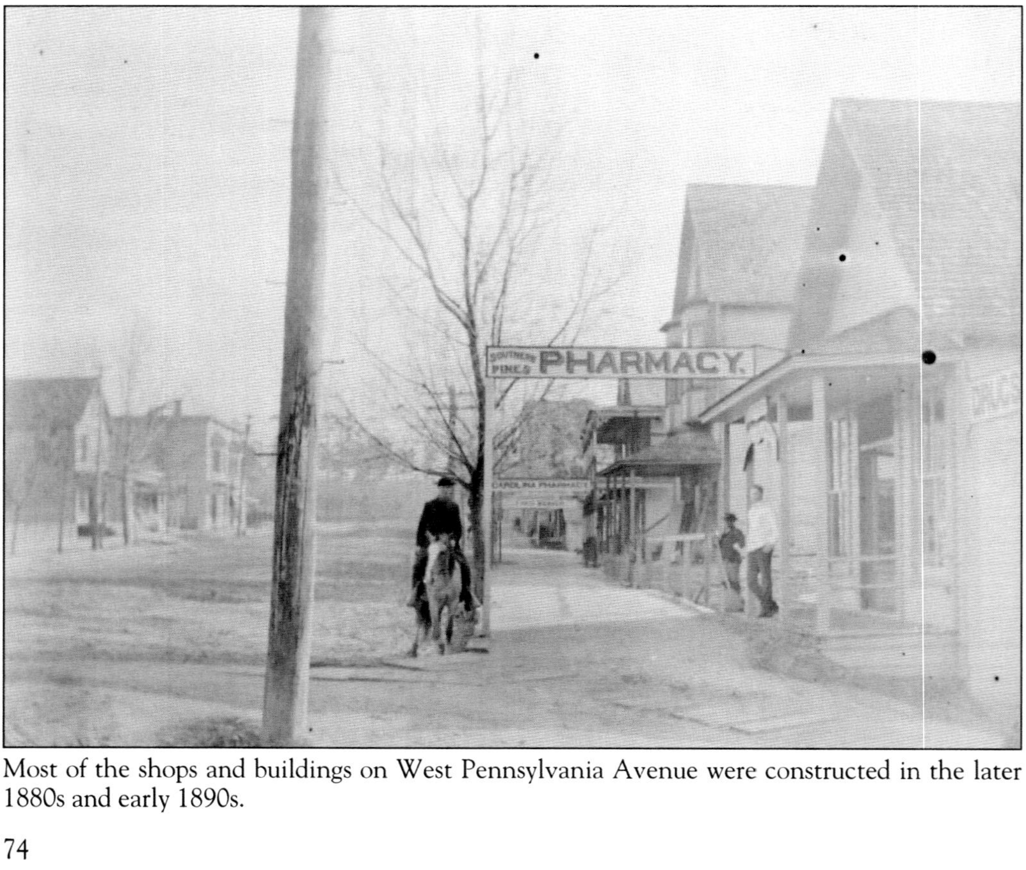

Most of the shops and buildings on West Pennsylvania Avenue were constructed in the later 1880s and early 1890s.

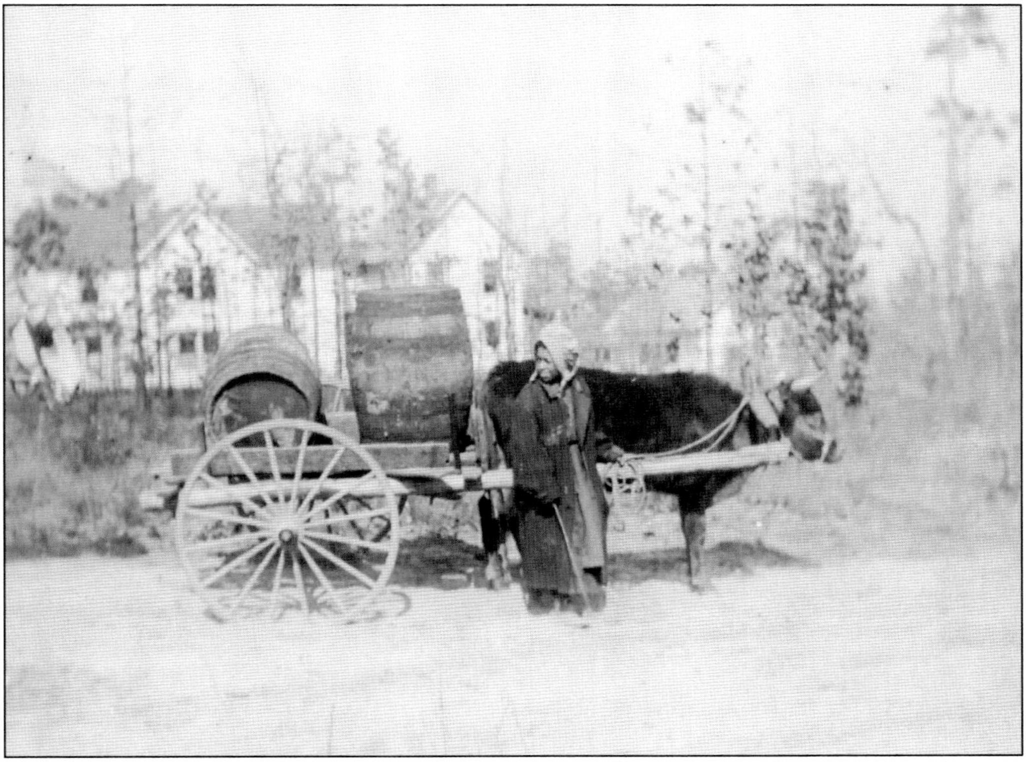

This young woman was photographed in front of an ox-drawn cart on East Vermont Avenue, with the Highland Lodge in the background. The lodge was built as a residence in 1897 and was converted into a boarding house in 1902.

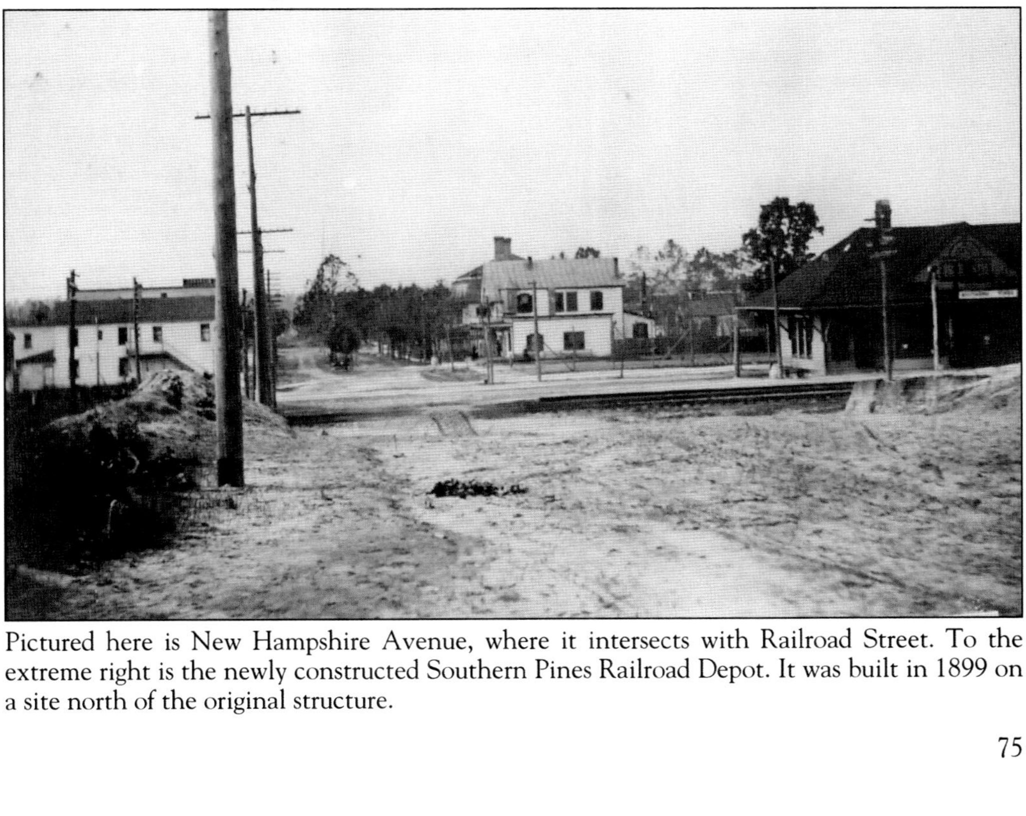

Pictured here is New Hampshire Avenue, where it intersects with Railroad Street. To the extreme right is the newly constructed Southern Pines Railroad Depot. It was built in 1899 on a site north of the original structure.

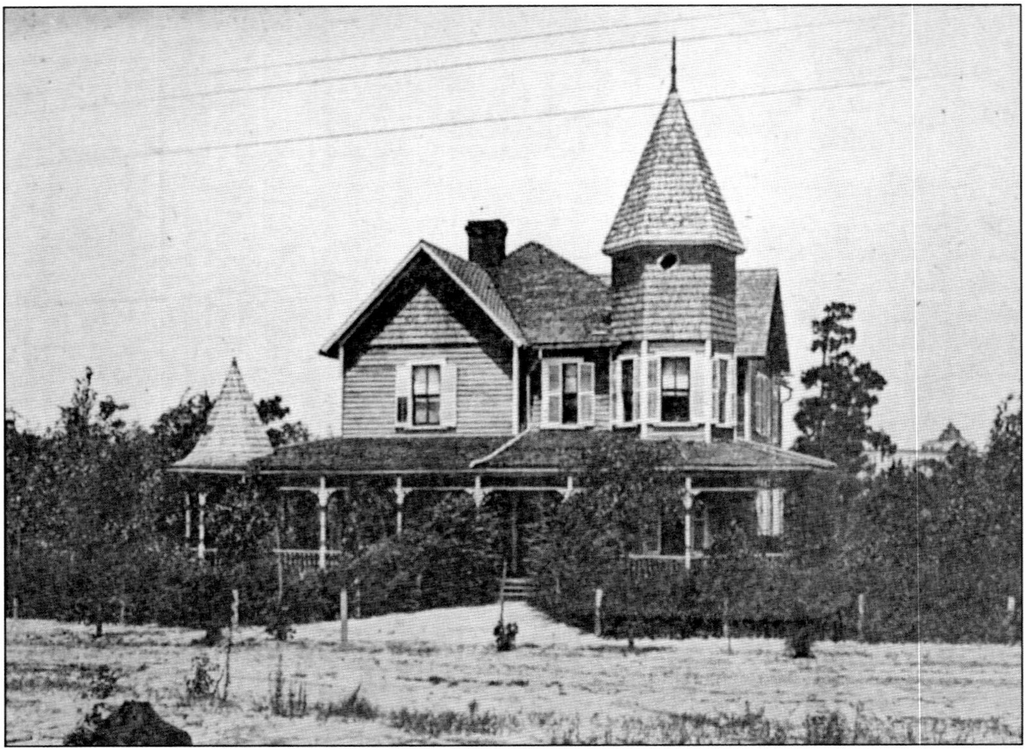

The Ferguson House was built in 1895 on Railroad Street for Dr. M.K. Ferguson, one of a handful of early doctors who moved to Southern Pines both to practice medicine and to enjoy the benefits of a health resort. Ferguson later became mayor of Southern Pines.

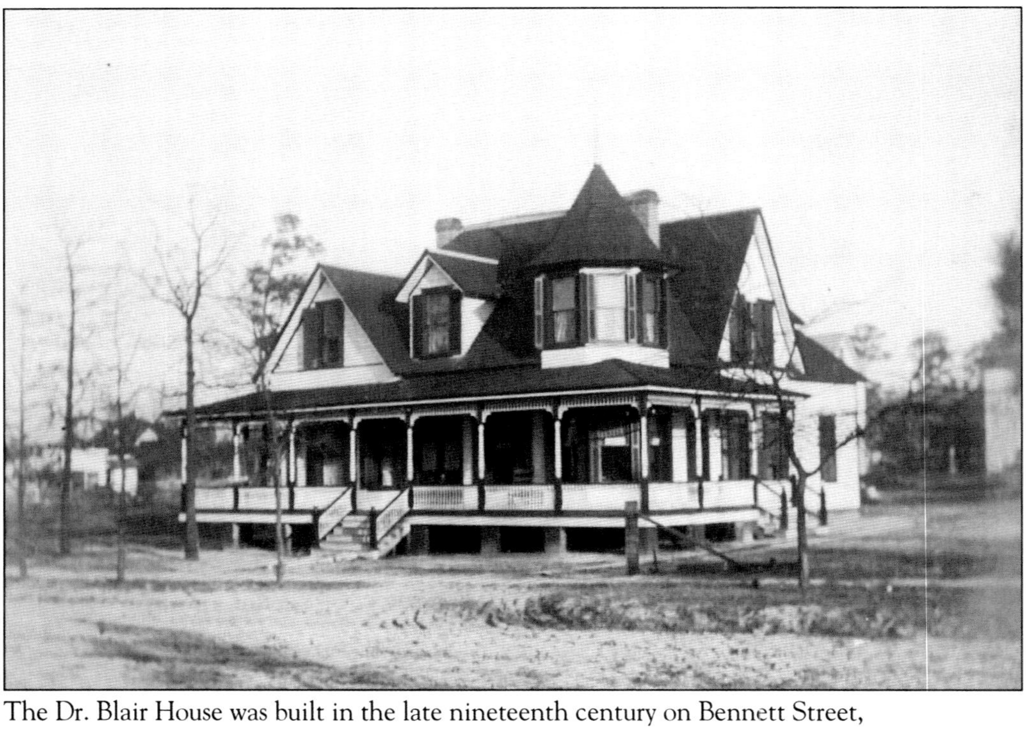

The Dr. Blair House was built in the late nineteenth century on Bennett Street,

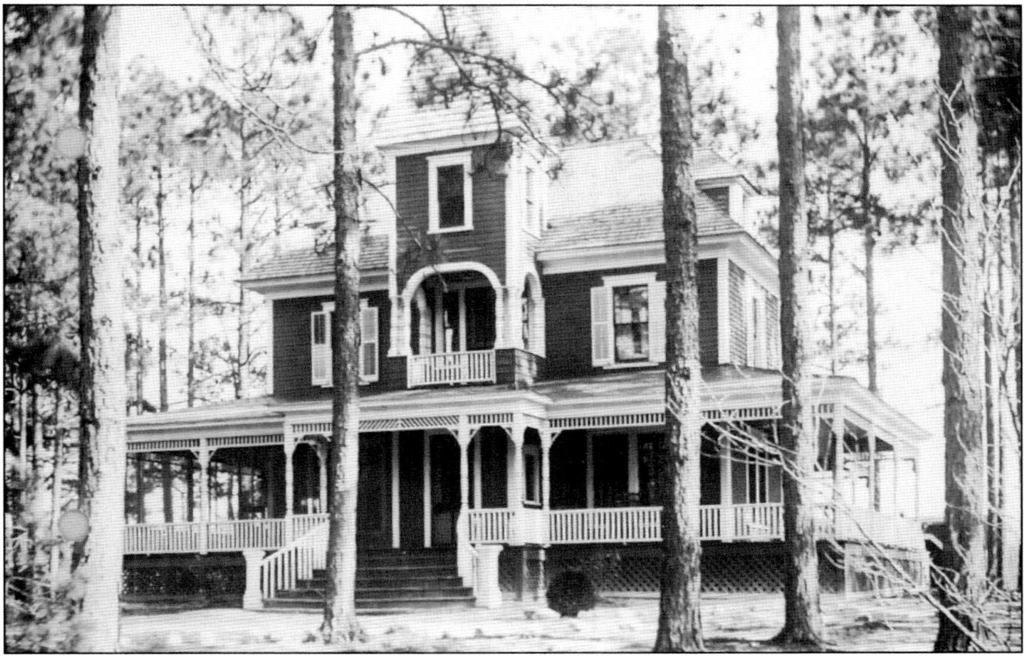

The Dr. Lasker House is pictured here, *c*. 1900.

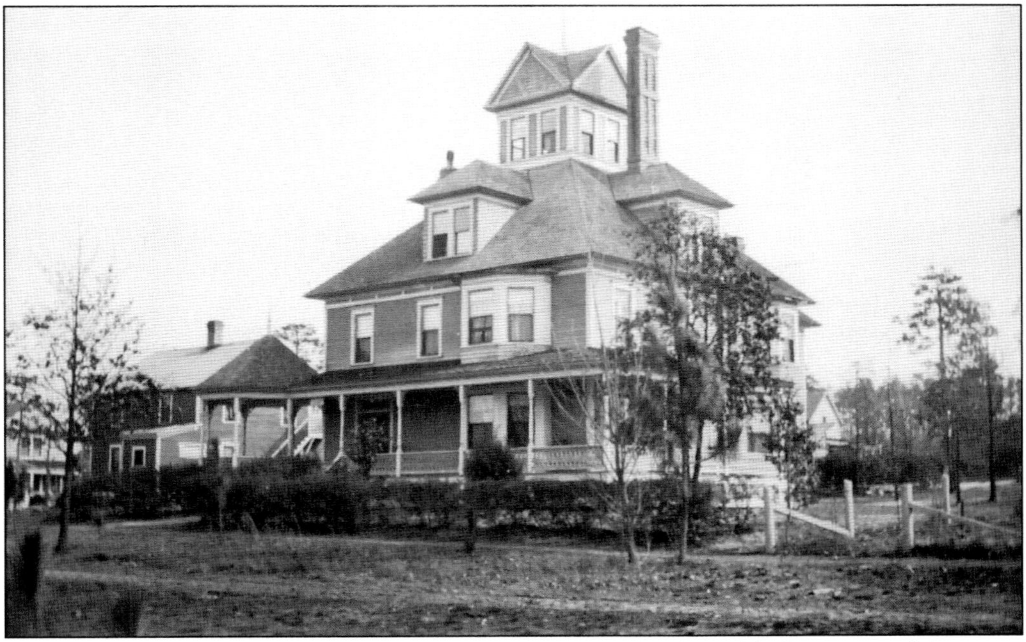

Mount Vernon was built in 1902 on Ashe Street and was clearly visible from most of the town. It served as an early boarding house.

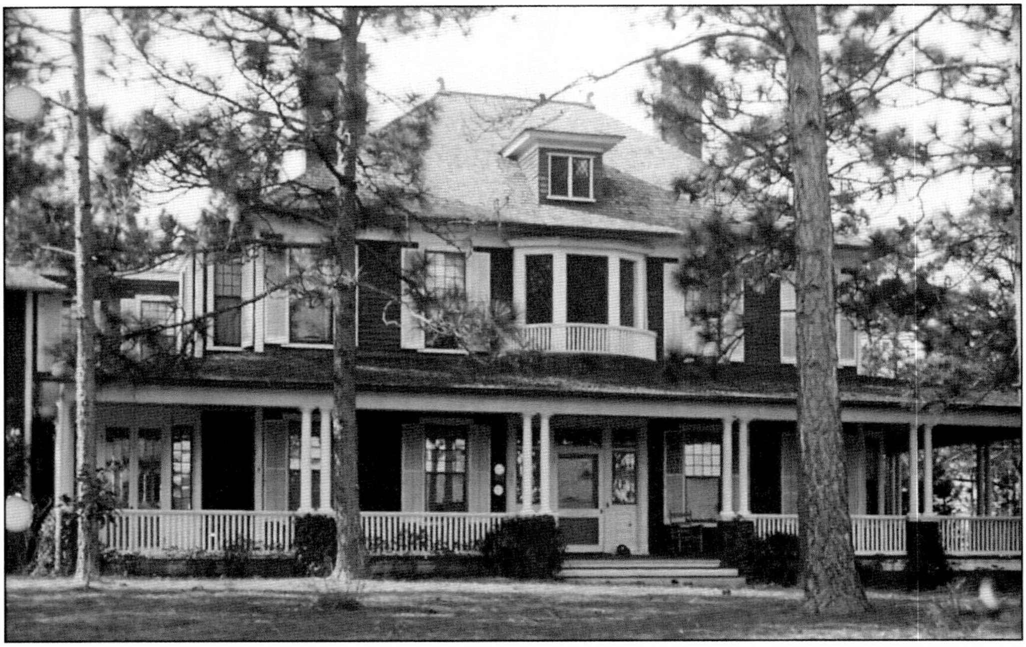

Weymouth Woods was built in 1905 for James Boyd, a retired Pennsylvania industrialist and grandfather of author James Boyd, on a 2,500-acre tract overlooking Southern Pines. Boyd played an instrumental role in the early affairs of the community and was largely responsible for the development of the Weymouth Heights subdivision. The house was replaced in 1922 by a much larger structure.

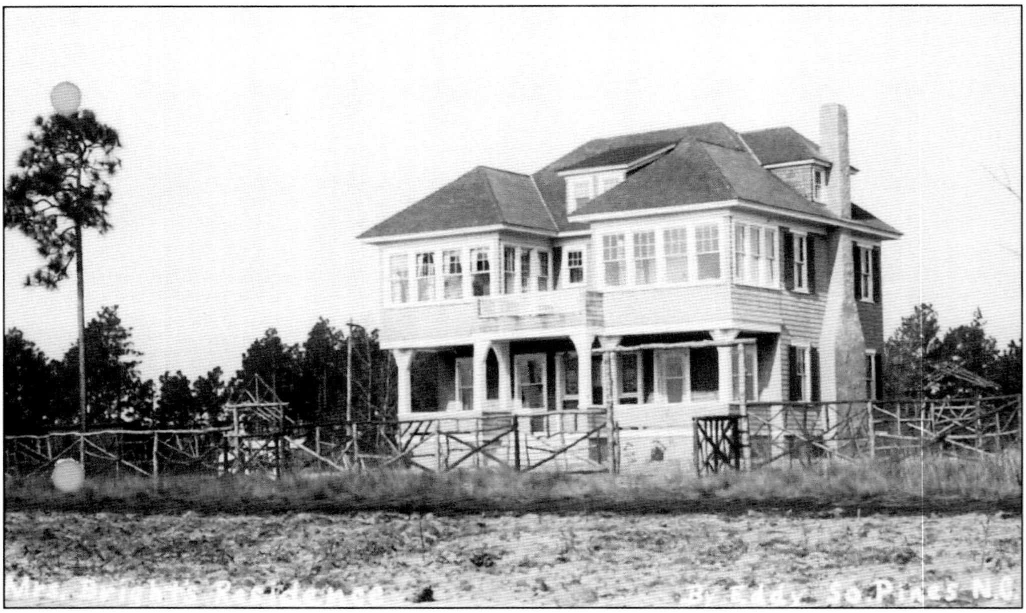

Pictured here is Mrs. Brights' house on South Ridge Street, *c.* 1900.

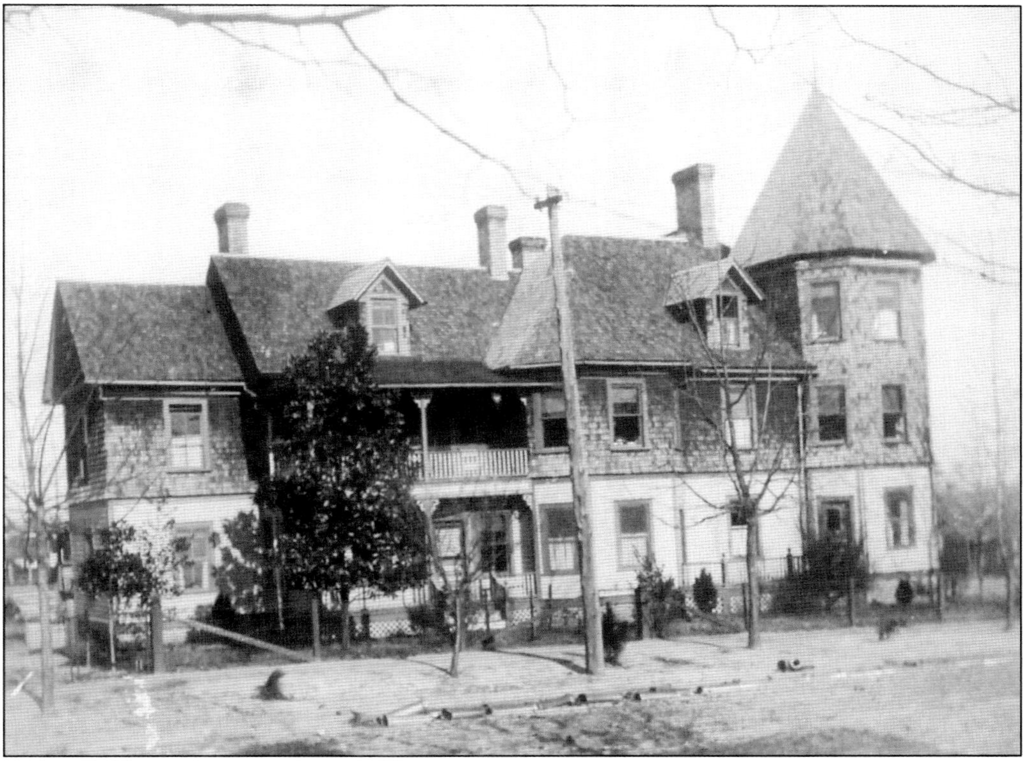

The Essex House was an early boarding house. Its shingled-style was a popular feature of many homes in Southern Pines.

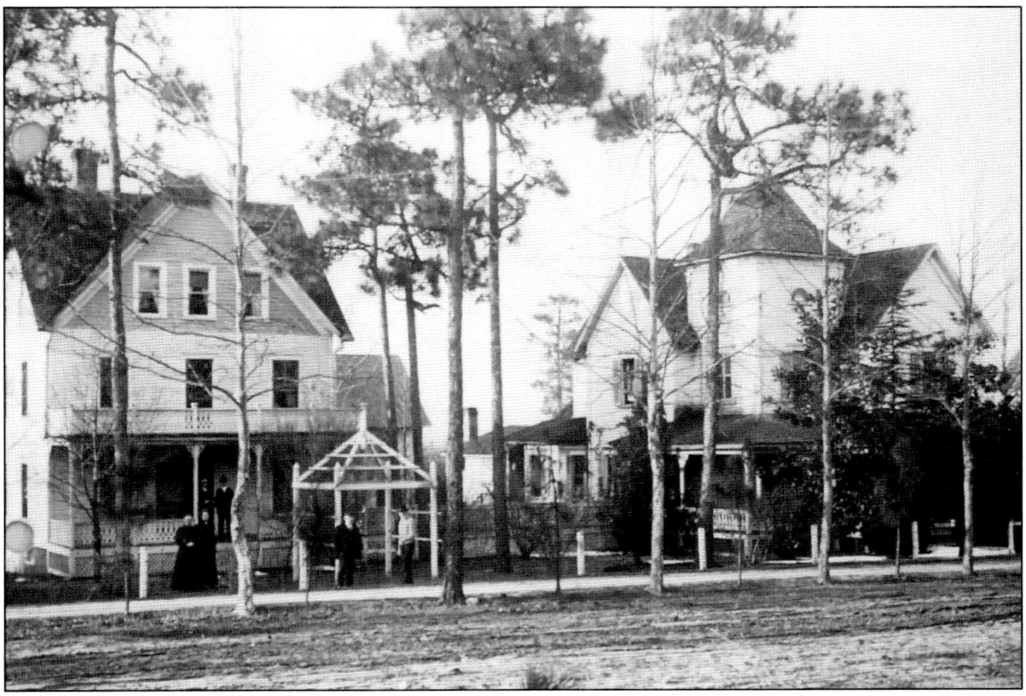

Pictured here are two early boarding houses on North Ashe Street.

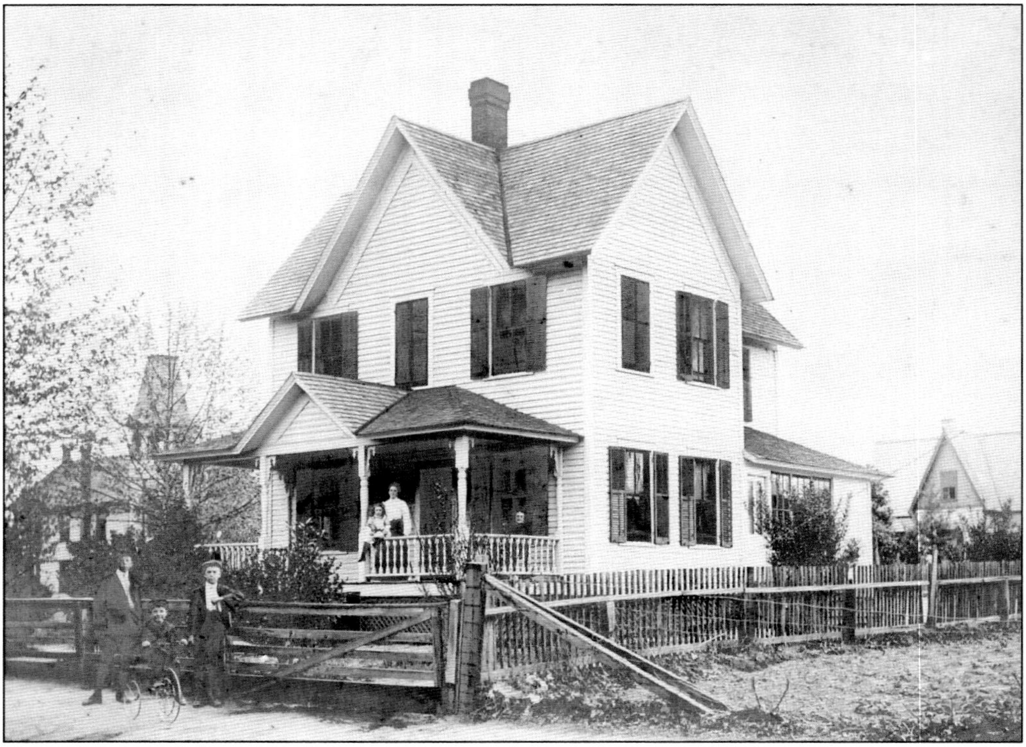

The parsonage of the Congregational church was built in 1896 on North Bennett Street for the church's first minister, the Reverend George R. Ransom. Pictured is the family of a later owner, William Goldsmith. In the left background is the King's Daughters' Hall, a community center which also served as an early school, library, and clubhouse.

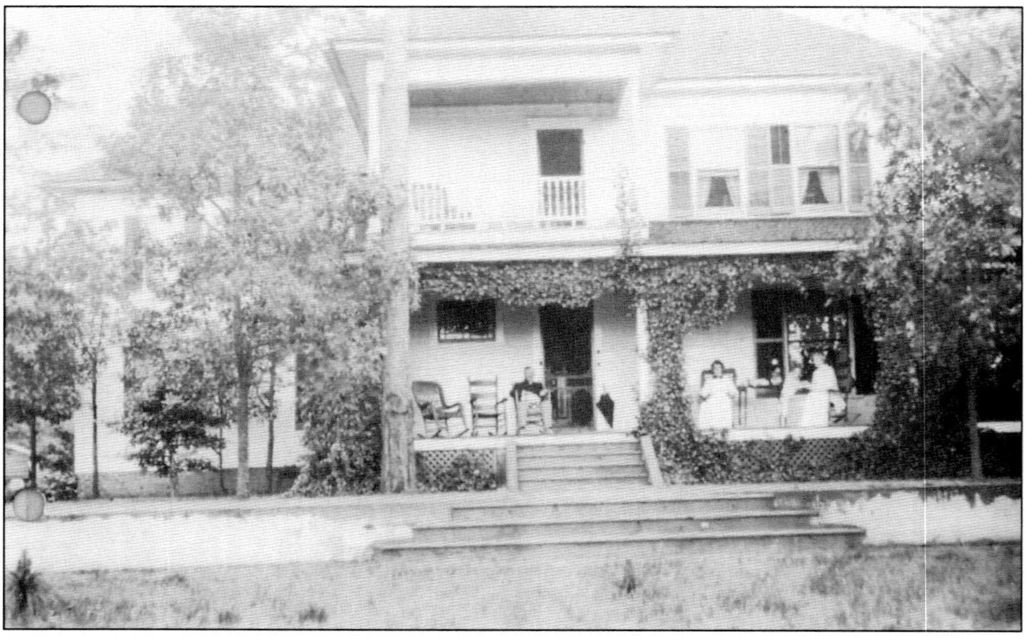

Burleigh Corner was constructed in 1906 on North May Street for Gilman Burleigh as a winter home. It was later opened as a boarding house.

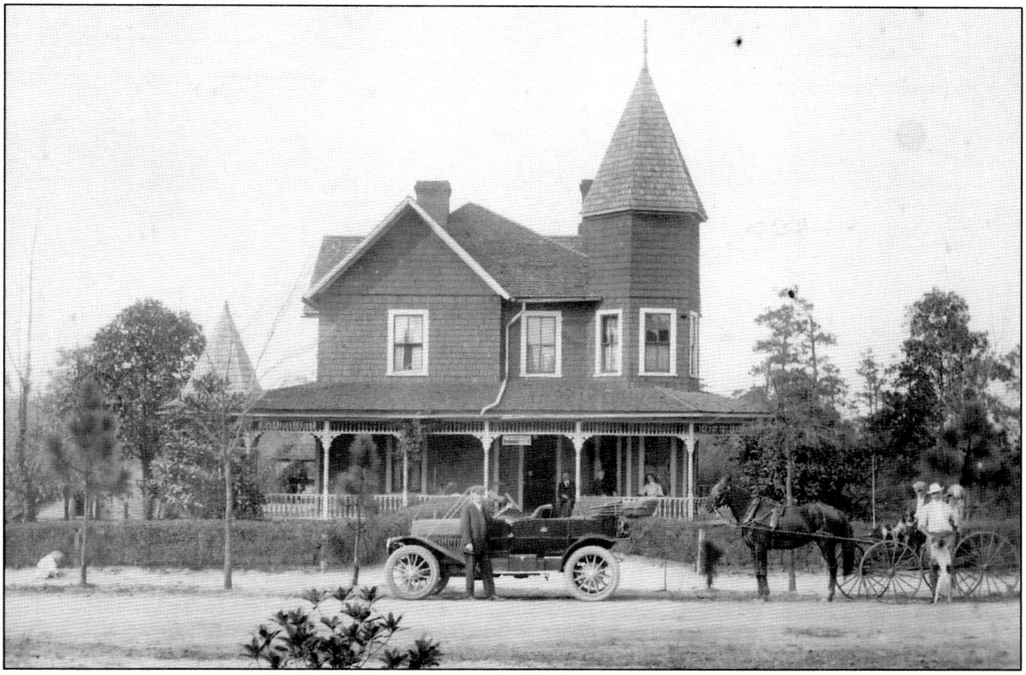

The New Haven House was built in the 1890s as a boarding house on Railroad Street. It was later used as a funeral home.

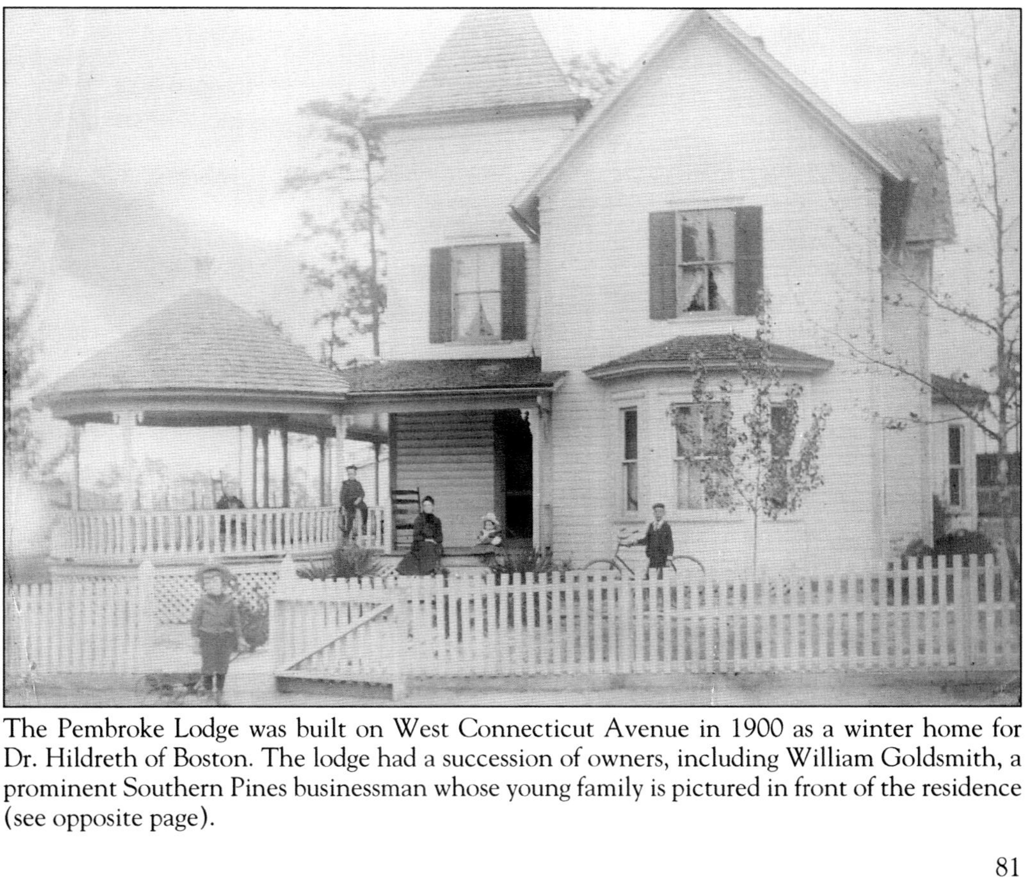

The Pembroke Lodge was built on West Connecticut Avenue in 1900 as a winter home for Dr. Hildreth of Boston. The lodge had a succession of owners, including William Goldsmith, a prominent Southern Pines businessman whose young family is pictured in front of the residence (see opposite page).

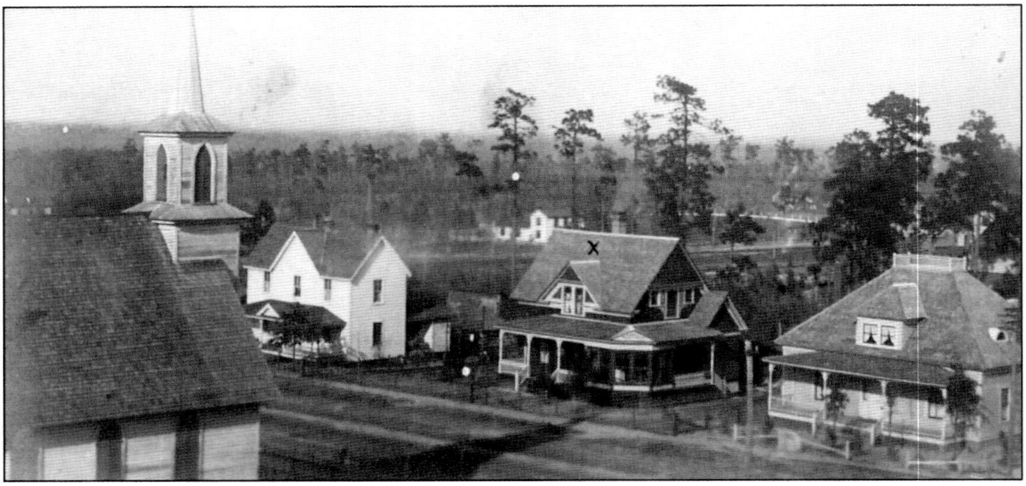

This is a 1905 view of East Vermont Avenue. Pictured in the center of the photograph is "Kandanarque," the resort cottage of Mrs. Vida Southerland from Kandanarque, New York.

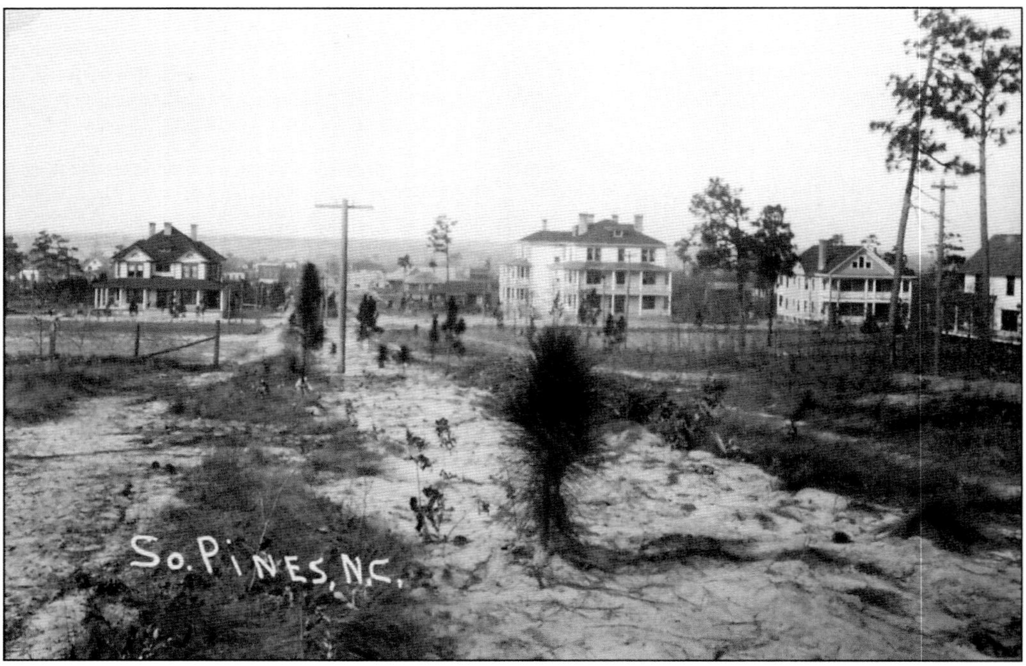

This is a view of North May Street, with the two Gould Apartment Buildings in the center of the photograph. The large frame structures were designed by Southern Pines architect Walter Flower.

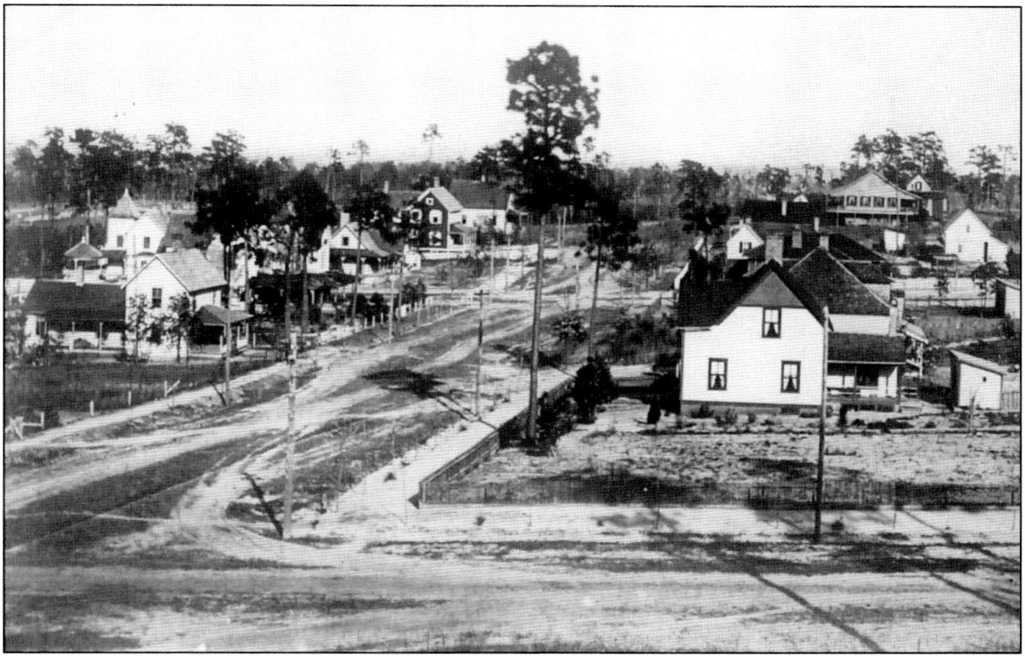

A 1904 photograph shows four residential blocks in west Southern Pines, with the tower of the Pembroke Lodge visible in the left of the picture. Most of the early homes were surrounded by fenced enclosures with outhouses.

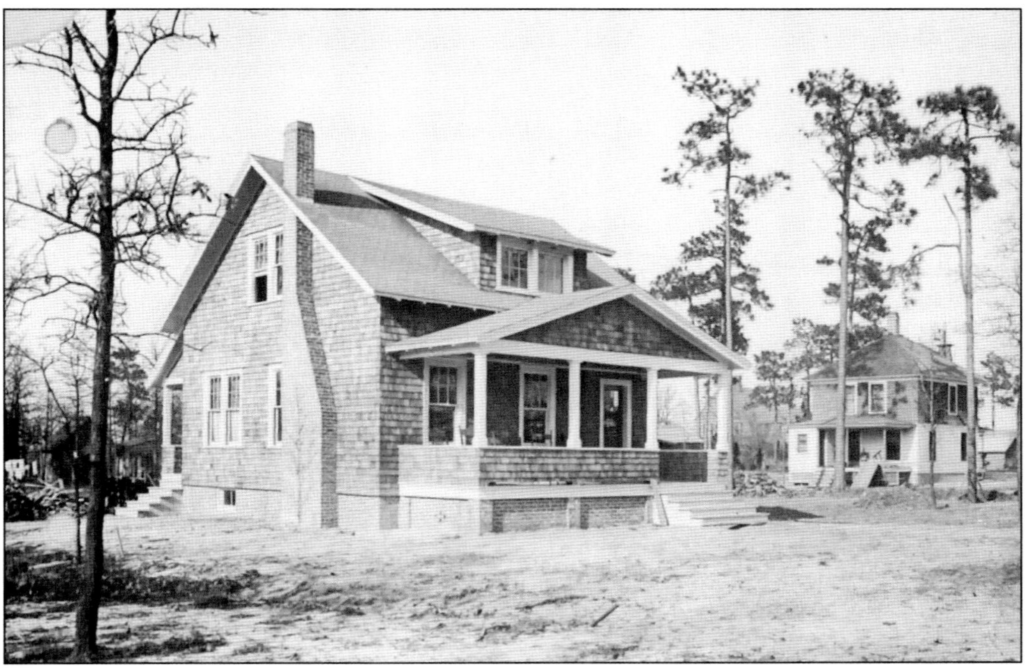

This photograph displays the newly constructed Walker and Merrill Houses on Ashe Street.

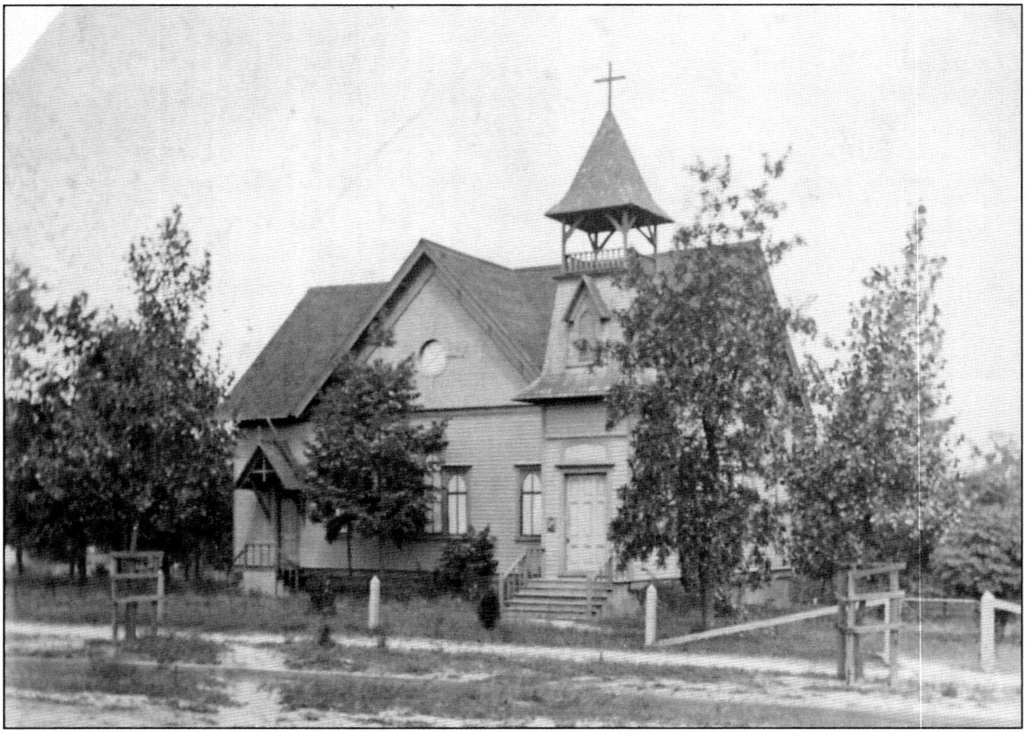

Emmanuel Episcopal Church, on the corner of Page Street and New Hampshire Avenue, was constructed in 1893 and was open only four to five months of the year. It was the first church built in Southern Pines.

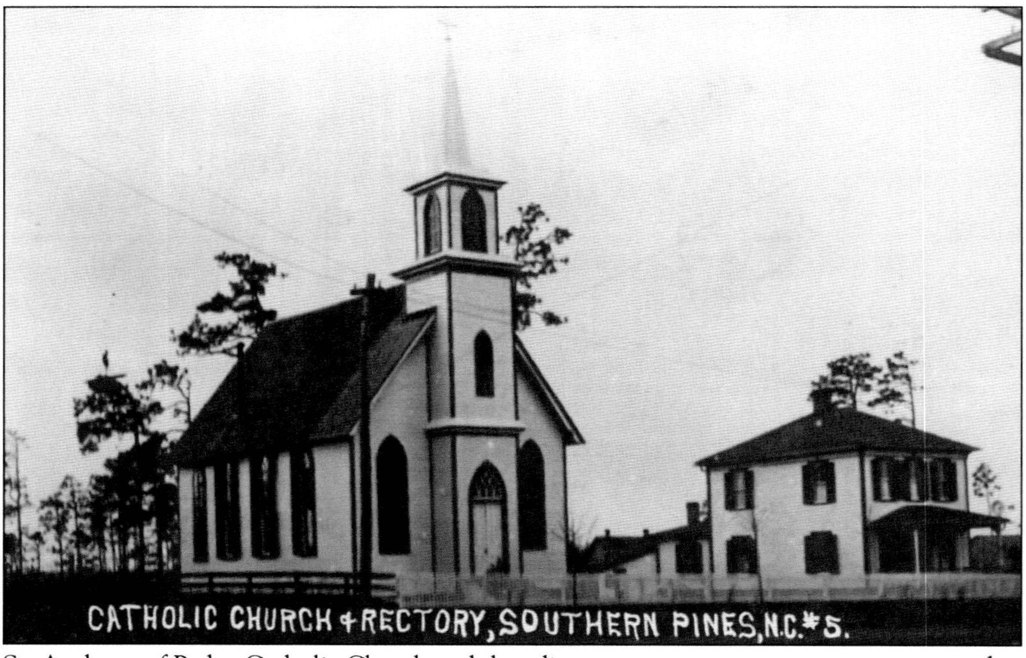

St. Anthony of Padua Catholic Church and the adjacent two-story rectory were constructed in 1895, on the corner of North Ashe Street and East Vermont Avenue. St. Anthony's was the first Catholic church built in Moore County.

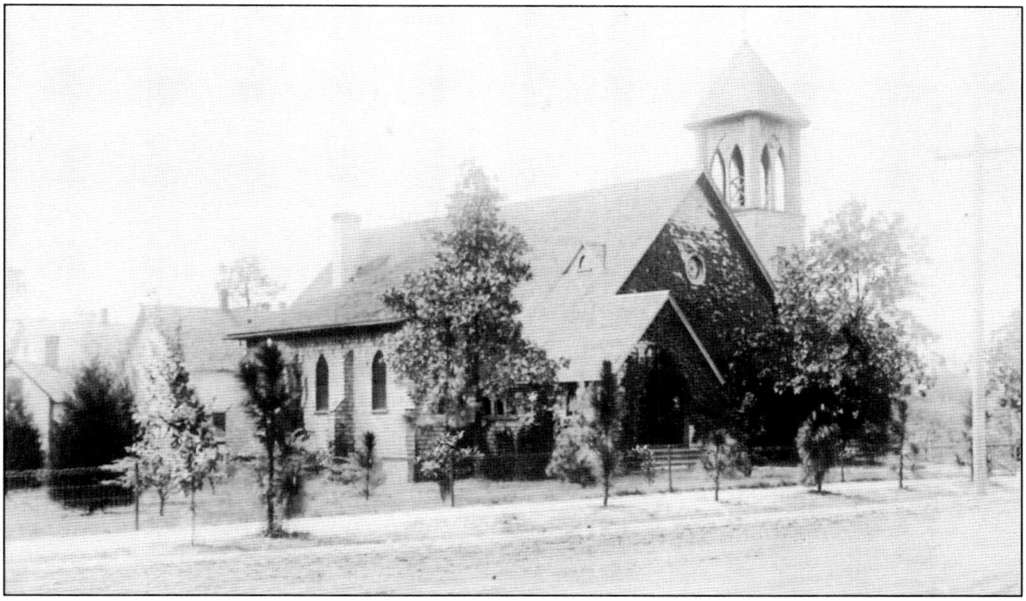

The Congregational Church was built in 1898 as the largest church in early Southern Pines. It stood on the corner of Bennett Street and New Hampshire Avenue.

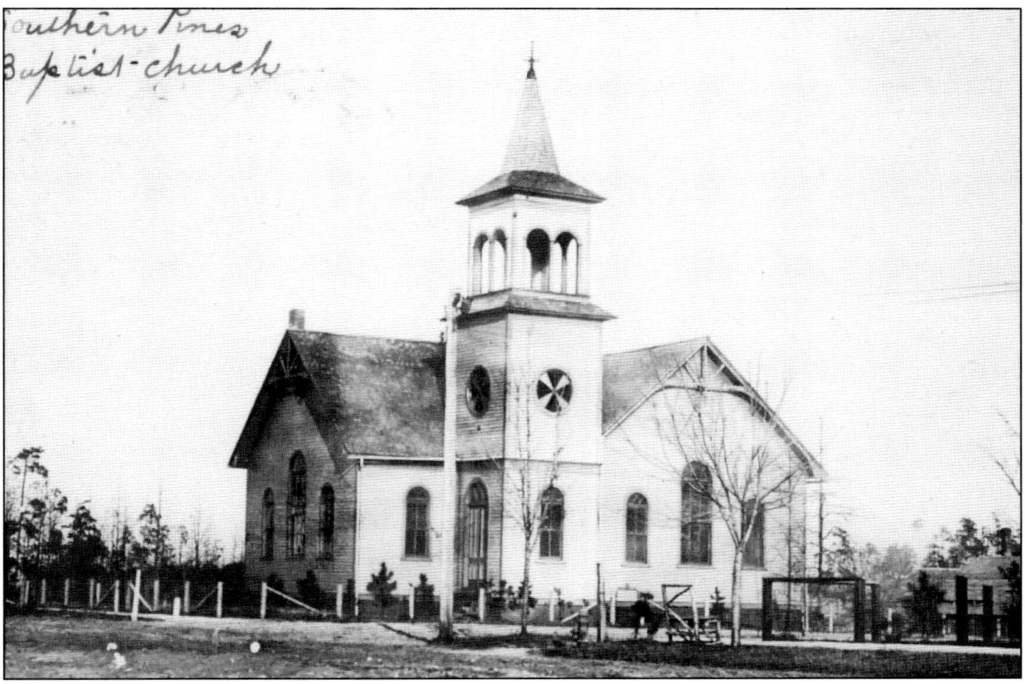

The First Baptist Church on Page Street was constructed in 1899 after the congregation moved from Manly. It was the fourth church built in Southern Pines before 1900.

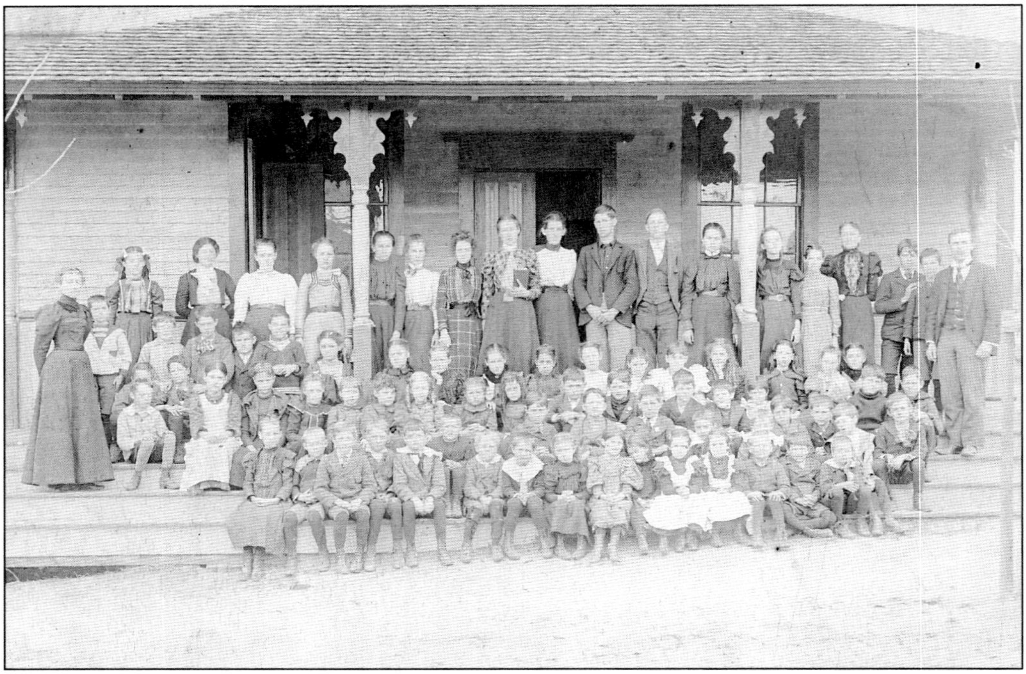

The entire class of the Southern Pines High School, 1898–1899, are pictured in front of King's Daughters Hall.

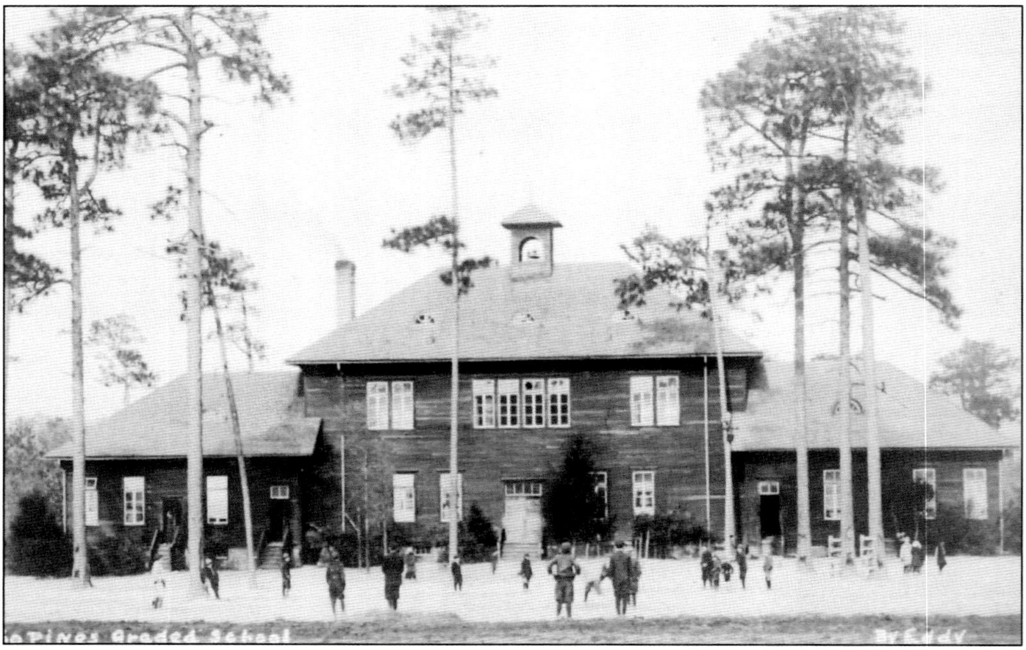

This photograph shows the first public school building constructed in Southern Pines.

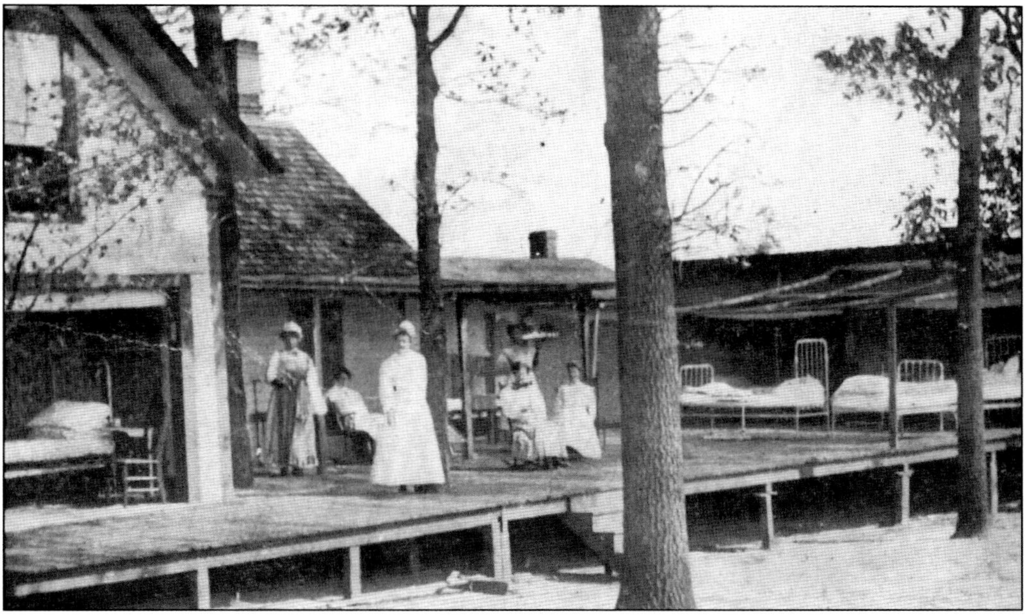
This photograph shows the Southern Pines Sanitarium.

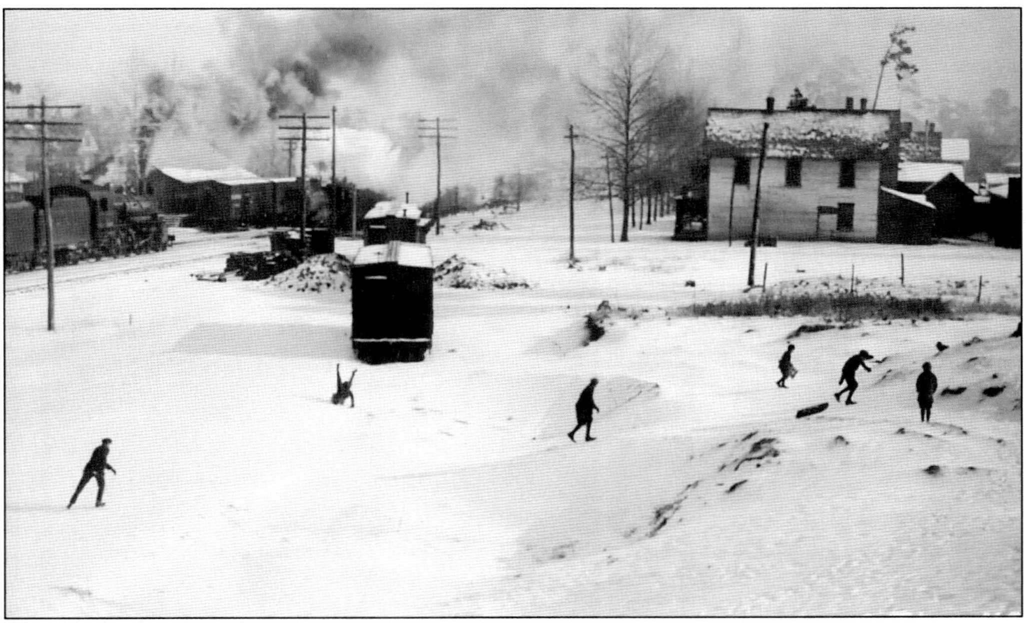
This is a photograph of Railroad Street covered in snow.

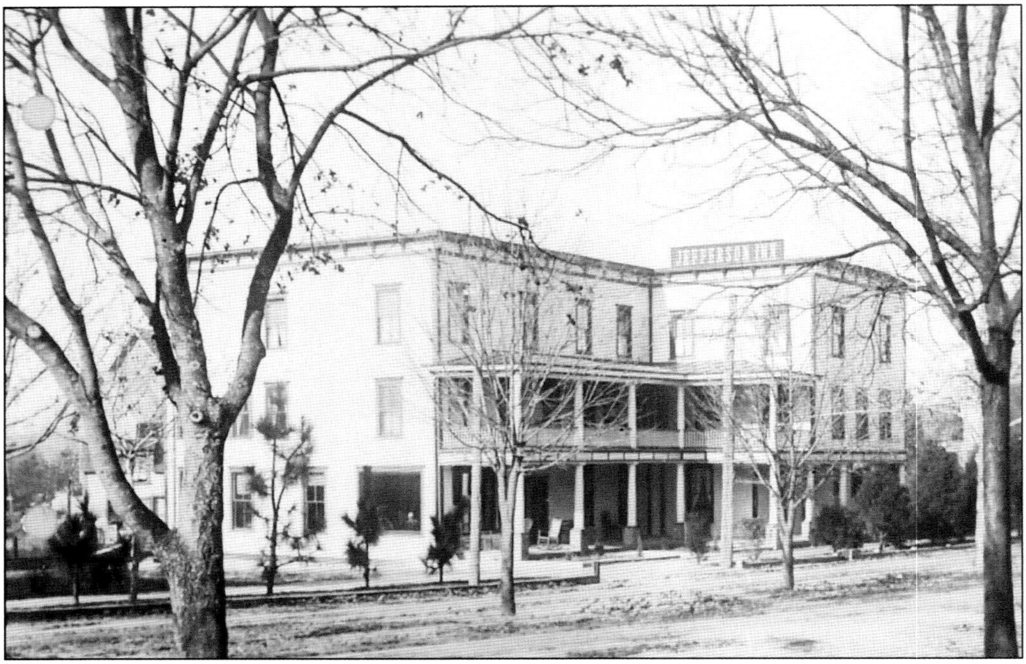

The Jefferson Inn on West New Hampshire Avenue was constructed in 1901 as a small two-story boarding house. In 1912, the Inn was significantly expanded to form the present three-story hotel. The Jefferson Inn had an elegant interior, with a paneled lobby and impressive central staircase.

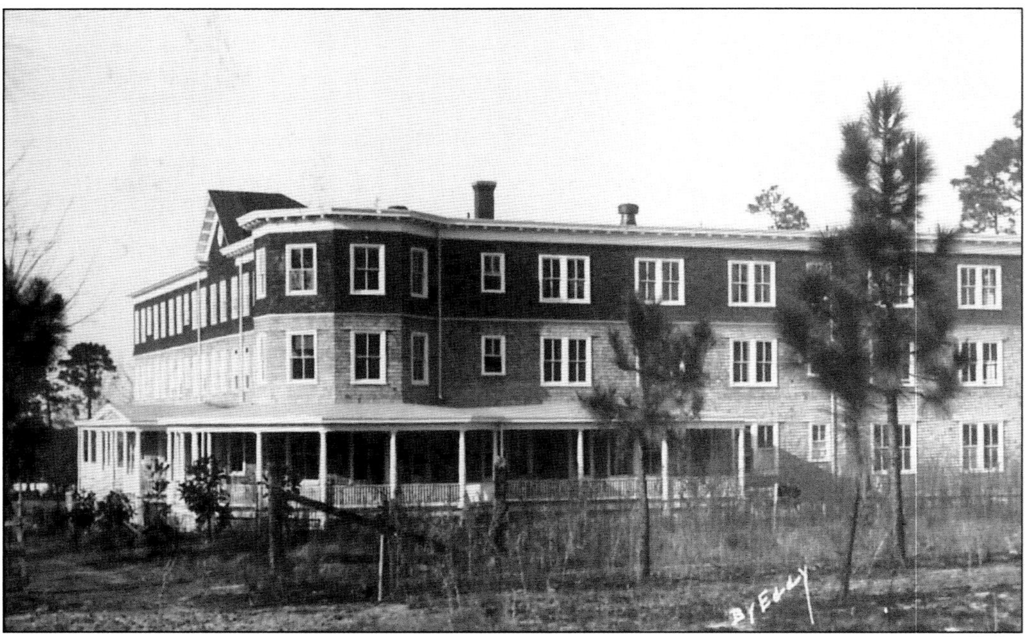

The Hollywood was a popular hotel built after the turn of the century. It was sheathed in shingle siding and had the characteristic flat-top roof so prevalent in many of the early structures in town.

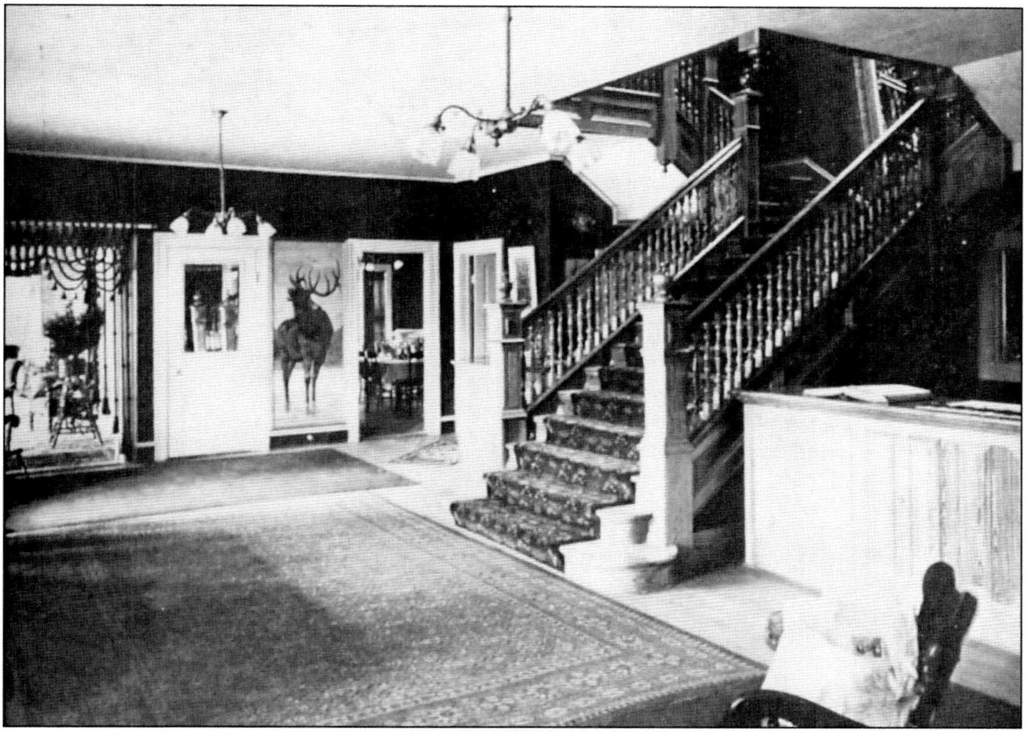

Pictured here are the staircase and foyer of the Southern Pines Hotel.

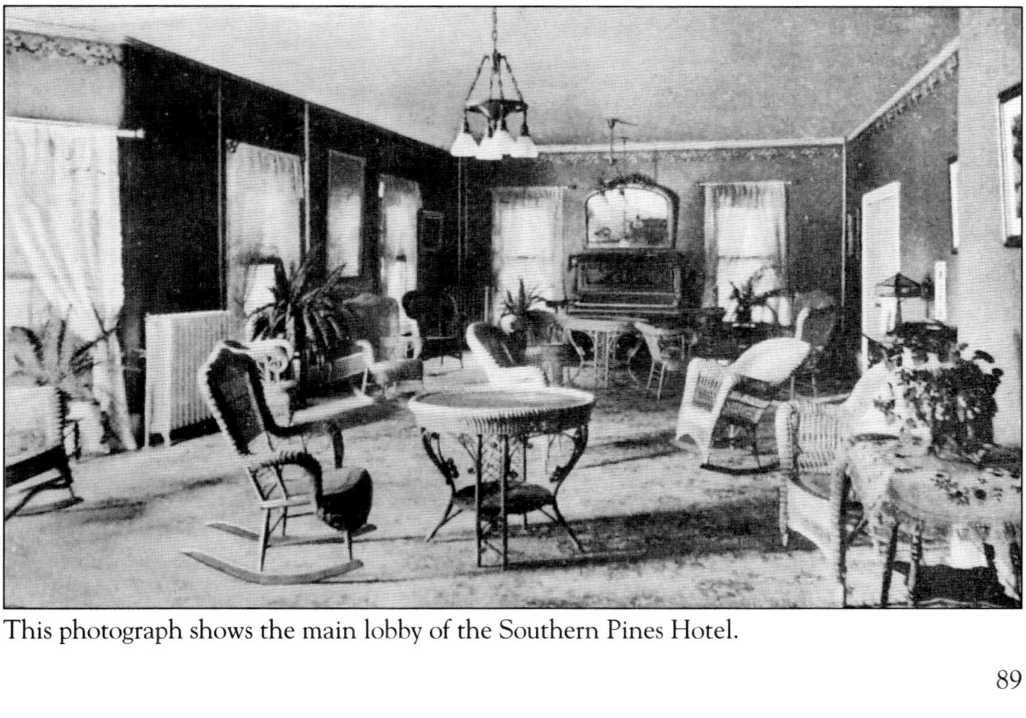

This photograph shows the main lobby of the Southern Pines Hotel.

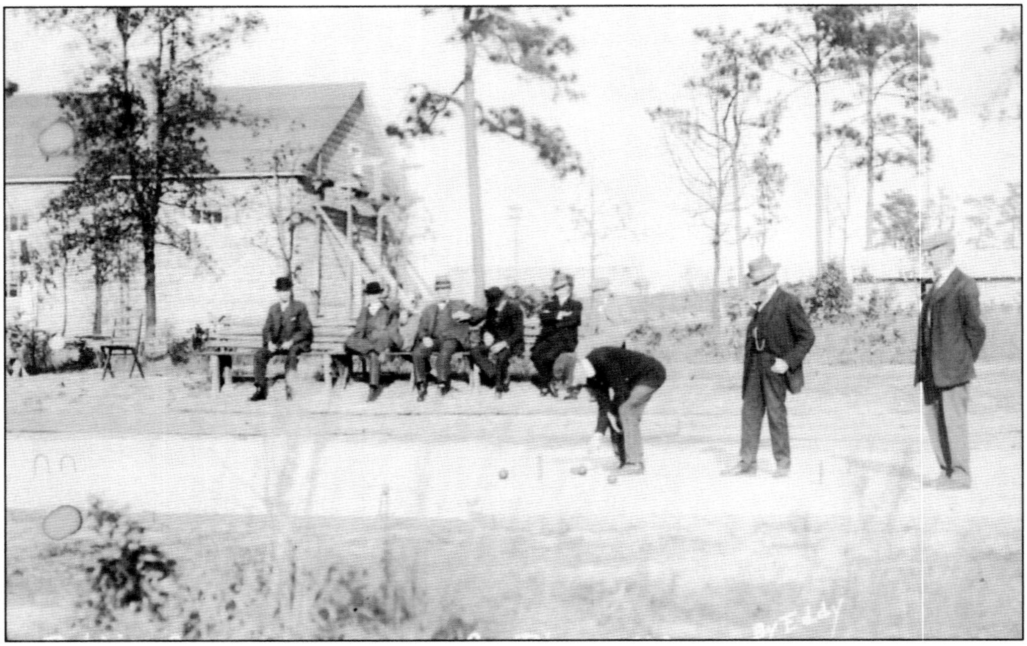

Croquet was a popular sport for many of the winter residents of Southern Pines. Shown is the public croquet court on Pennsylvania Avenue.

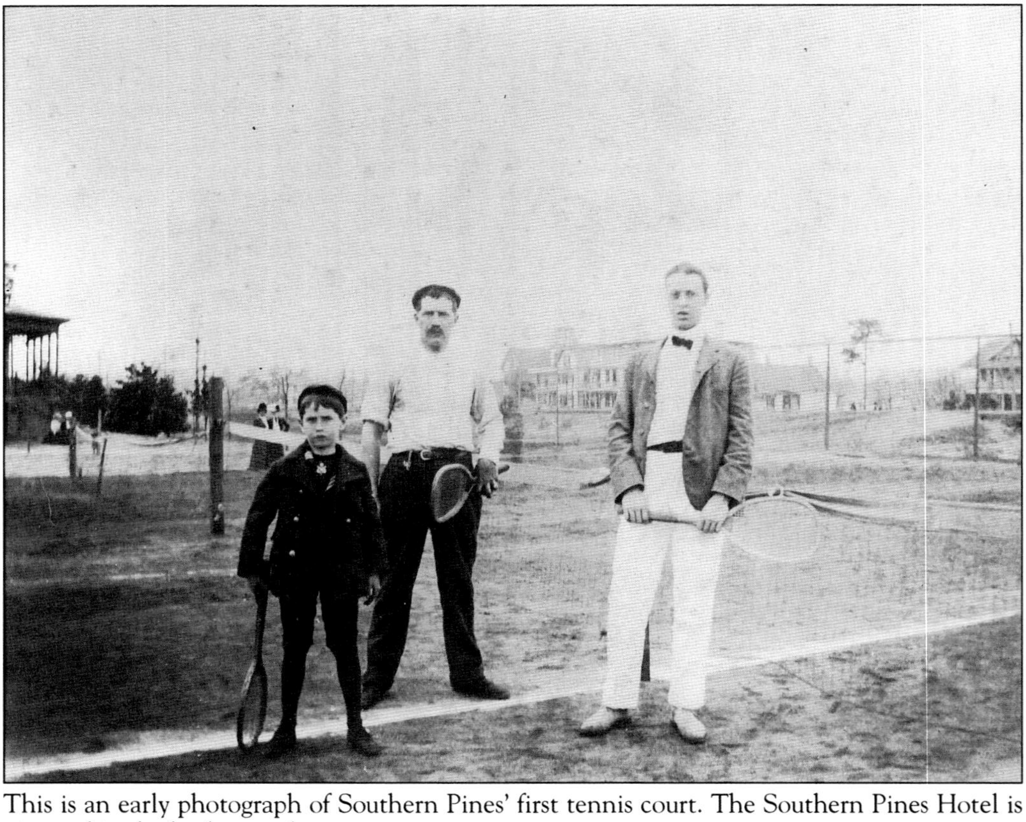

This is an early photograph of Southern Pines' first tennis court. The Southern Pines Hotel is pictured in the background.

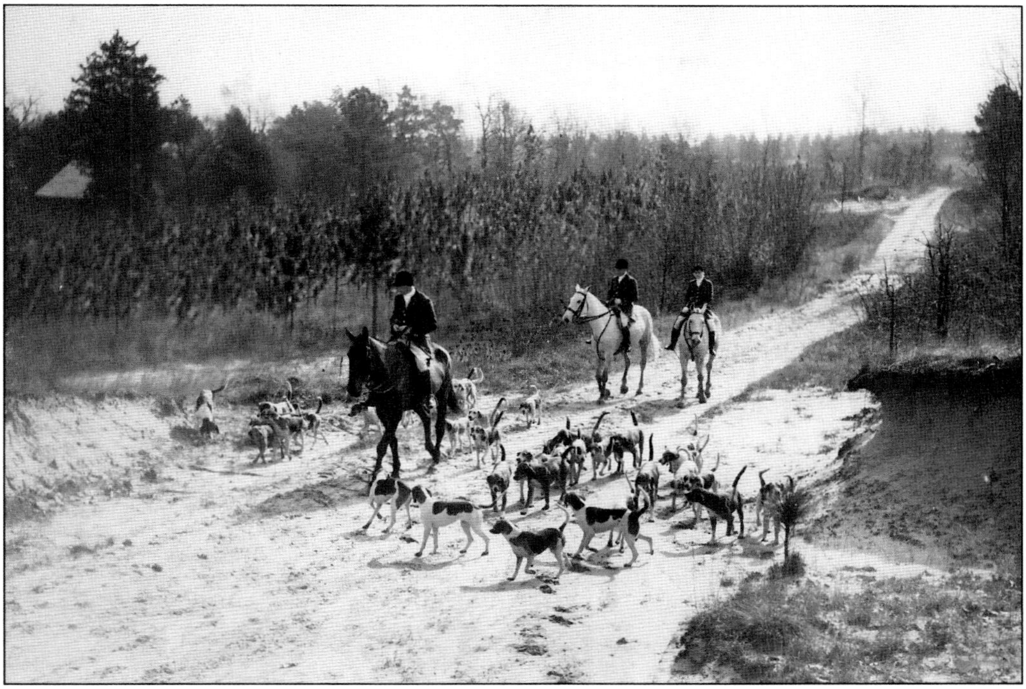

Fox hunting was a sport eagerly promoted by the Boyd family in Southern Pines. Pictured on their way back to the kennels on East Indiana Avenue (from left to right) are Jackson Boyd, Will Stratton, and Margaret Keilly.

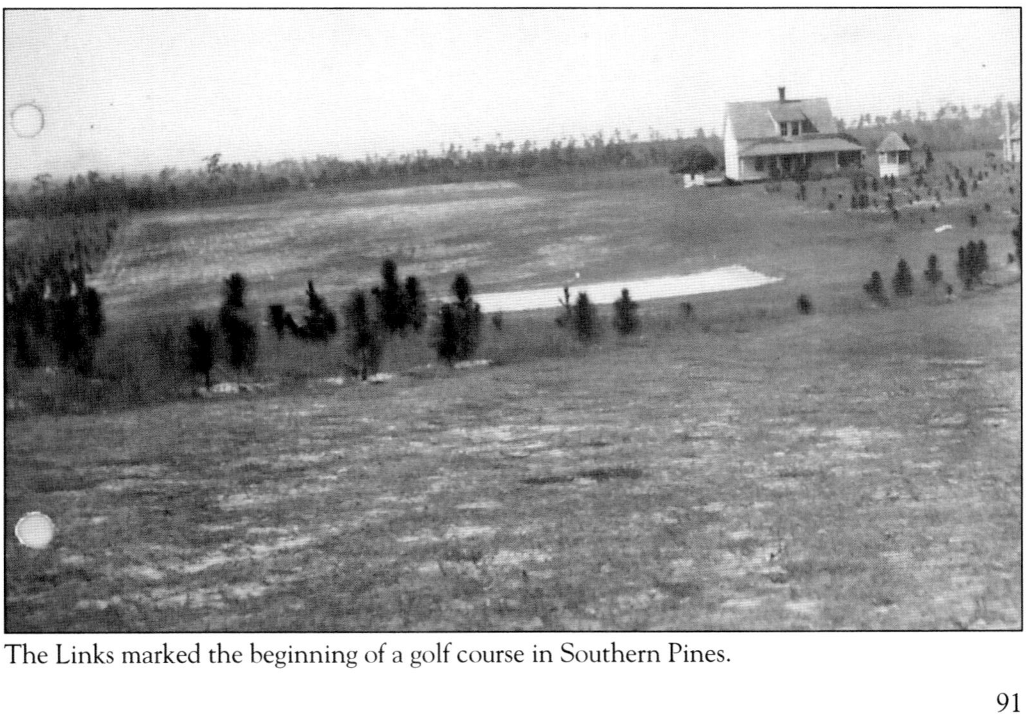

The Links marked the beginning of a golf course in Southern Pines.

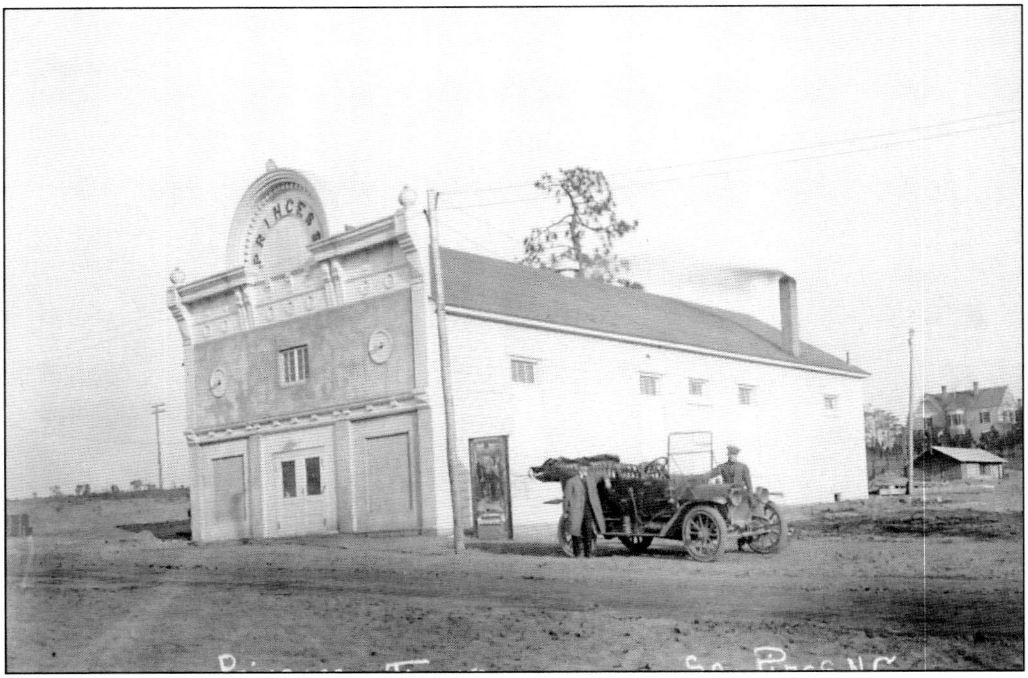

The Princess Theatre was a fashionable gathering spot for early residents of the town. It provided live theatre and first-run movies for nearly four decades.

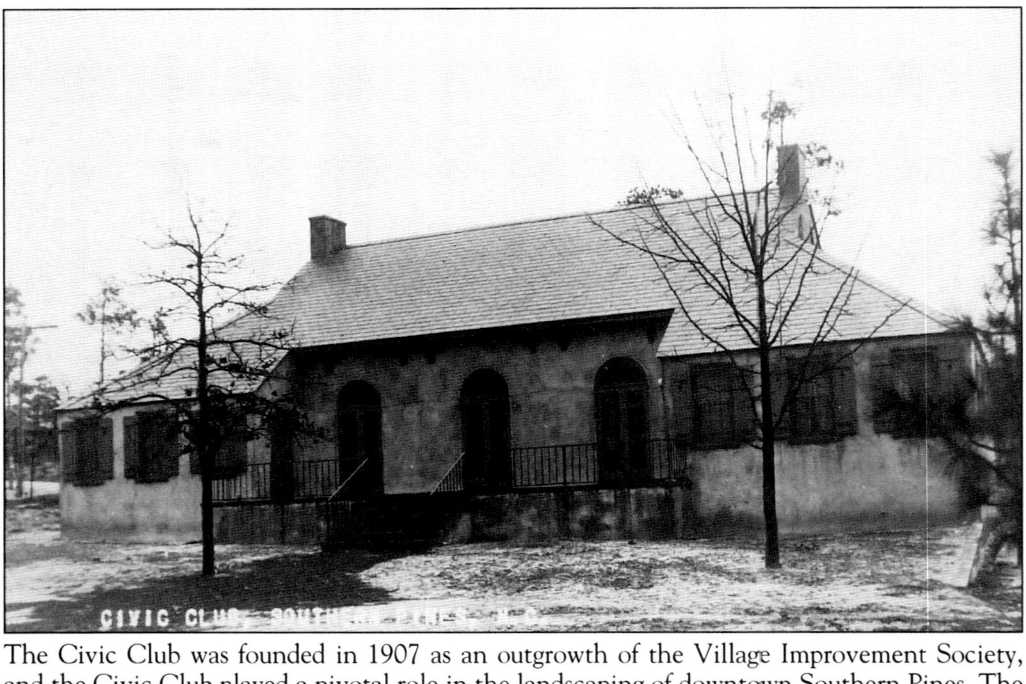

The Civic Club was founded in 1907 as an outgrowth of the Village Improvement Society, and the Civic Club played a pivotal role in the landscaping of downtown Southern Pines. The building was designed by noted landscape architect A.B. Yeomans.

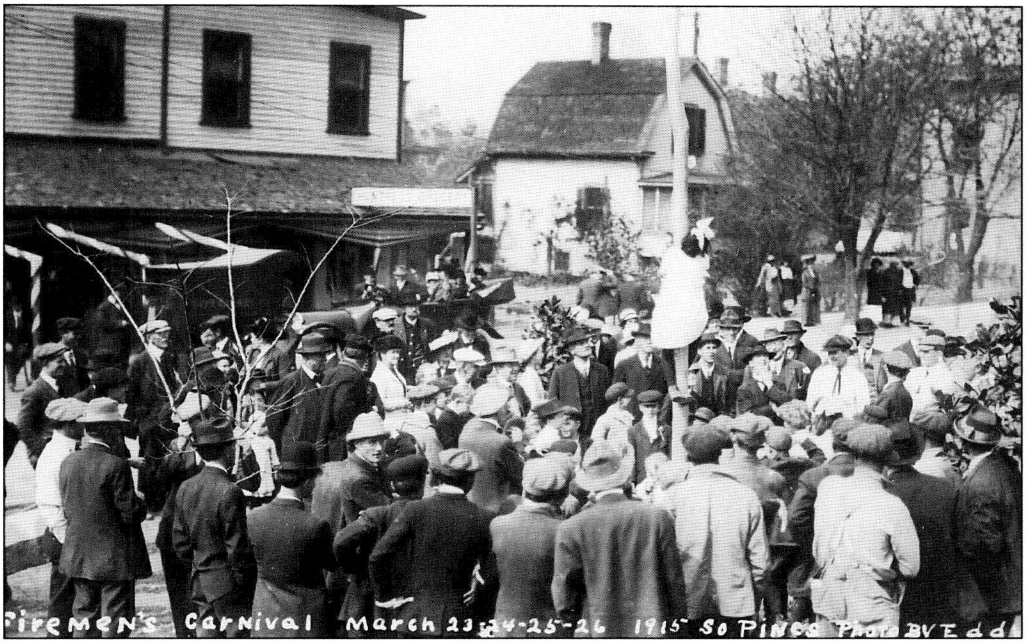

The Firemen's Carnival was an annual four-day event celebrated by residents and tourists alike. Pictured is a crowd of onlookers gathered around a young girl trying to climb the May Pole.

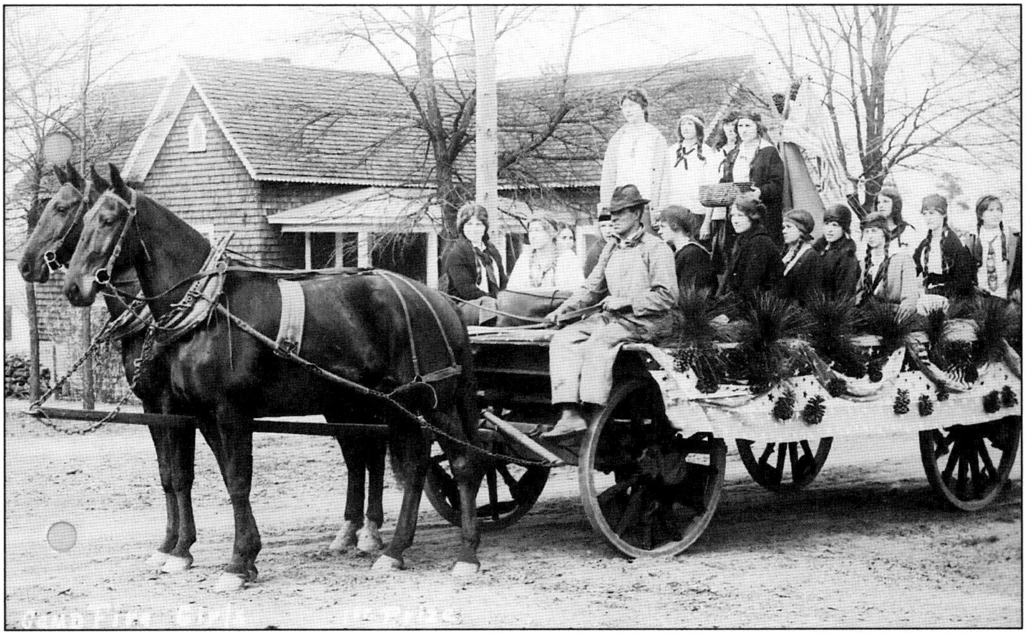

Pictured here is a float for the Camp Fire Girls at the annual festival. In the background is the 1884 Marks Cottage, one of the first houses built in Southern Pines.

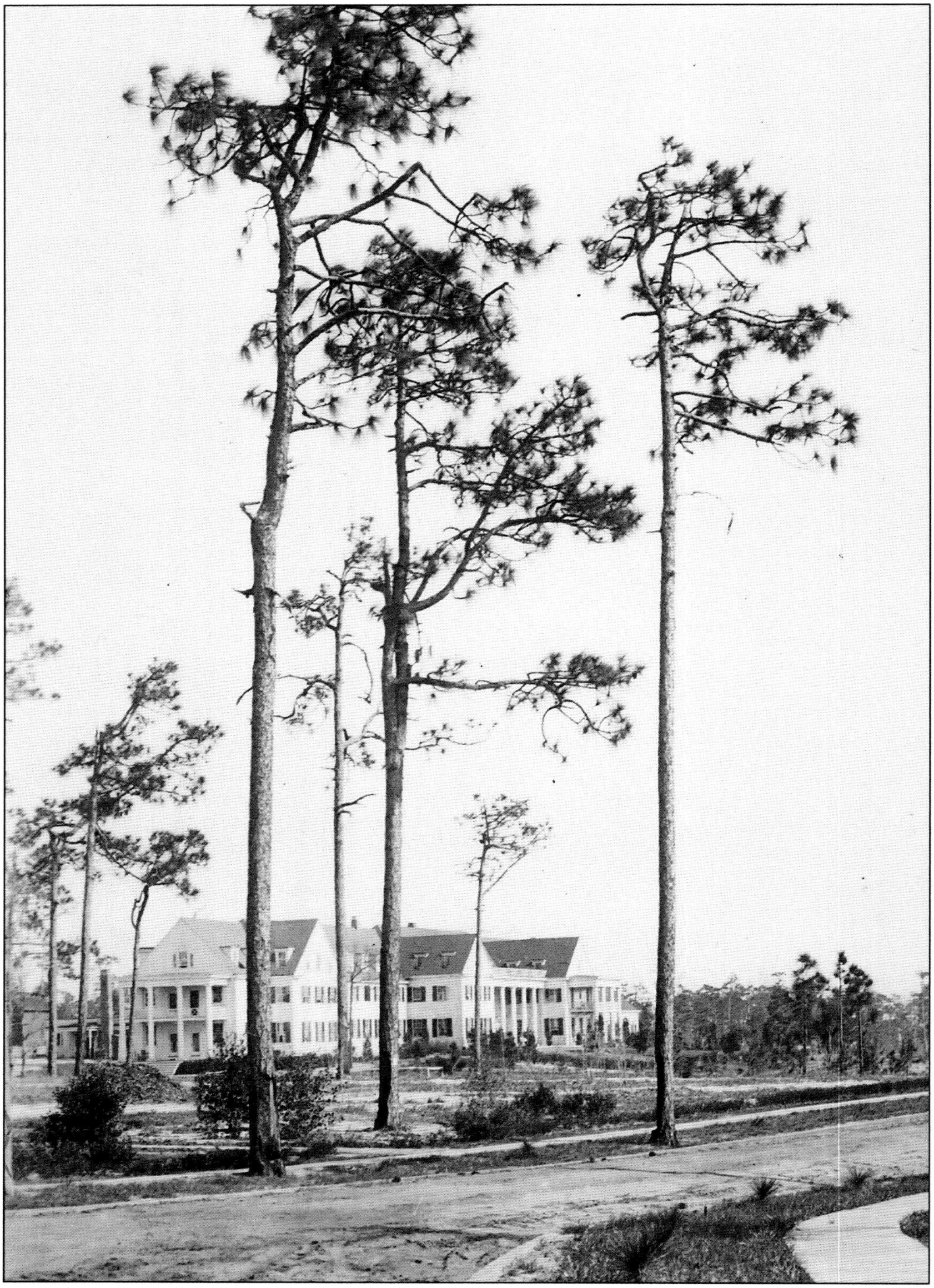

The Colonial Revival Highland Pines Inn was designed by Aymar Embury II and built in 1912 amidst a 500-acre subdivision known as Weymouth Heights. Its elaborate design and the physical layout of the streets around it signaled the end of Southern Pines' early renown as a health resort. It would soon become an acclaimed winter retreat known primarily for its equestrian activities.

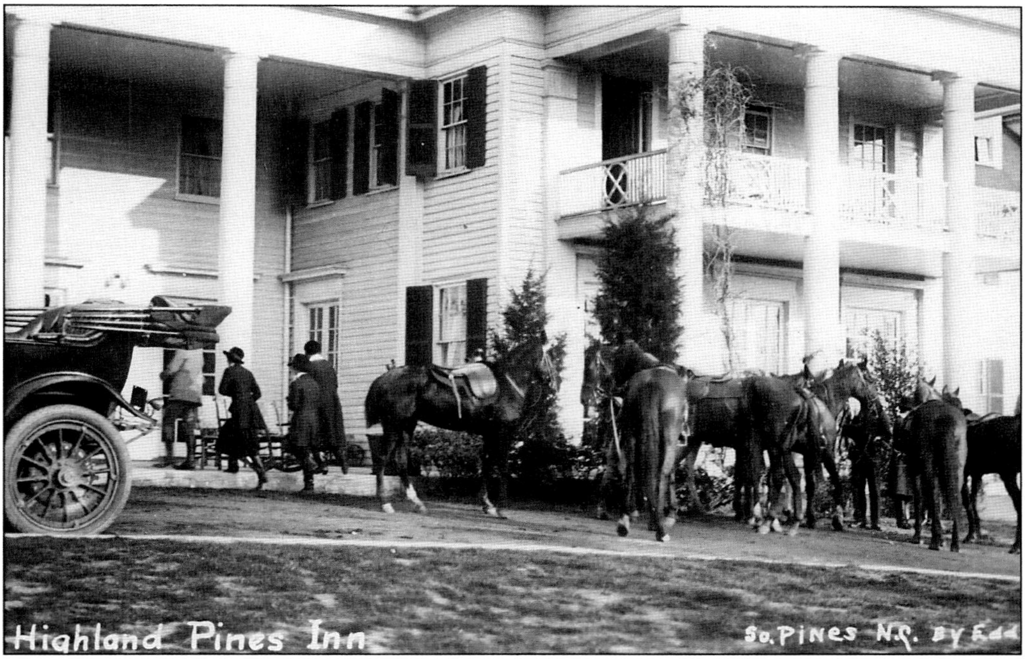

A group of riders enter the Highland Pines Inn after a fox hunt. The hotel was a popular watering spot for horsemen and nearly residents.

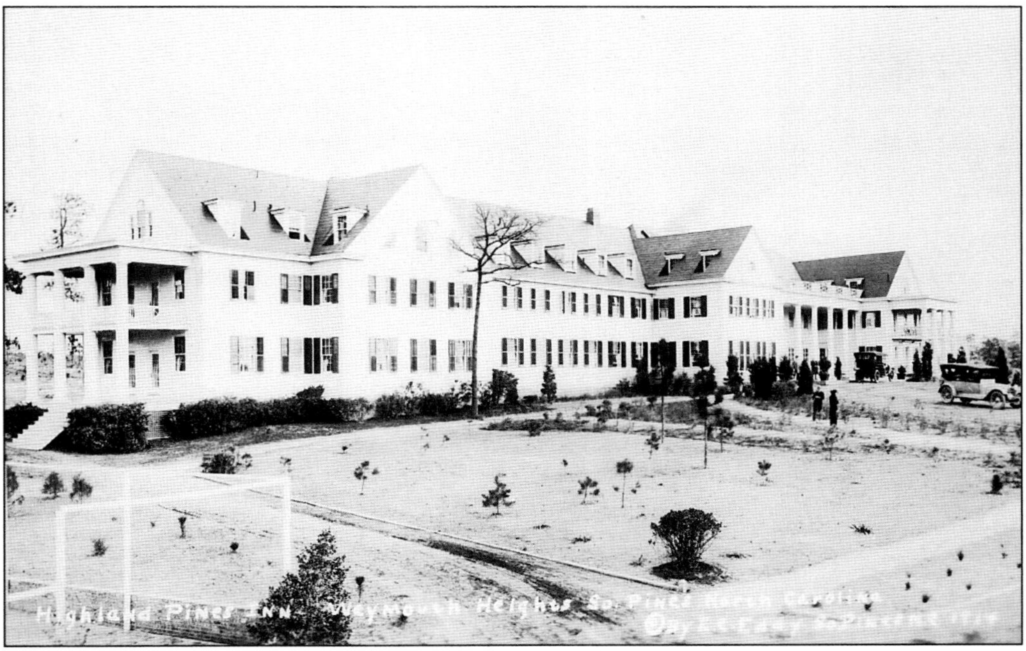

The Highland Pines Inn was a functional building, with tall white-columned porticoes opening onto panoramic views of the countryside. It offered a variety of entertainment, including music from big-name bands, tennis, riding, and golf. The surrounding subdivision featured large landscaped lots with winter homes for wealthy patrons from the New England and Middle Atlantic states.

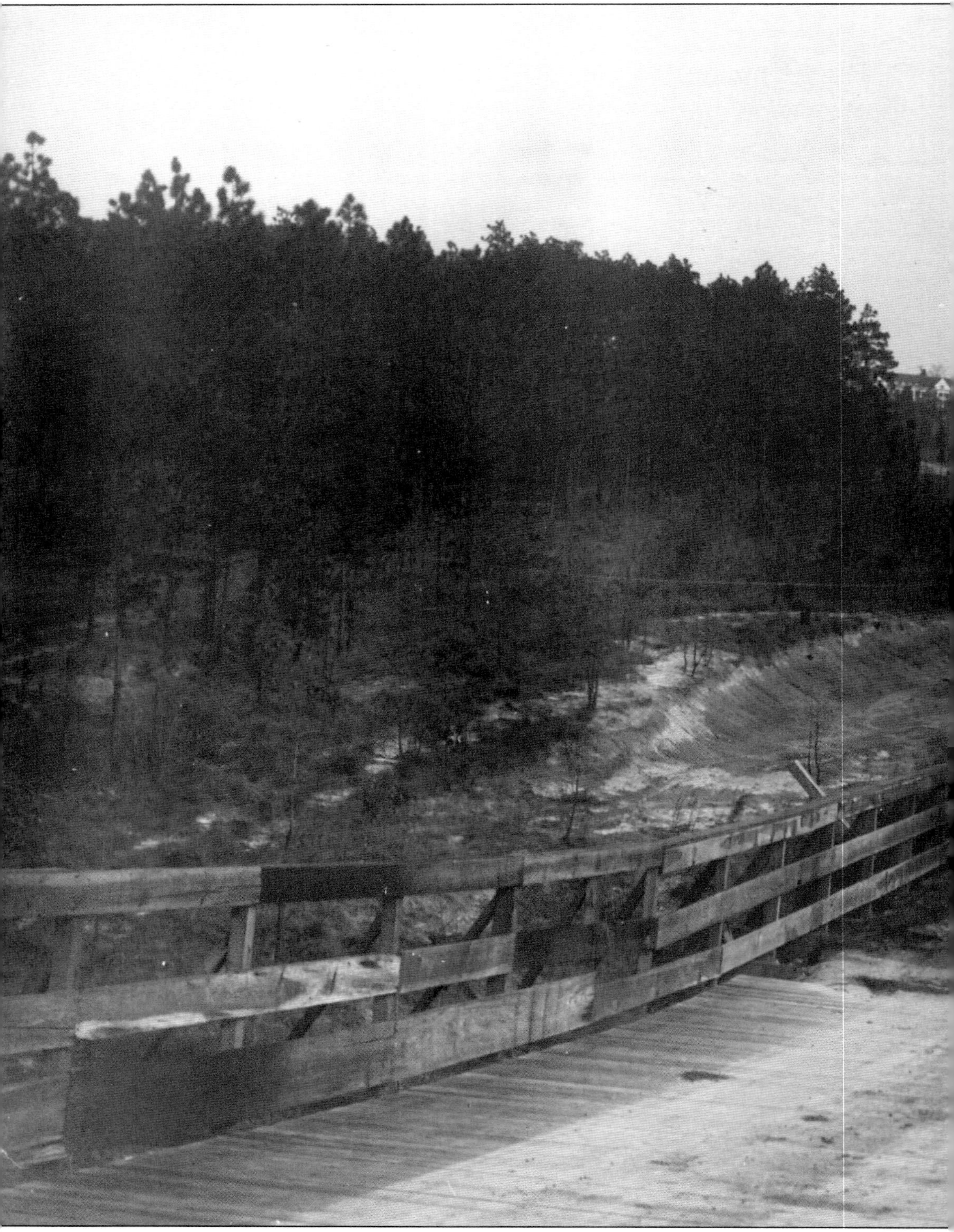

A group of riders cross the railroad bridge on Old Morgantown Road. The Highland Pines Inn is barely visible in the background. Pictured in front (from left to right) are riders James,

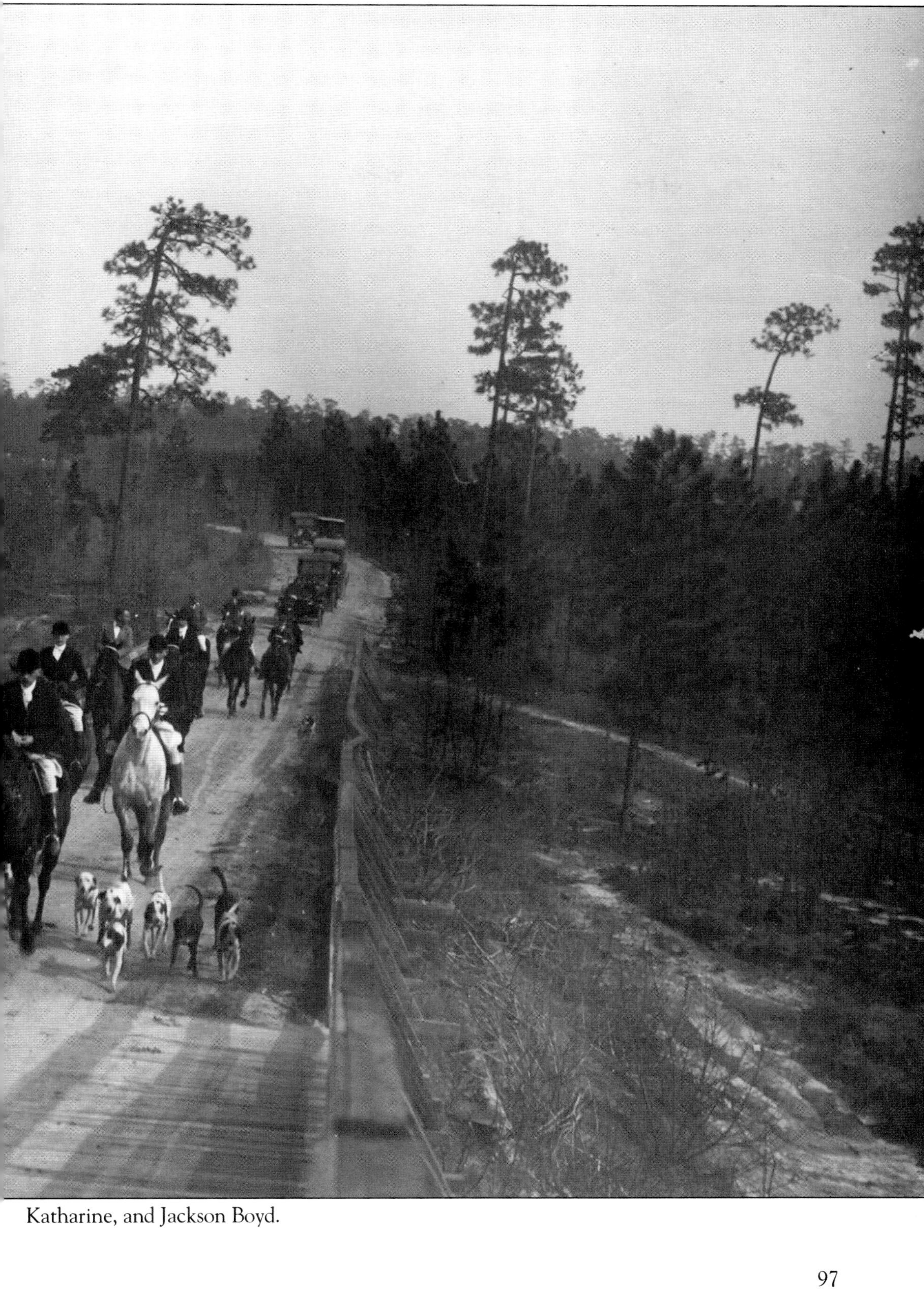

Katharine, and Jackson Boyd.

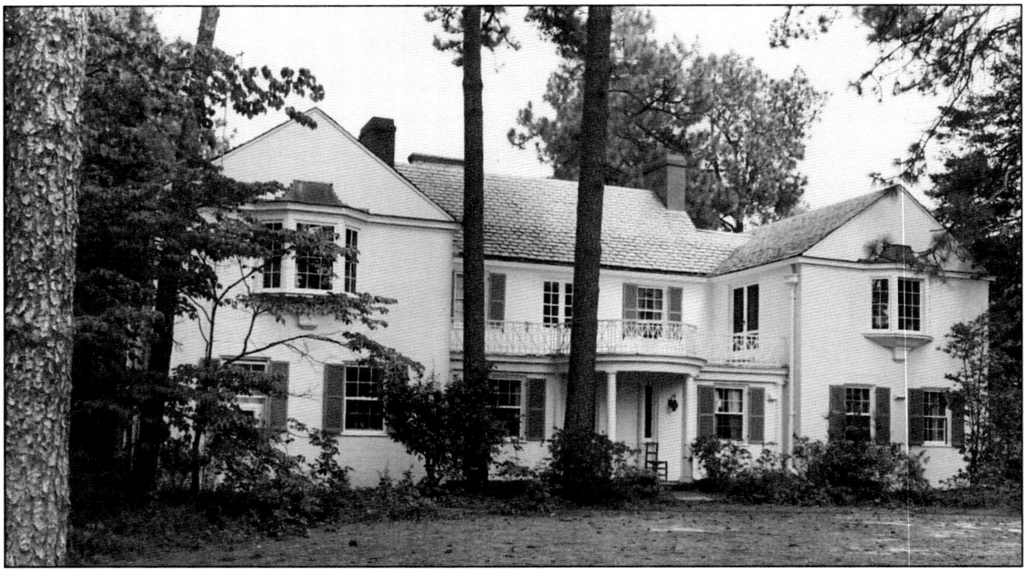

Weymouth Woods was designed by Aymar Embury II and constructed in 1922 for famed author James Boyd. It was erected on the site of a smaller structure built in 1905 for Boyd's grandfather amidst a sprawling 2,500-acre estate. Boyd played a leading role in the early development of Southern Pines and co-founded the Moore County Hounds in 1914.

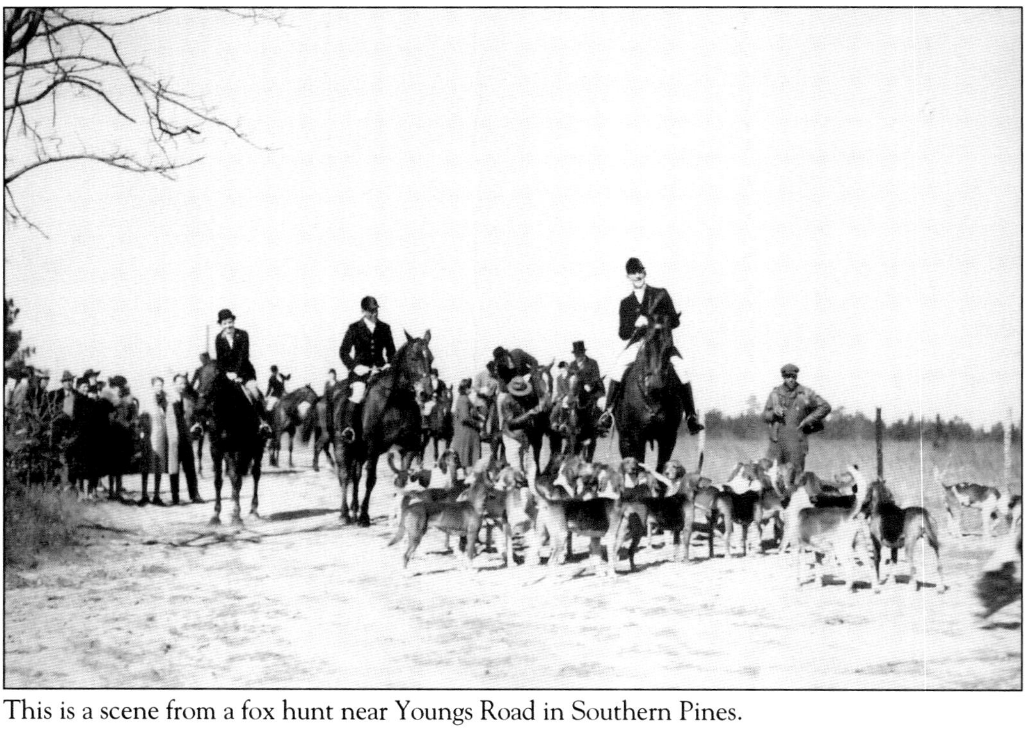

This is a scene from a fox hunt near Youngs Road in Southern Pines.

Dear Sir:-

At a single stroke your powerful newspaper has destroyed my happiness and ruined my reputation. Although for nearly thirty years I have been a citizen of Southern Pines, you described me as coming from Pinehurst. The difference is immense.

Pinehurst is a resort visited by golfers; Southern Pines is a town inhabited by fox hunters. In the summer, Pinehurst ceases to exist. It is merely a deserted village haunted by the ghosts of departed golfers. But all the year round, Southern Pines may be seen vigorously flourishing, its noble civic life distinguished by sectarian disputes, town dogs, corner loafers, Kiwanians, caucuses, tax-dodgers, boot-leggers, dead-beats, rummage sales, law suits, chiropractors, literary gents, beauty shoppes and all the other attributes of organized metropolitan society.

You can, therefore, conceive my grief at your misapprehension. Especially when I tell you that I am a fox-hunter, and that all fox hunters are ex-officio Nature's noblemen whose lustre no amount of lying, liquor and vaingloriousness can dim. If it could, that lustre would have been dimmed long ago.

Golf, on the other hand, is merely the most expensive and depressing form of pedestrianism. It renders its victims on the one hand gloomy and self-pitying, and, on the other, tediously and interminably loquacious. I know of no other practice, except the purchase and consumption of bad liquor, wherein good money can be spent for so pitiable a result.

James Boyd
Southern Pines, N. C.

The letter above was written by author James Boyd in 1927 in response to a newspaper article published in the *Raleigh News and Observer* which mistakenly identified him as a resident of nearby Pinehurst.

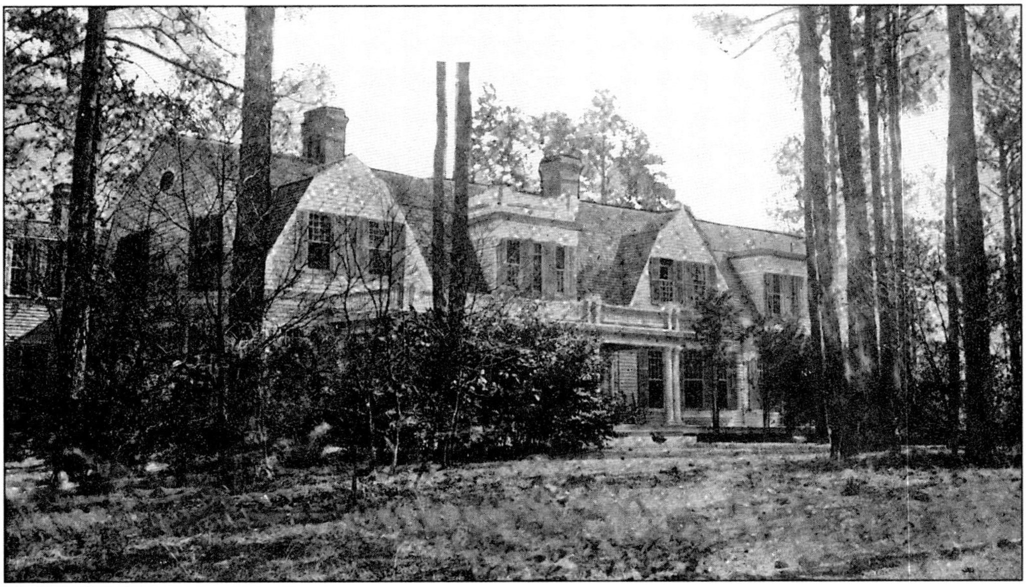

Hibernia was built in 1900 and extensively renovated in 1926 by A.B. Yeomans for author Struthers Burt, a close friend of James Boyd. The 42-acre estate bordered Weymouth Woods and became a popular meeting place for such authors as John Galsworthy, F. Scott Fitzgerald, Sherwood Anderson, and Thomas Wolfe.

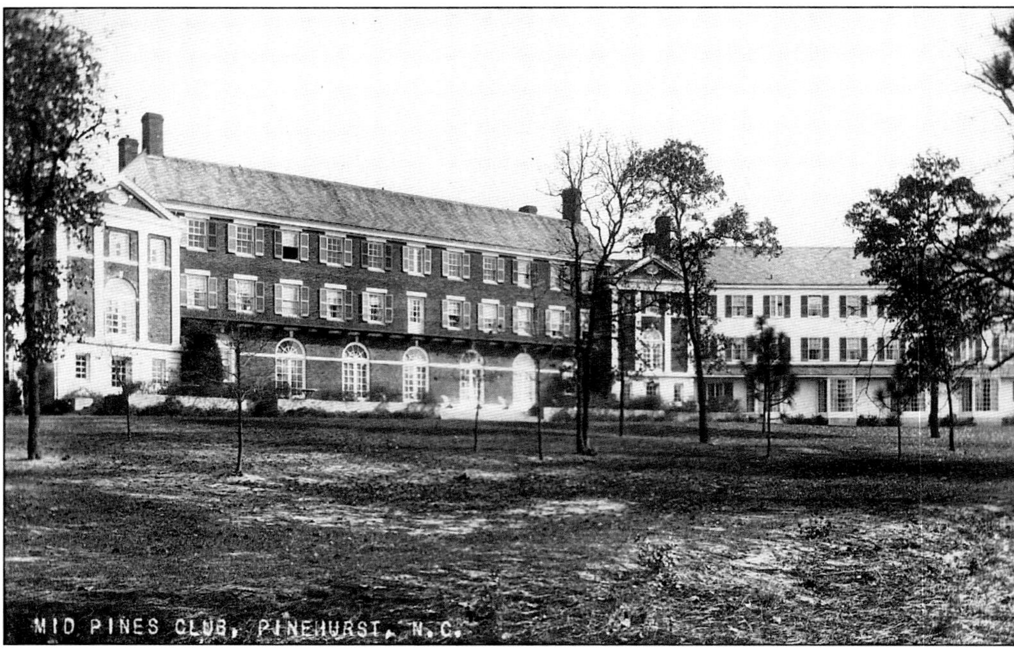

Mid Pines Club was designed by Aymar Embury II and built in 1921 as the centerpiece of Knollwood, an exclusive residential subdivision similar to Weymouth Heights. It featured grand entrances and an impressive circular lobby flanked by Corinthian columns. The surrounding golf course was designed by internationally acclaimed golf course architect Donald Ross.

Seven

PINEBLUFF

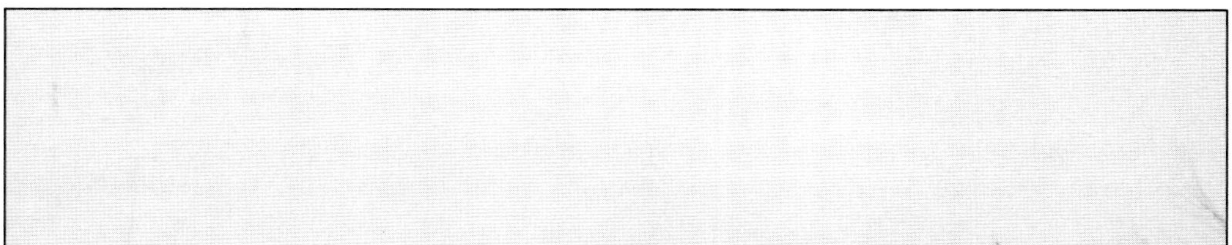

Pinebluff was located 7 miles south of Southern Pines, along the route of the Raleigh and Augusta Railroad. It was founded in 1884 as a resort and originally featured 100-foot-wide streets with an elaborate system of diamond-shaped islands at each intersection. Shown is Currant Street, the town's main thoroughfare, with the Pinebluff Inn to the extreme right.

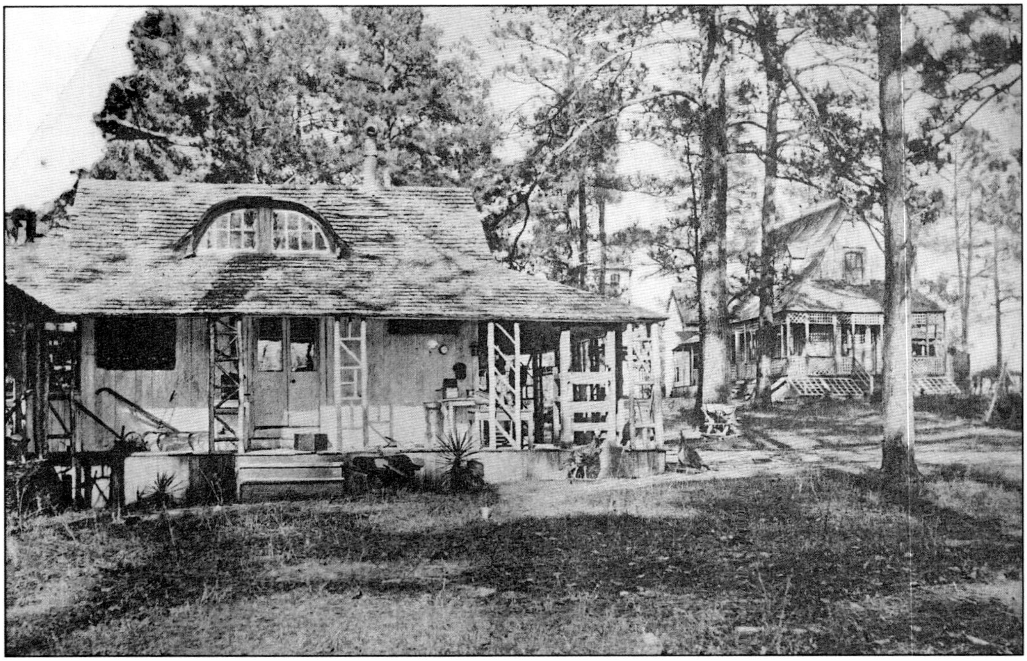

Pictured here is the workshop and two-story plantation home of Pinebluff's founder, John T. Patrick. It was called Patrick's Plantation and was located east of the resort village, nestled amongst rolling hills, streams, lakes, and virgin longleaf pine forests.

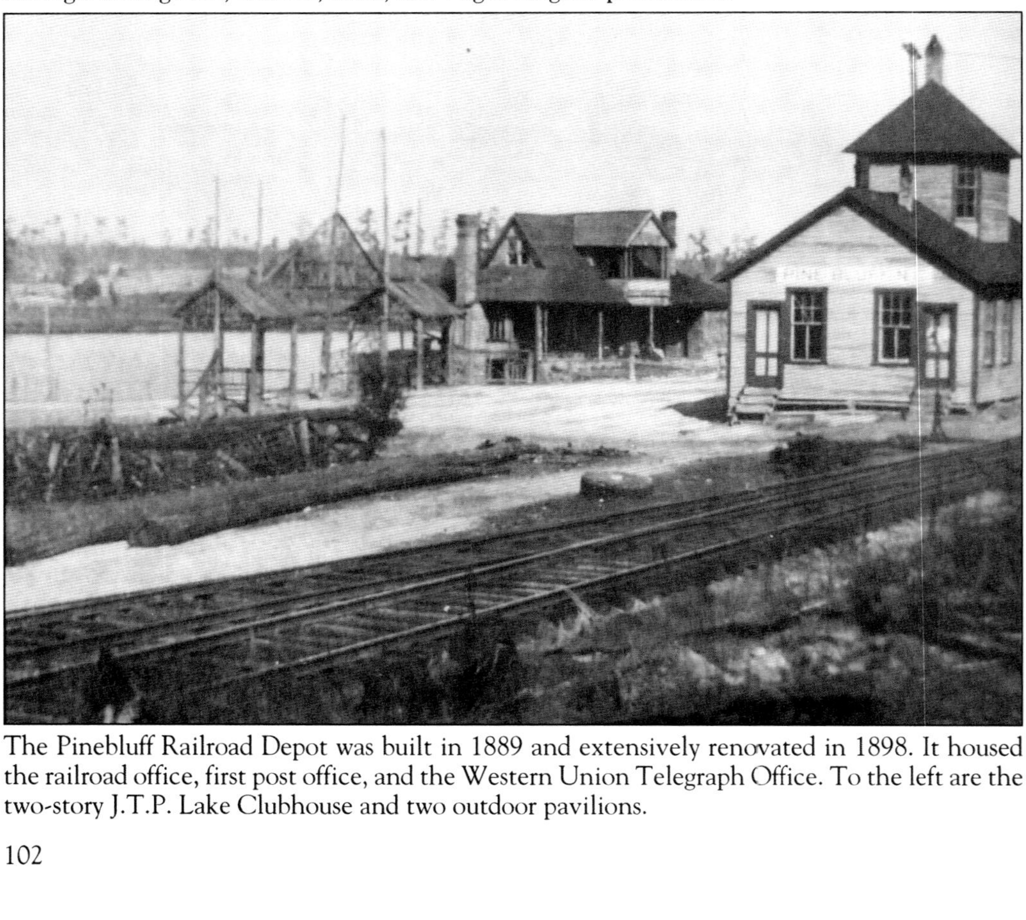

The Pinebluff Railroad Depot was built in 1889 and extensively renovated in 1898. It housed the railroad office, first post office, and the Western Union Telegraph Office. To the left are the two-story J.T.P. Lake Clubhouse and two outdoor pavilions.

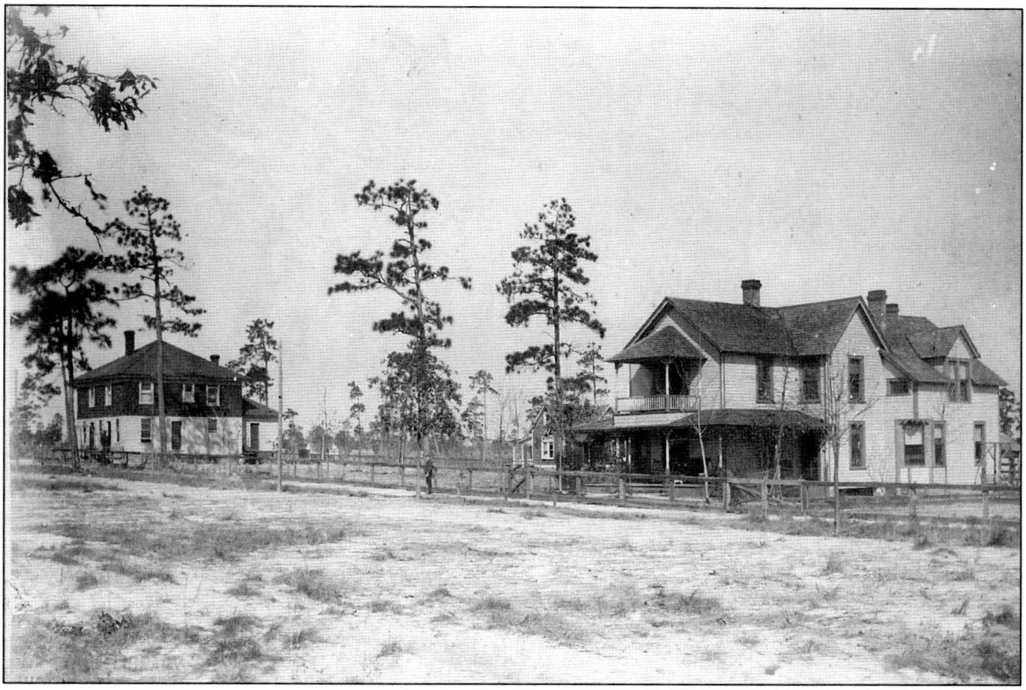

This 1898 photograph of an early Pinebluff street scene shows the C.G. McMinn House to the extreme left. The building housed the Sherman and Adams Grocery store and second Pinebluff post office on the ground floor.

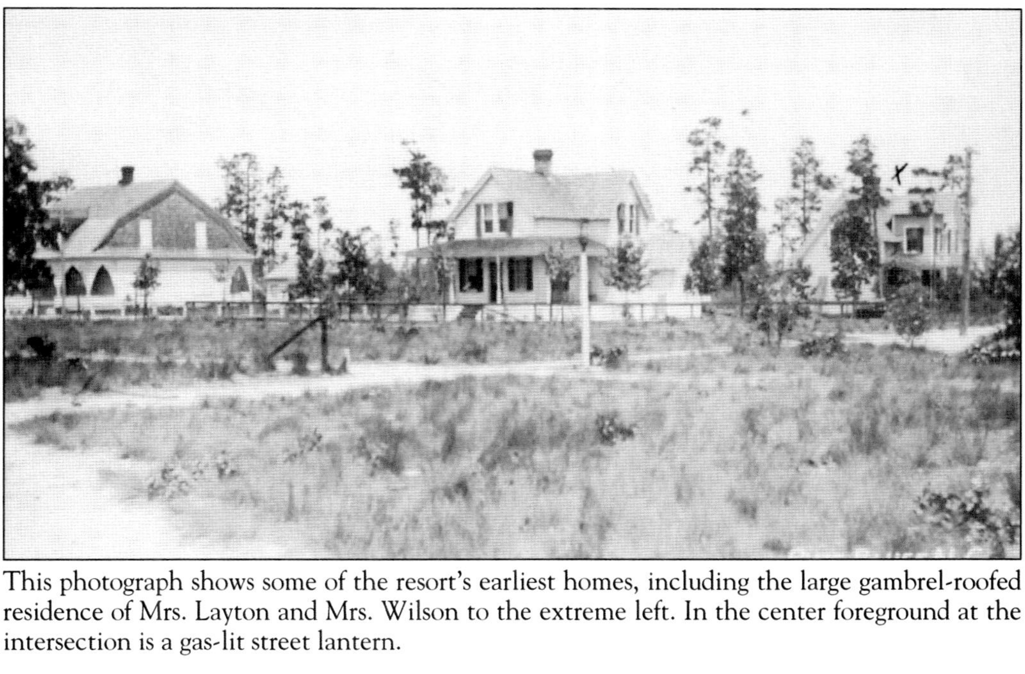

This photograph shows some of the resort's earliest homes, including the large gambrel-roofed residence of Mrs. Layton and Mrs. Wilson to the extreme left. In the center foreground at the intersection is a gas-lit street lantern.

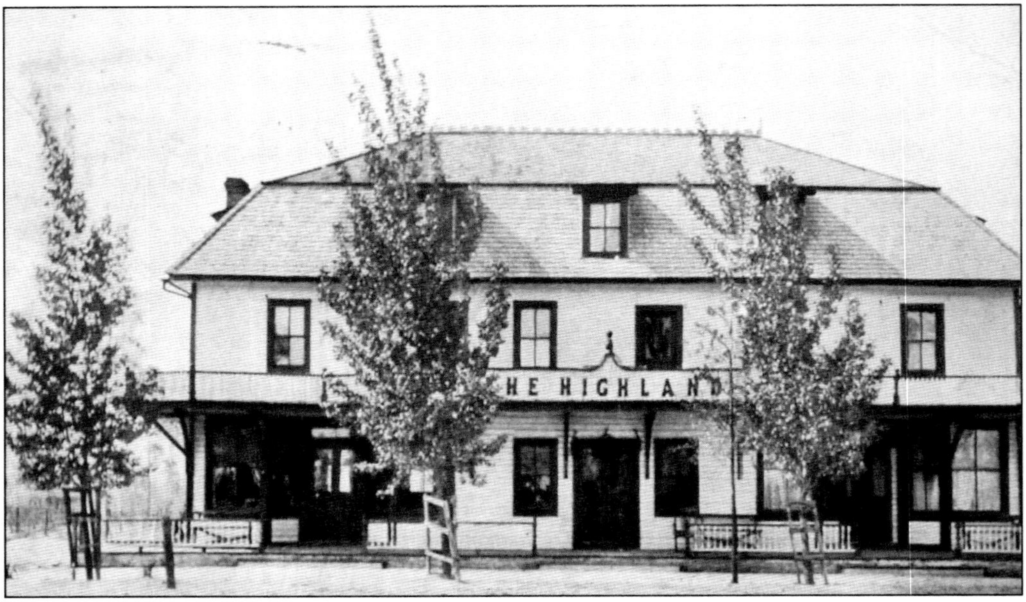

The Highland Hotel was built in 1899 and was originally called Bryan's Hotel. It stood on the northeast corner of New England Avenue and Currant Street.

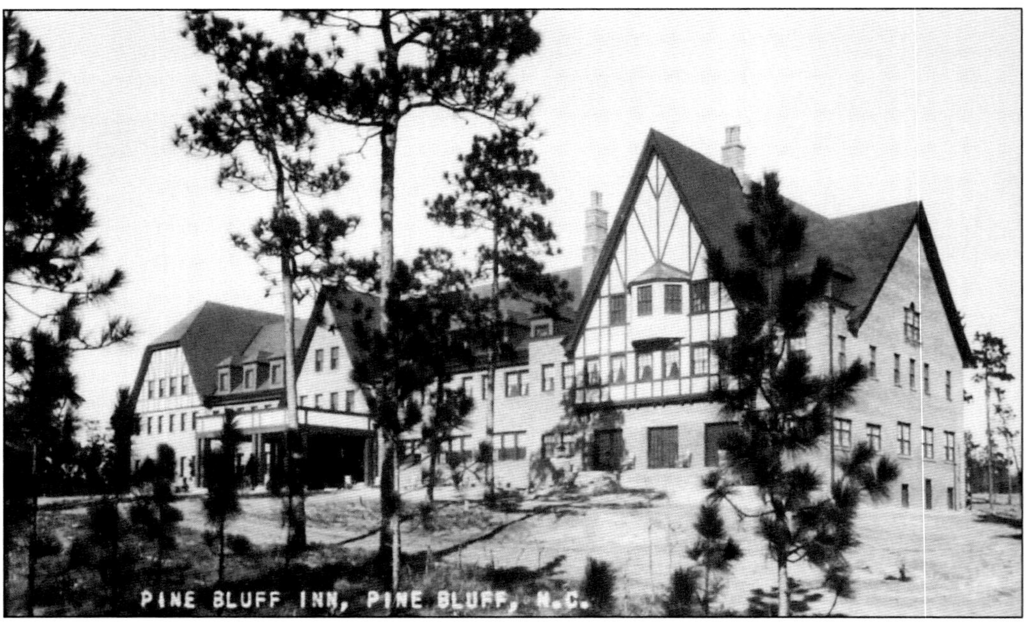

In 1925, the second Pinebluff Inn was constructed over the site of the original inn, built in 1903. The Pinebluff Inn later became the Pinebluff Sanitarium.

Eight

Pinehurst

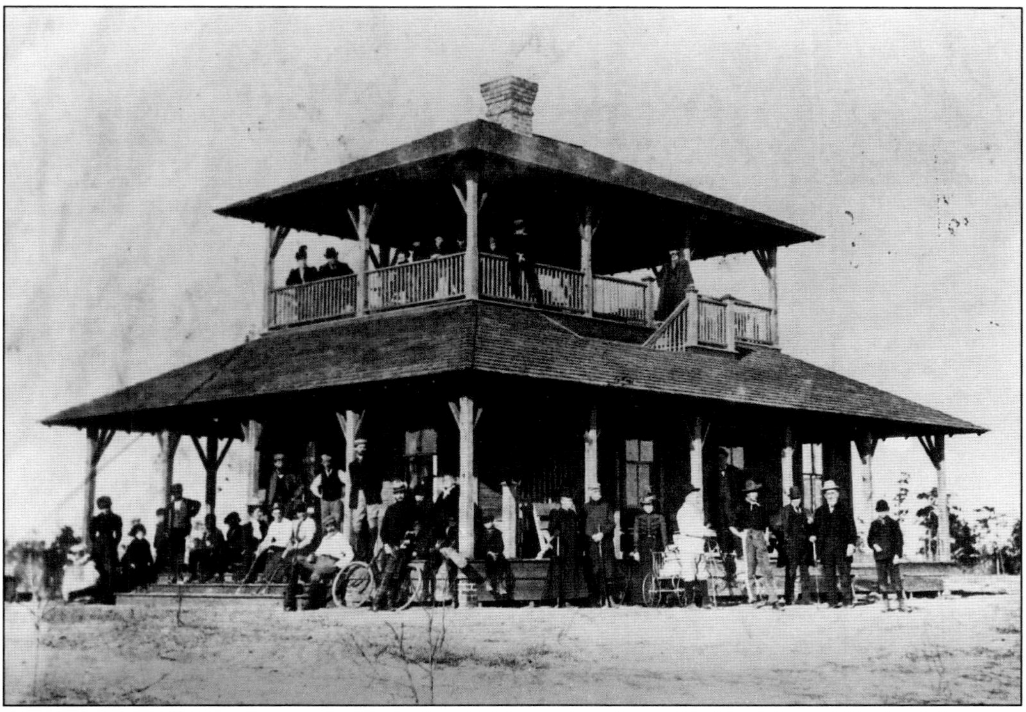

The first golf clubhouse was constructed in 1899 on a knoll overlooking the golf links. It became the nucleus of the Pinehurst Country Club.

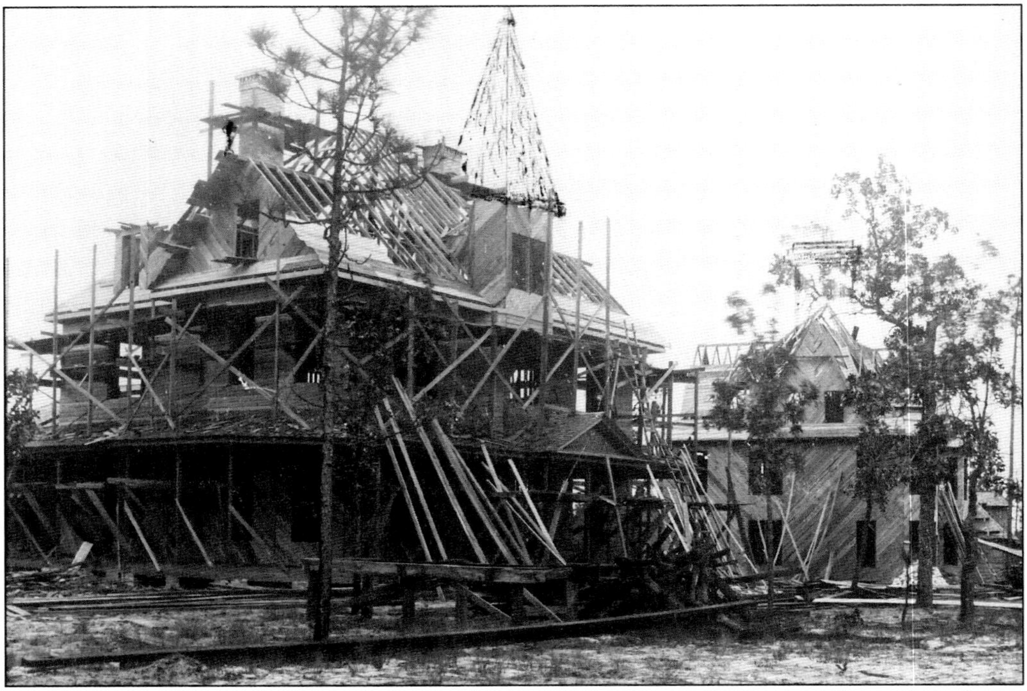

A massive building campaign began in June of 1895 to construct the resort village of Pinehurst. By November 27 of that year, the first hotel, a store, three large rooming houses, and eighteen cottages were completed.

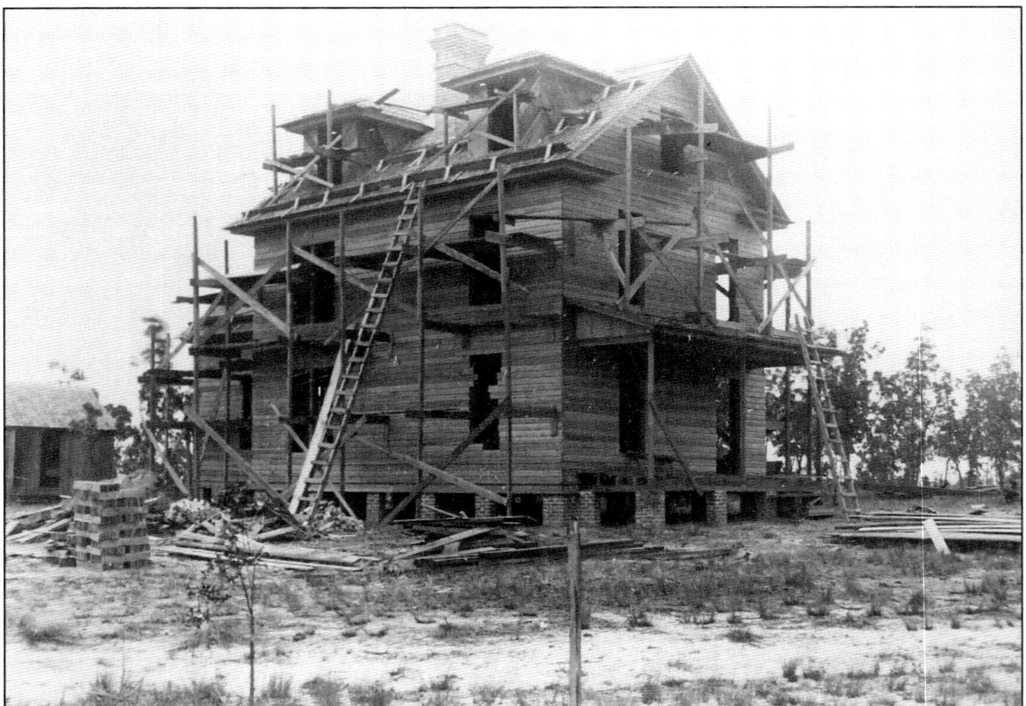

Here, an early cottage is shown while still under construction. The community was initially planned as a health resort for persons afflicted with tuberculosis and other respiratory ailments.

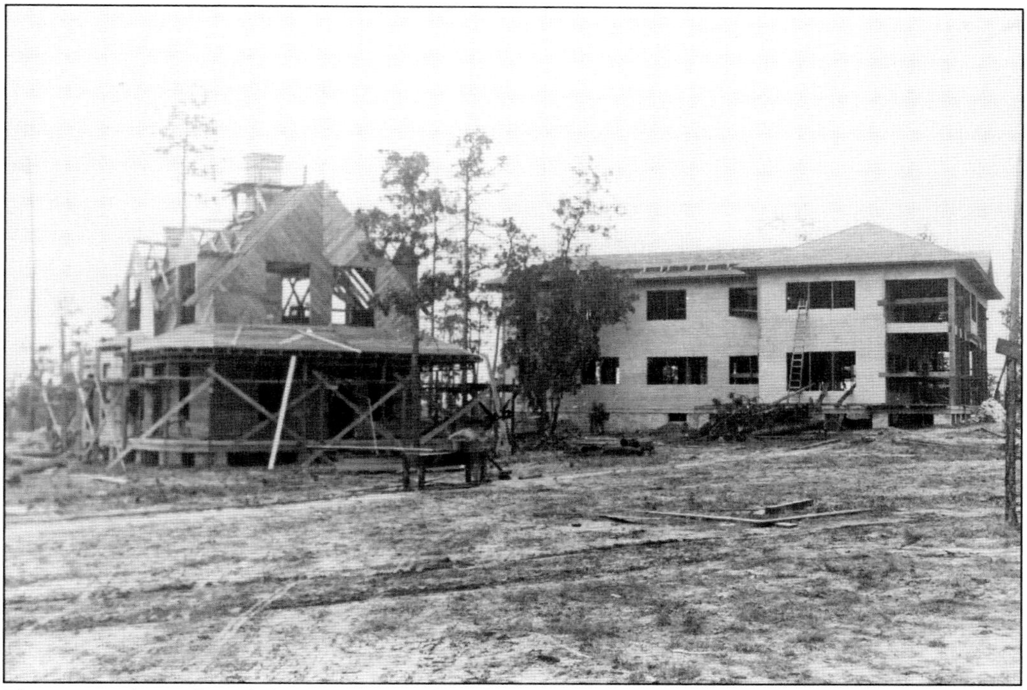

Shown in the right of this picture is the almost completed Casino Building. The structure housed a restaurant, reading room, billiard room, and smoking room. It was later known as the Pinehurst General Office Building.

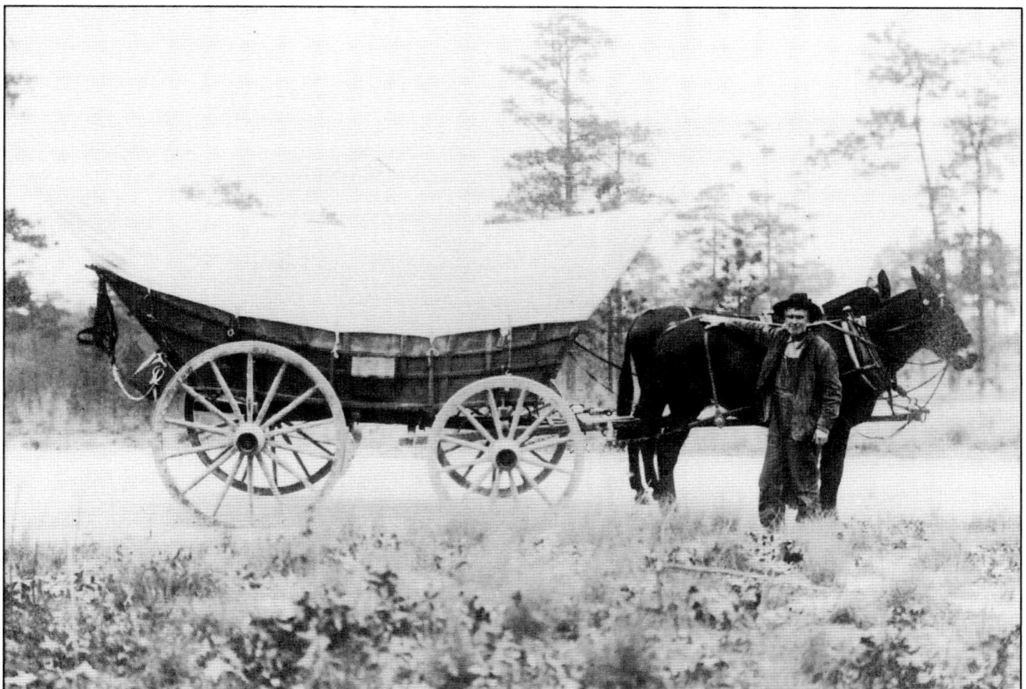

This photograph of a schooner was taken outside the village. Its boat-shaped hull enabled it to ford the region's sometimes swollen rivers and streams.

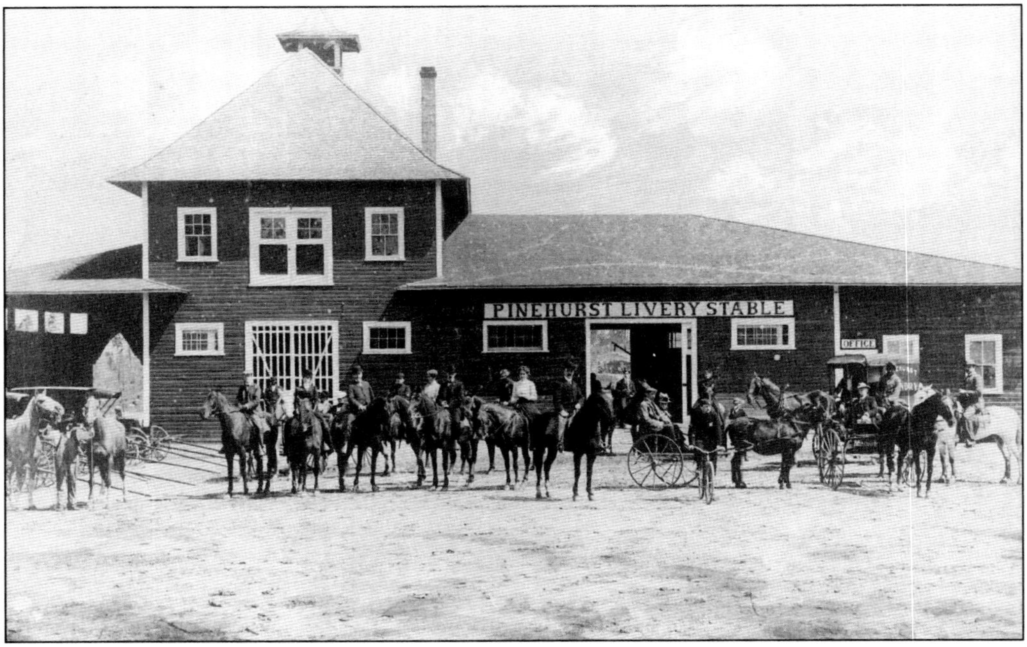

Pictured here is the Pinehurst Livery Stable.

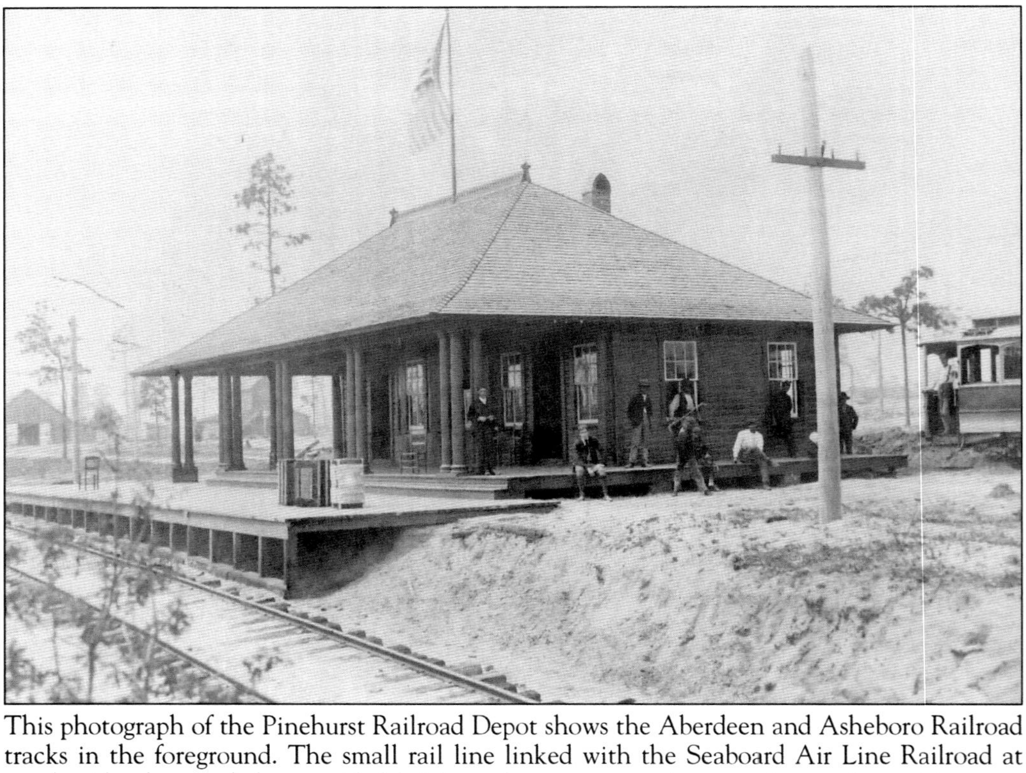
This photograph of the Pinehurst Railroad Depot shows the Aberdeen and Asheboro Railroad tracks in the foreground. The small rail line linked with the Seaboard Air Line Railroad at nearby Aberdeen and also provided freight and passenger service to major northern cities.

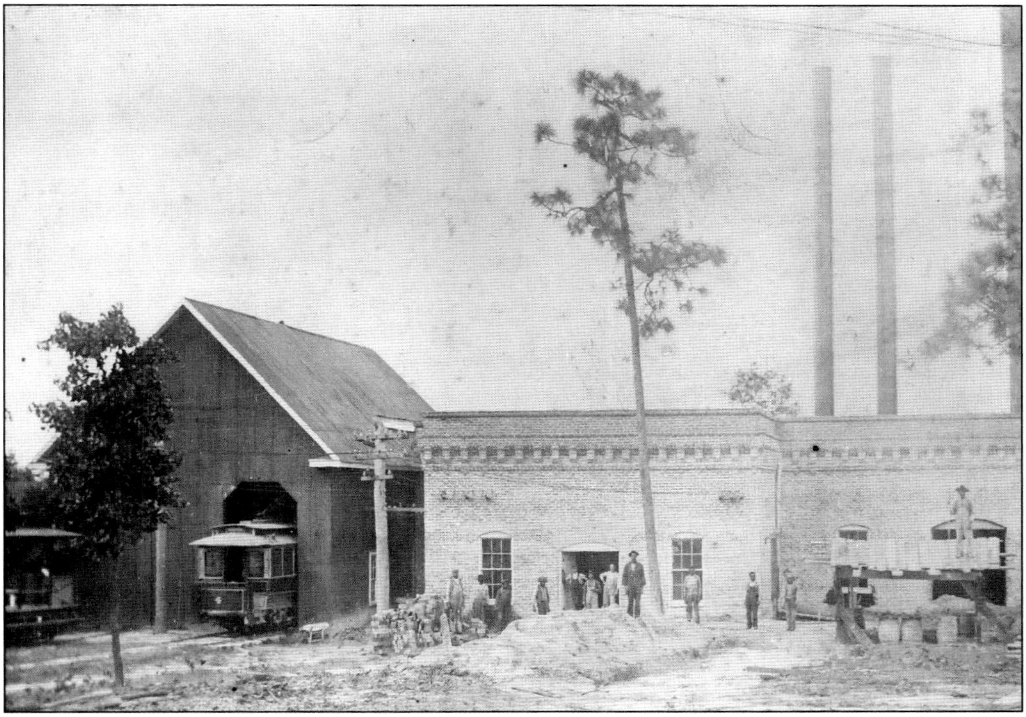

This early photograph of the trolley barn shows the newly constructed brick powerhouse to its right. Electric power came to Pinehurst in 1896.

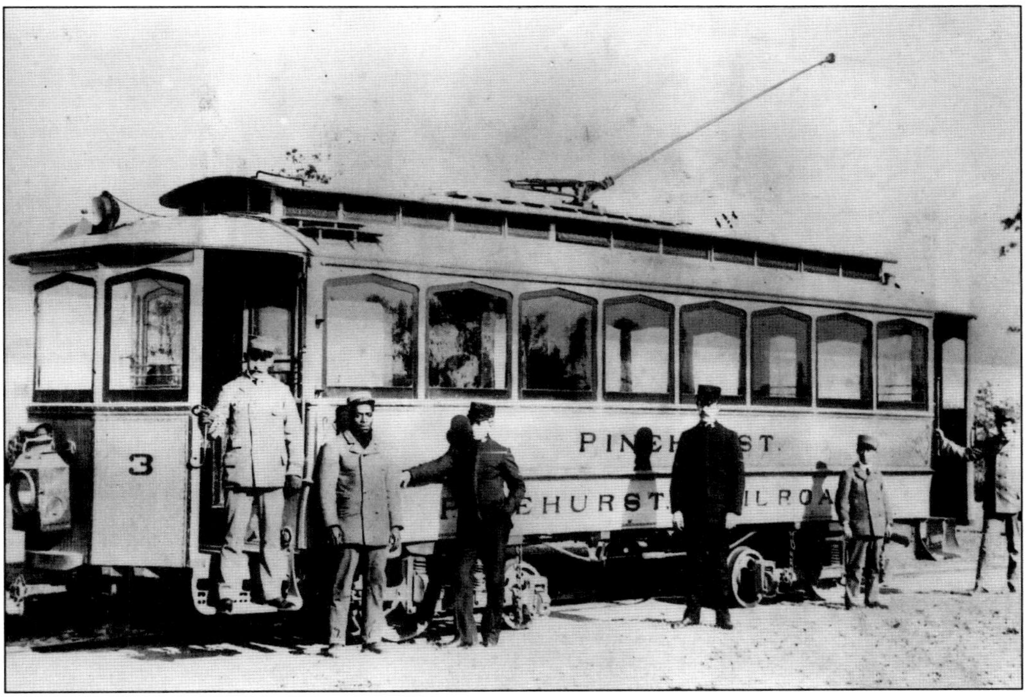

The trolley offered a daily passenger shuttle to Southern Pines and was used by residents and tourists alike. Pictured here are a group of workers, including Clarence Clendenin, reputedly the smallest man in Pinehurst.

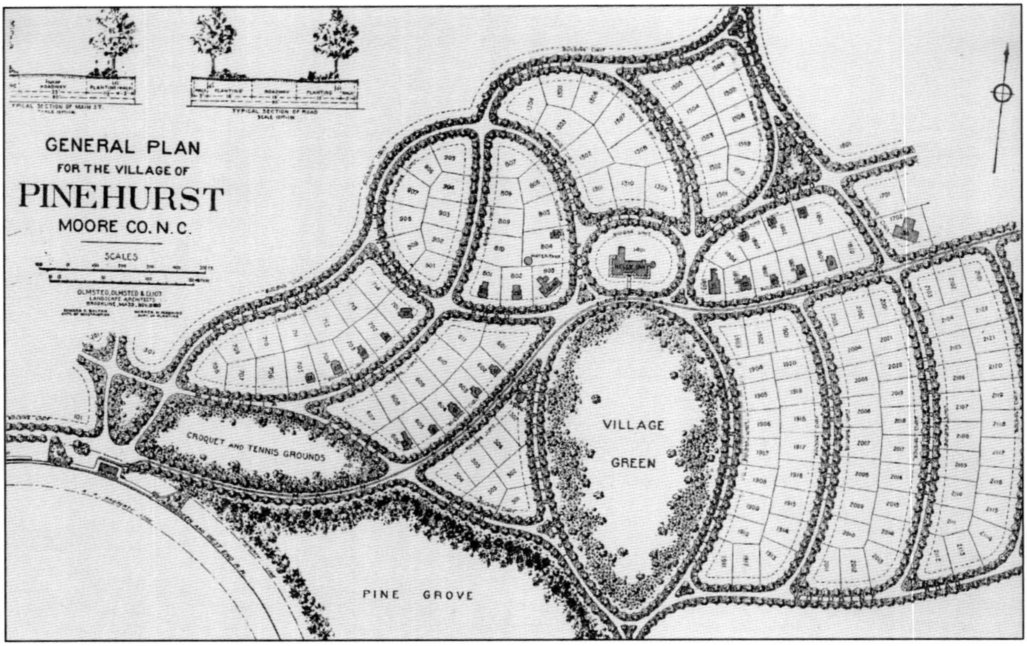

This is a map of the village of Pinehurst.

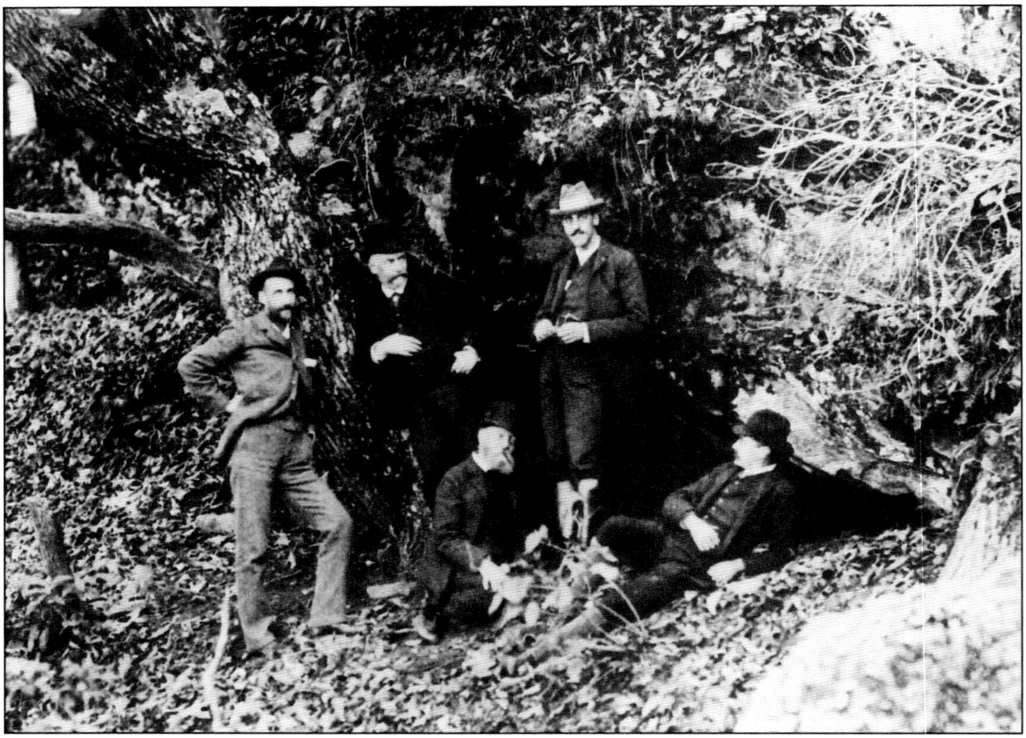

The famed architectural landscape firm of Olmsted, Olmsted, and Eliot was hired by Pinehurst founder James Walker Tufts to design the layout of the village. Pictured in the center of the photograph is Frederick Law Olmsted (sitting), with George W. Vanderbilt to his right.

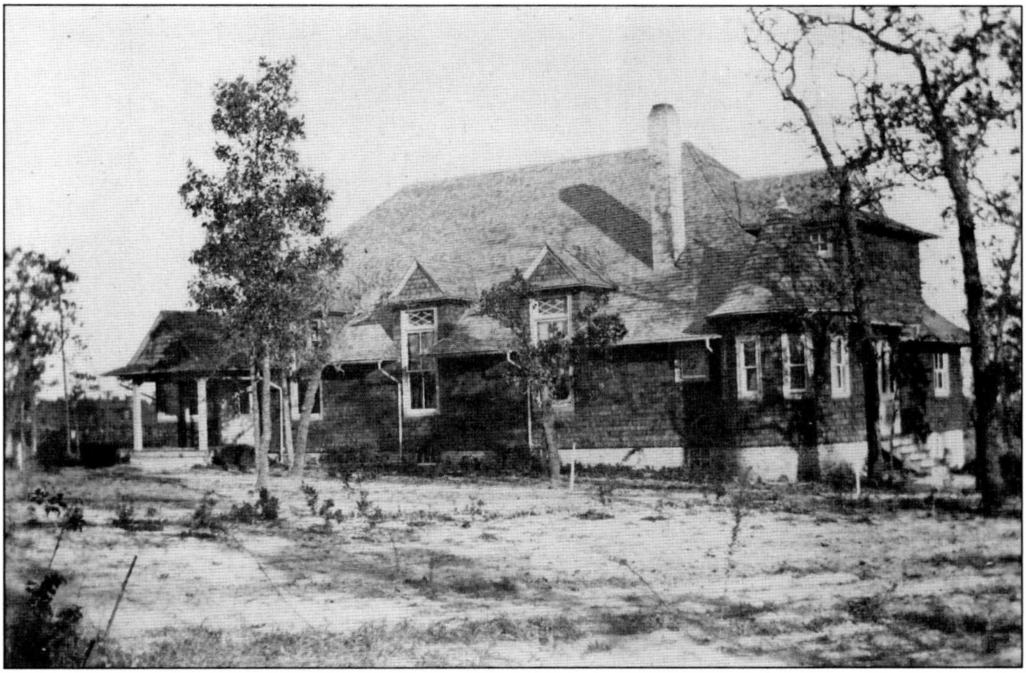

The village hall was an early social center where residents and guests participated in amateur dramas, musicals, and poetry readings. The hall was located near the Holly Inn, facing the village green.

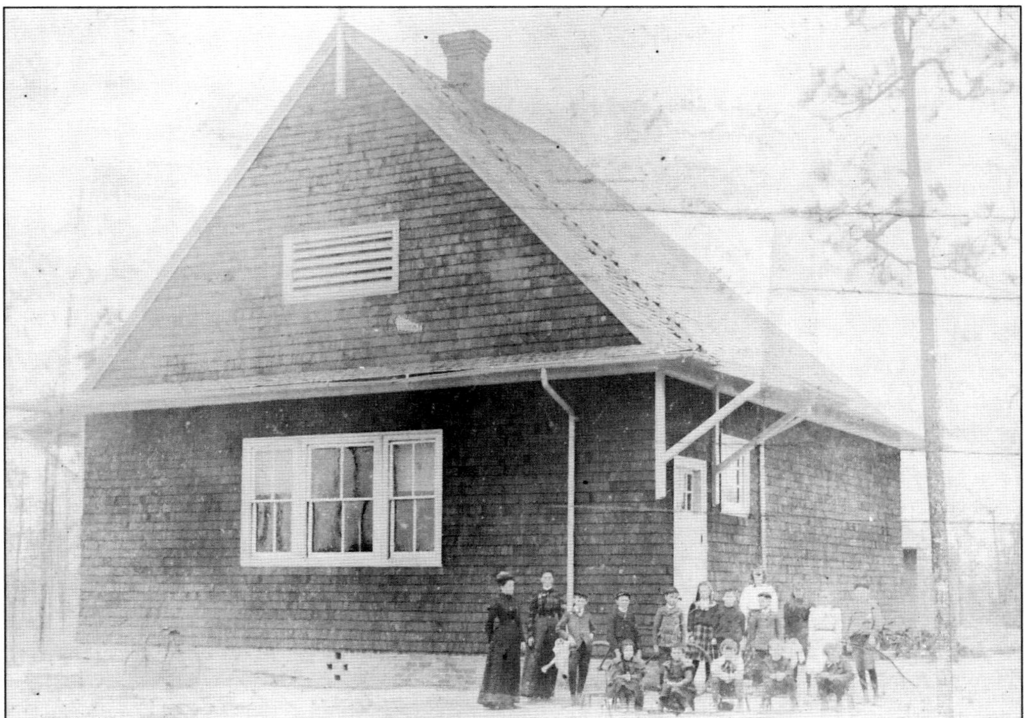

This is an 1895 photograph of the first one-room schoolhouse in the village. Pictured are a group of students with their teachers in the left foreground.

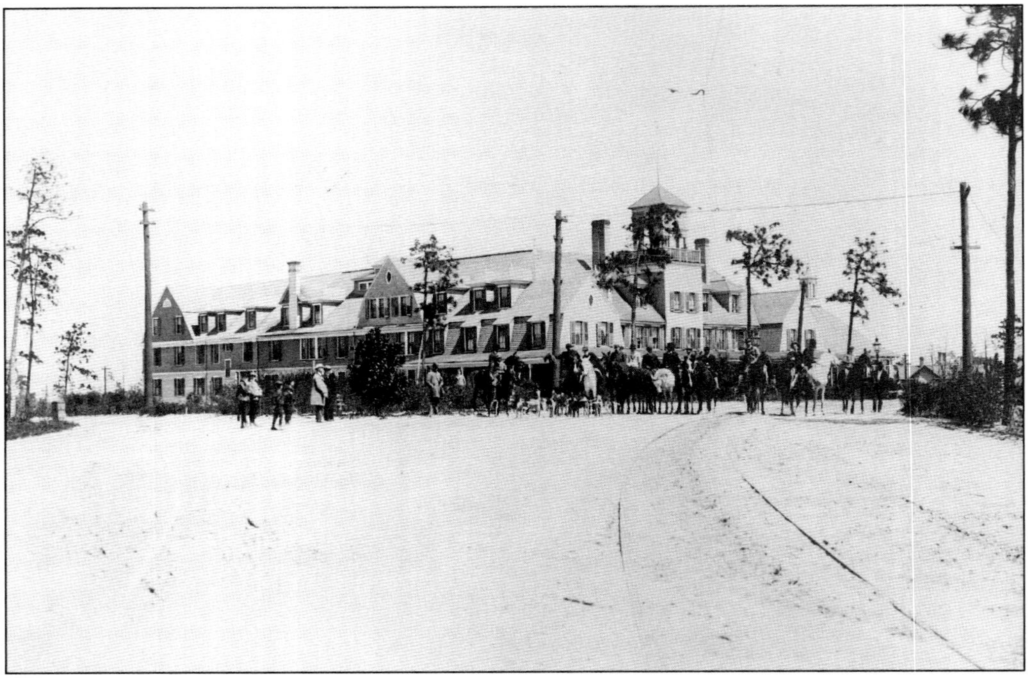

The Holly Inn was built in 1895 as the first hotel and was enlarged almost annually to accommodate the increasing number of guests. In this picture, a group of riders are in front of the building.

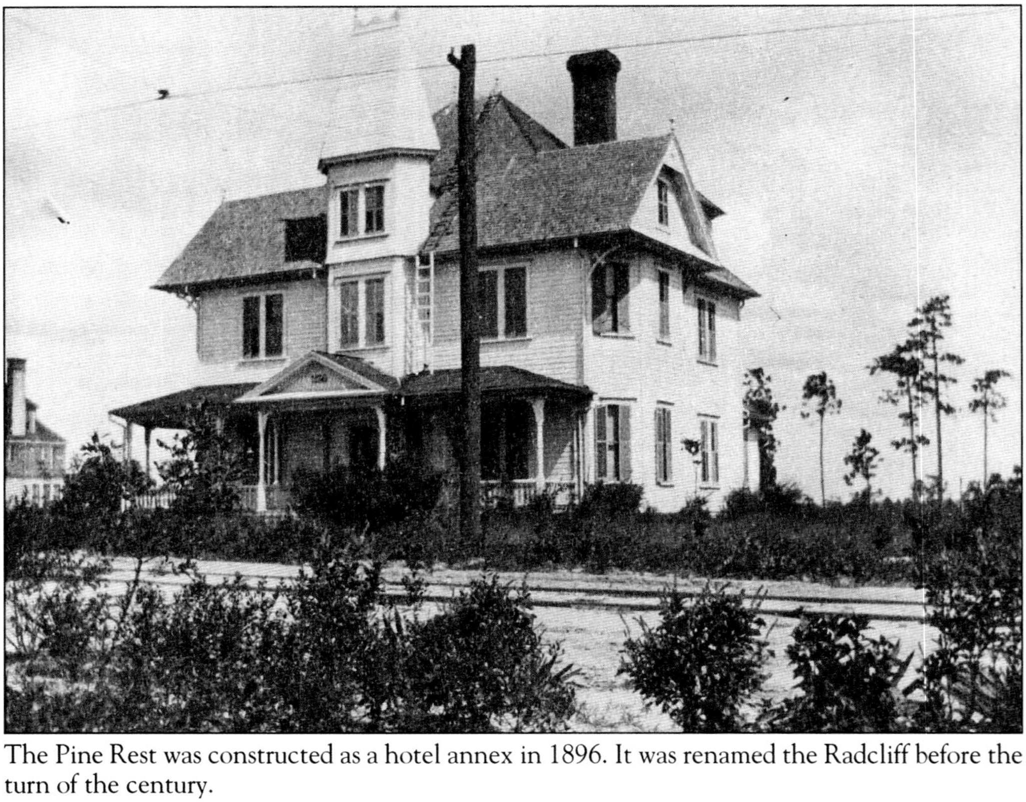

The Pine Rest was constructed as a hotel annex in 1896. It was renamed the Radcliff before the turn of the century.

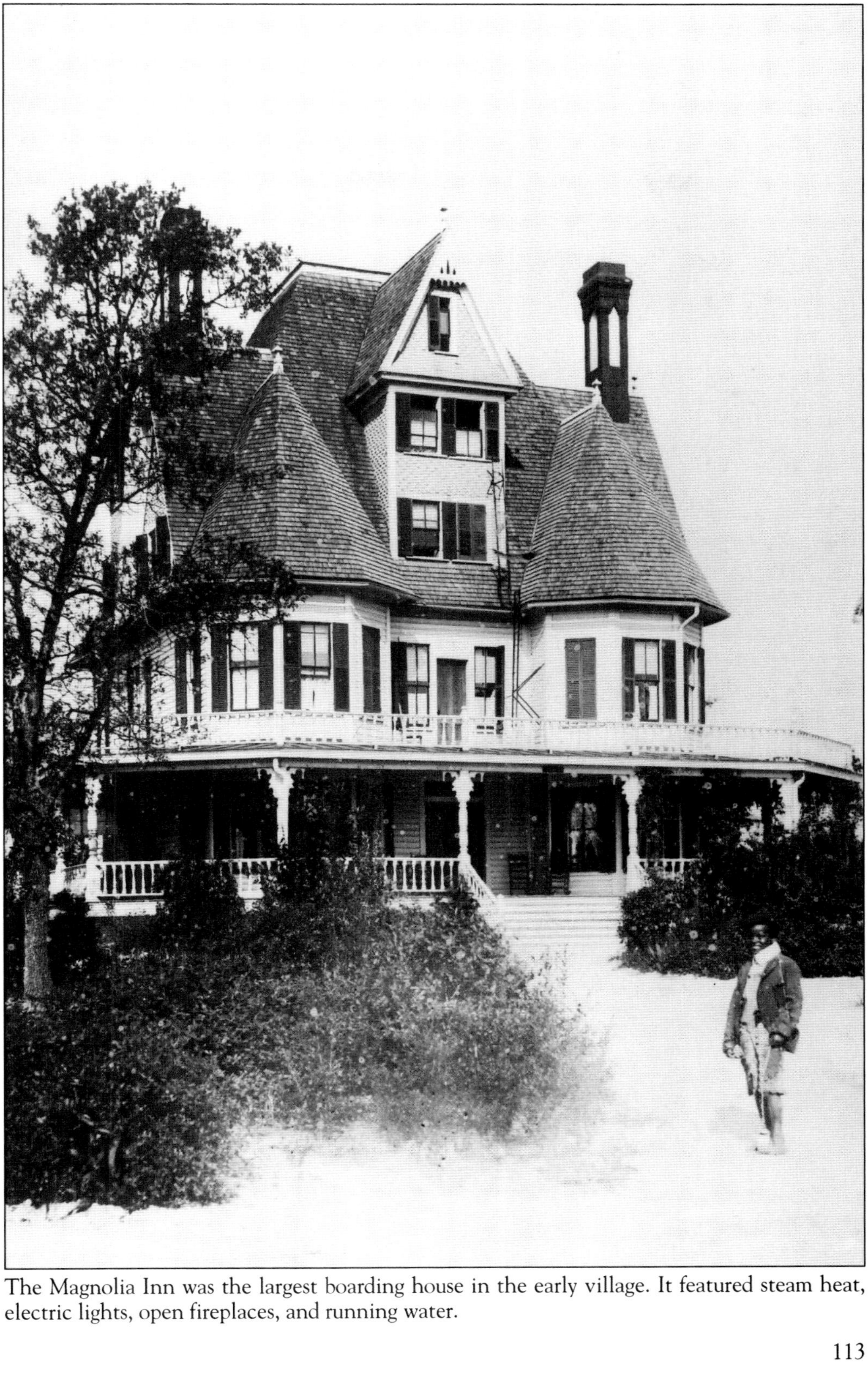

The Magnolia Inn was the largest boarding house in the early village. It featured steam heat, electric lights, open fireplaces, and running water.

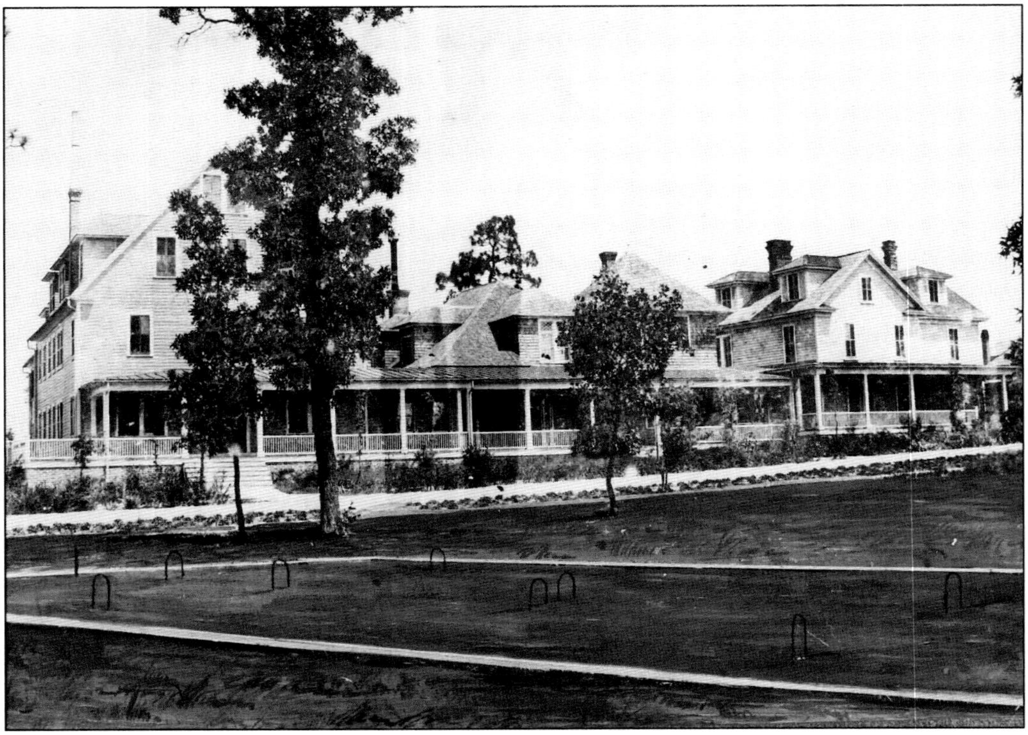

The Berkshire was formed in 1898 by connecting two cottages with a central one-story lobby and gabled second-floor passageway. It housed sixty guests, and advertised rooms at $2 a night.

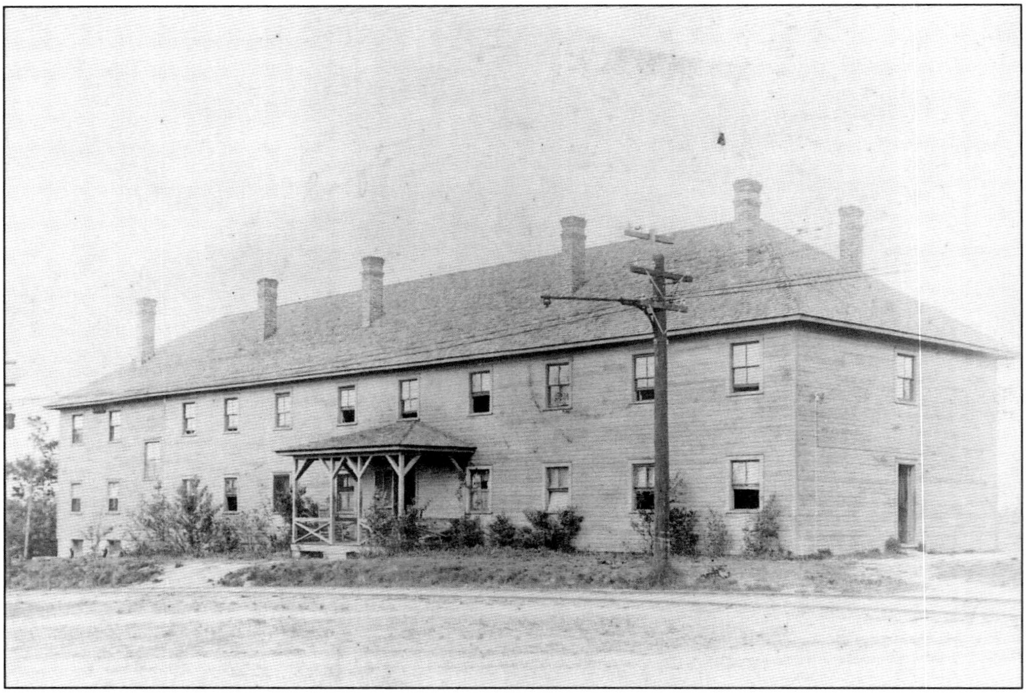

The Lexington was constructed in 1899 as an apartment house for hotel employees. It was used during the summer months by workers from the nearby peach orchards.

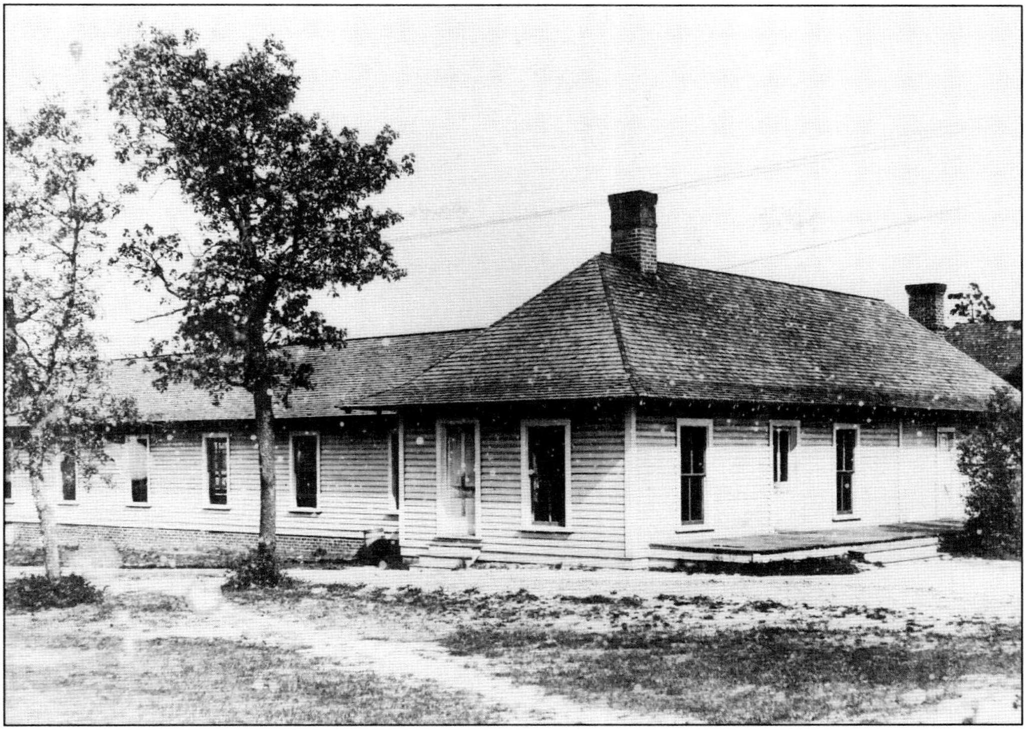

The Bowling Alley was constructed in 1898 in back of the Casino Building. It featured two inlaid maple alleys and "a commodious room fitted up as a barber shop" on the front side of the building.

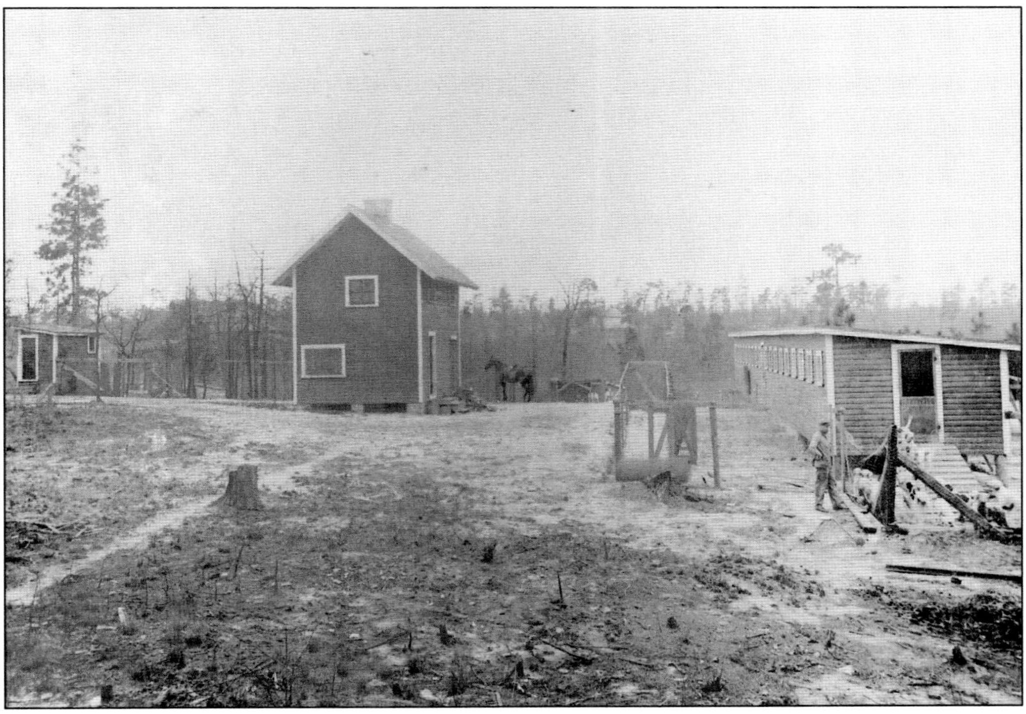

This is an early photograph of the Pinehurst kennels.

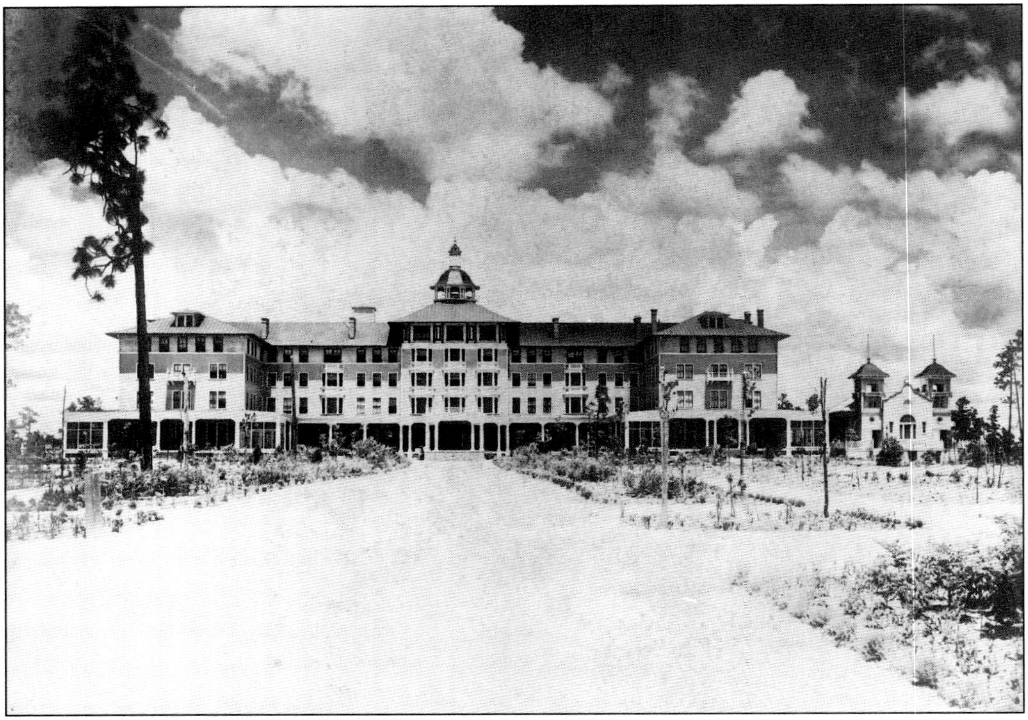

The Carolina Hotel was constructed in 1899–1900 and featured two hundred and fifty rooms, including forty-nine suites with separate baths. The turreted Mission-style building to the right was the music hall.

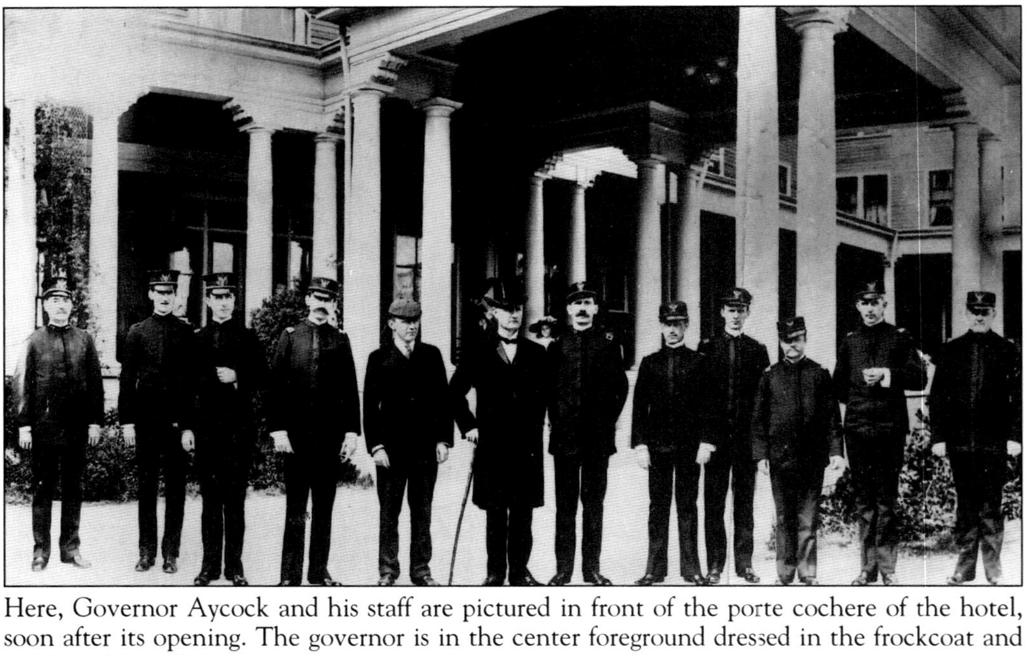

Here, Governor Aycock and his staff are pictured in front of the porte cochere of the hotel, soon after its opening. The governor is in the center foreground dressed in the frockcoat and wearing the top hat.

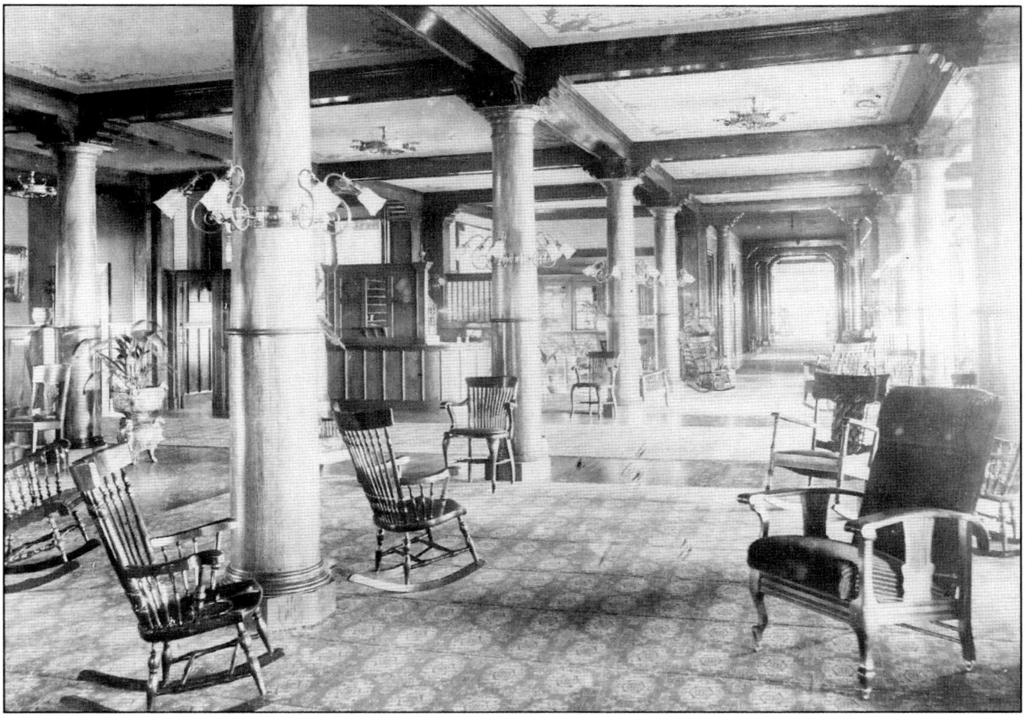

This photograph of the main lobby of the hotel shows the colonnaded cross hall.

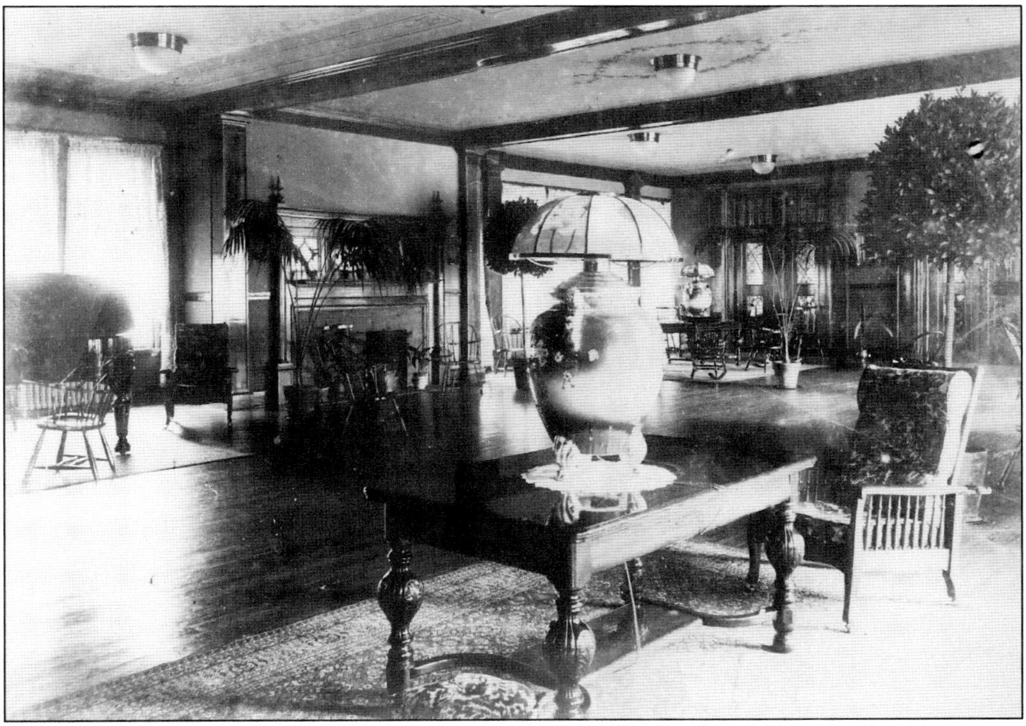

This is a view of one of the large community rooms of the Colonial Revival-styled hotel. Interior furnishings were magnificent

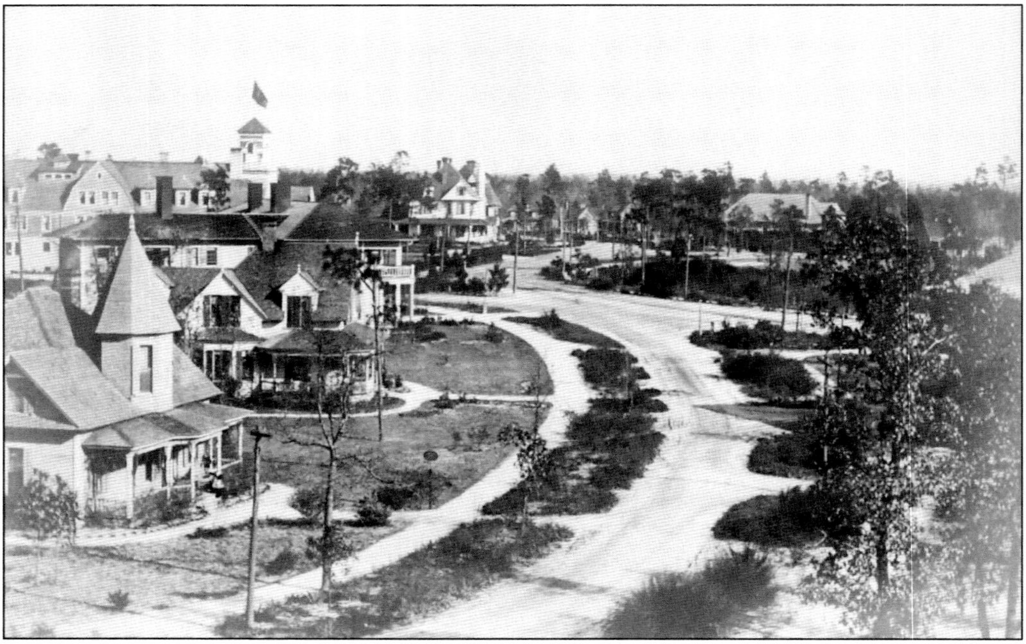

This is an early photograph of Magnolia Road looking northeast.

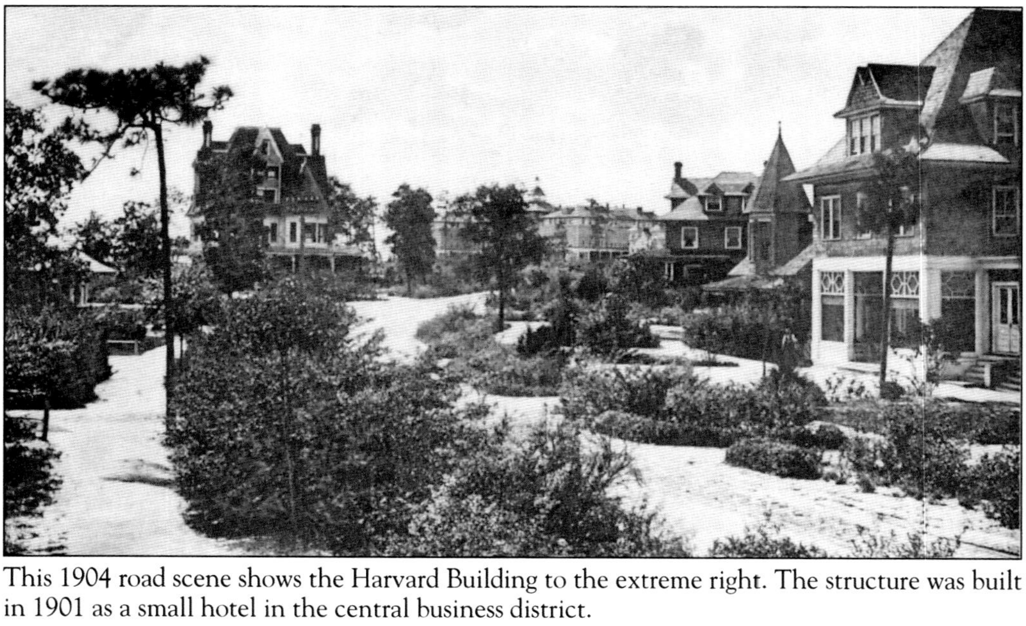

This 1904 road scene shows the Harvard Building to the extreme right. The structure was built in 1901 as a small hotel in the central business district.

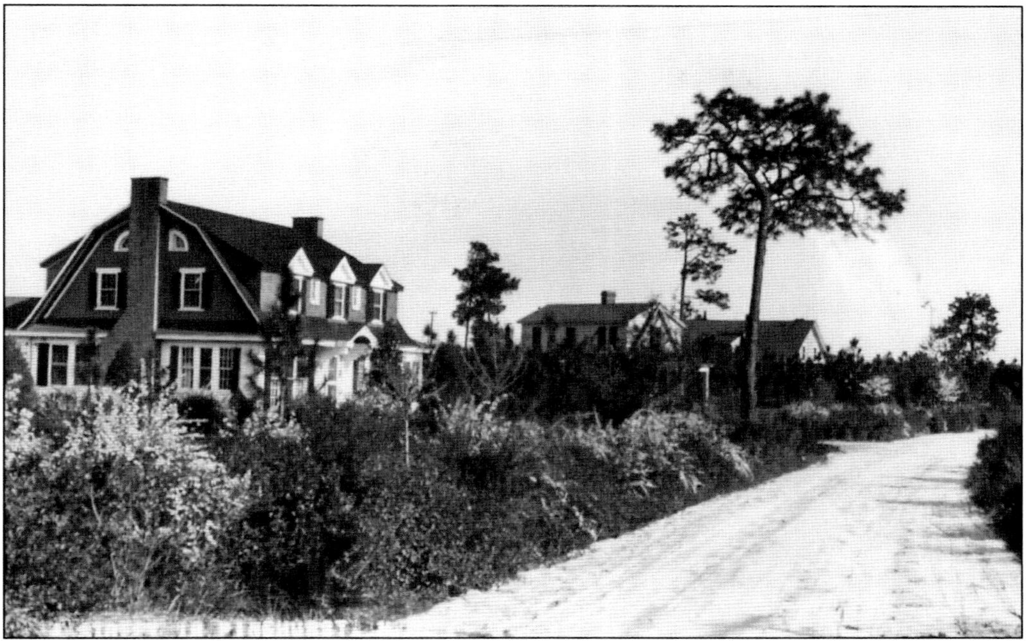

This photograph shows some of Pinehurst's early cottages.

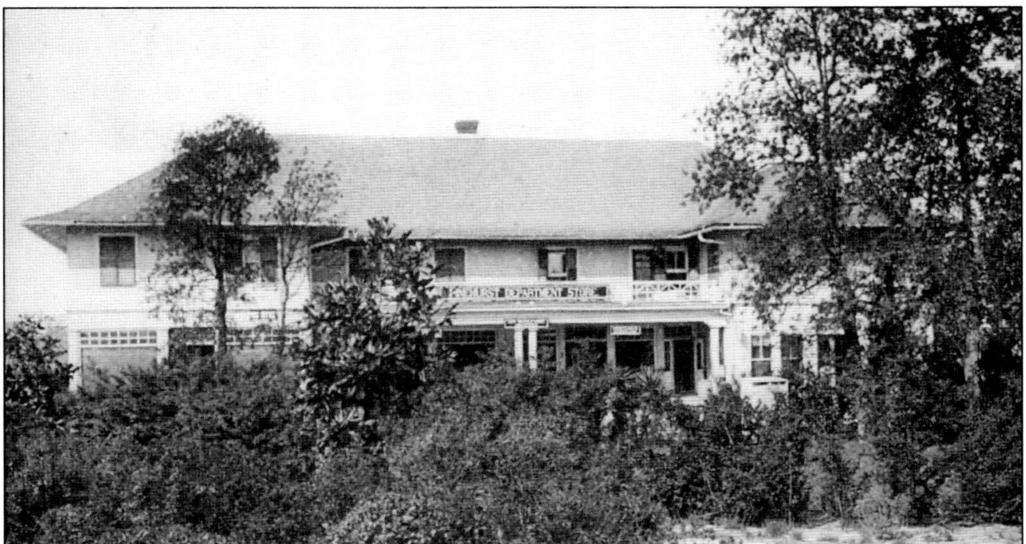

The Pinehurst Department Store was built in 1897 as the largest department store in Moore County. It offered a variety of goods, including crockery and glassware, "Proprietary Medicines," meat and fish, and fine furniture.

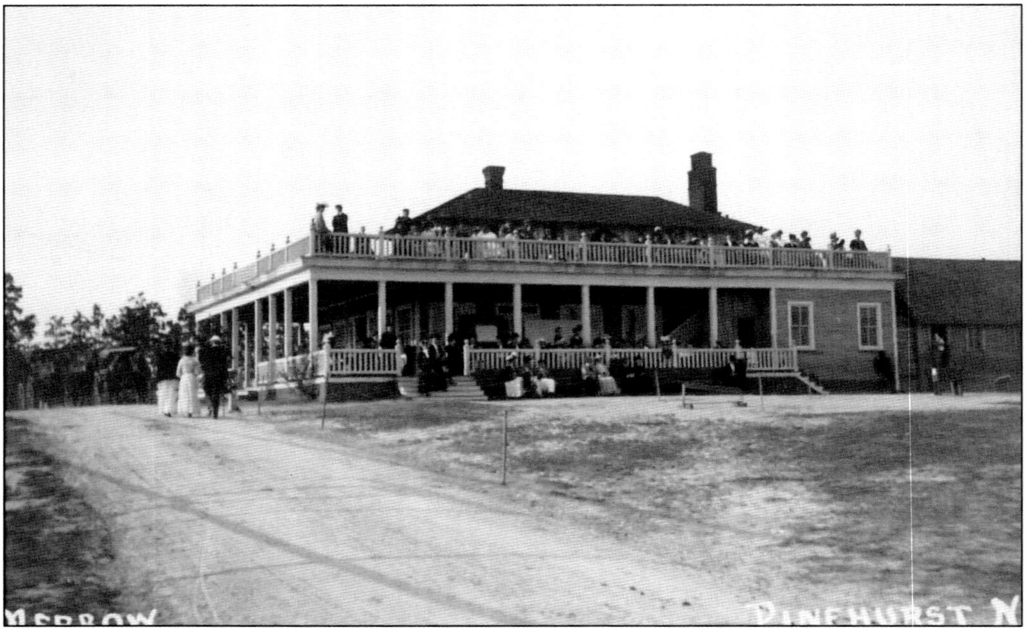

Golf was introduced to Pinehurst in 1897, and the first clubhouse was constructed in 1899. The building was enlarged several times between 1902 and 1910 to accommodate the increasing number of golfers and guests.

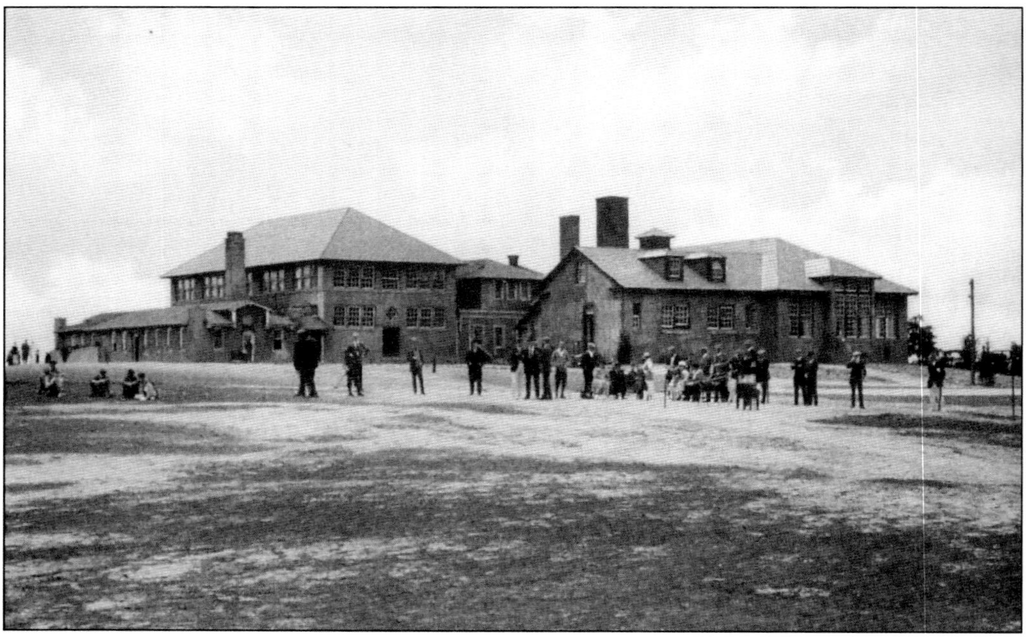

Construction of this Mediterranean-style clubhouse started in 1910. The large three-story building, flanked by its two wings in the left of the picture, was built as an annex to the original frame structure.

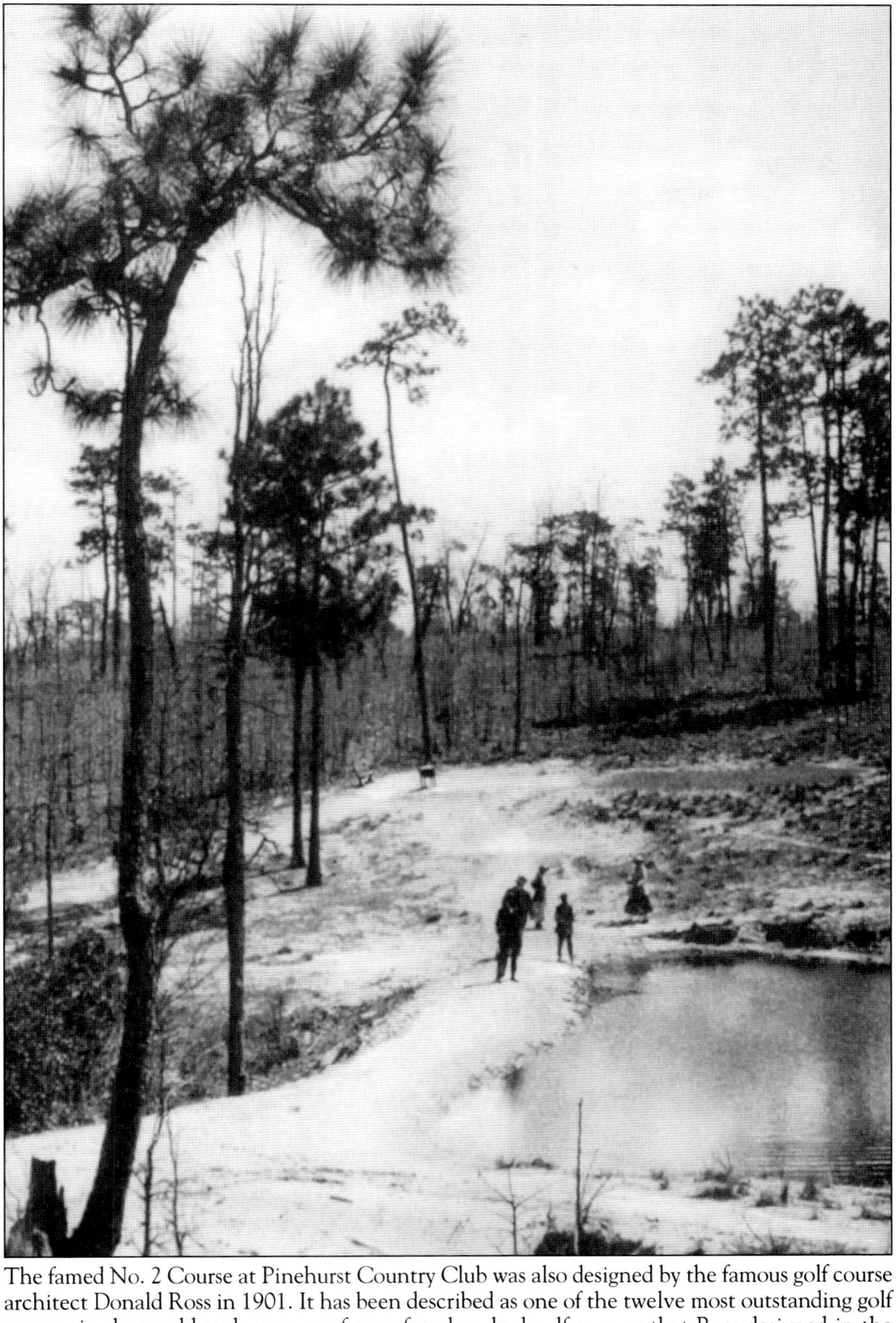

The famed No. 2 Course at Pinehurst Country Club was also designed by the famous golf course architect Donald Ross in 1901. It has been described as one of the twelve most outstanding golf courses in the world and was one of over four hundred golf courses that Ross designed in the United States.

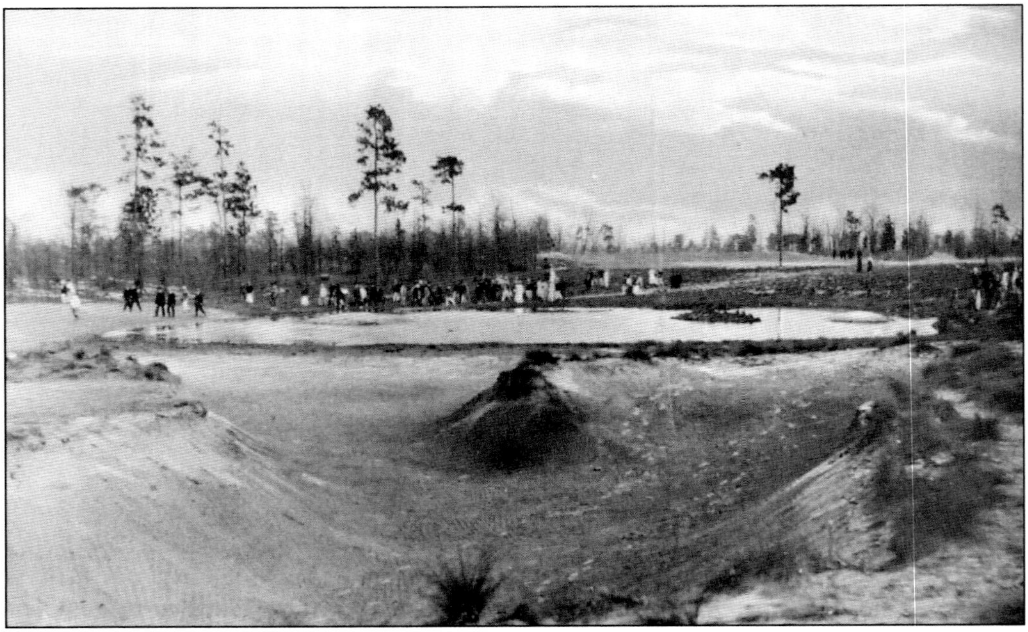

This photograph shows the sixteenth hole at the No. 2 Course at Pinehurst Country Club.

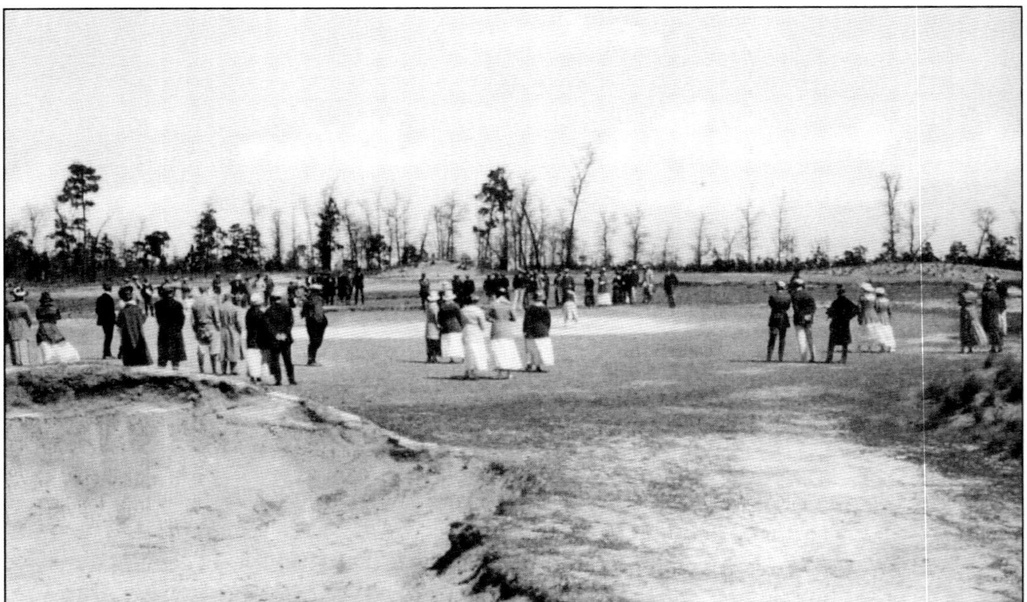

Pictured here is the twelfth green at the No. 2 Course.

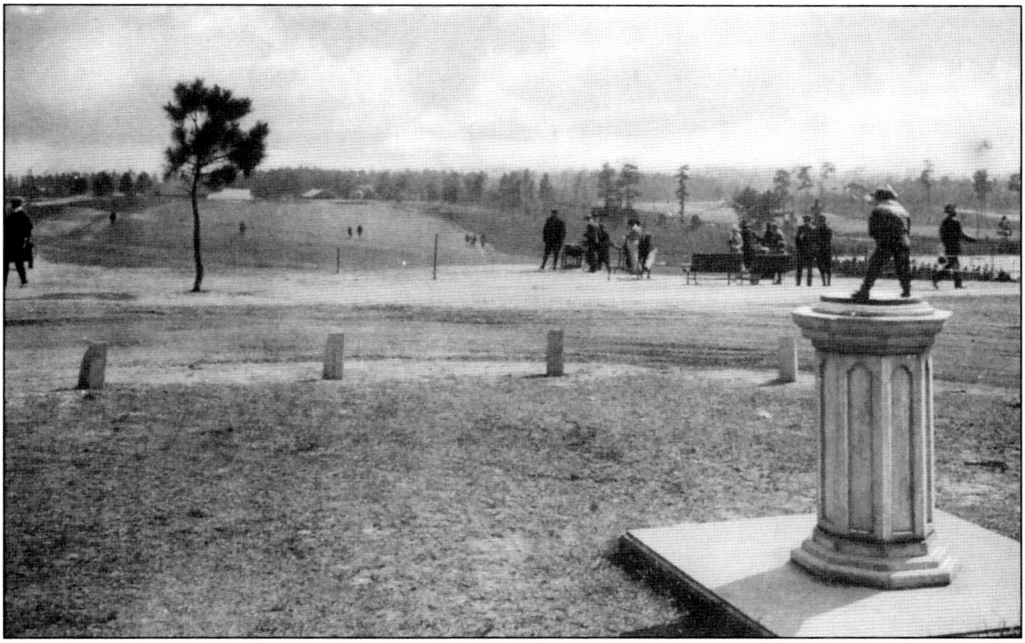

The No. 1 Course at Pinehurst Country Club was originally laid out by golf course architect D. Leroy Culver in 1897 and was completely redesigned by Donald Ross in the early years of the twentieth century. It has been described as "short but tight, tree-lined, and often rolling." Pictured is the first tee, with a bronze statue of Donald Ross visible in the right foreground.

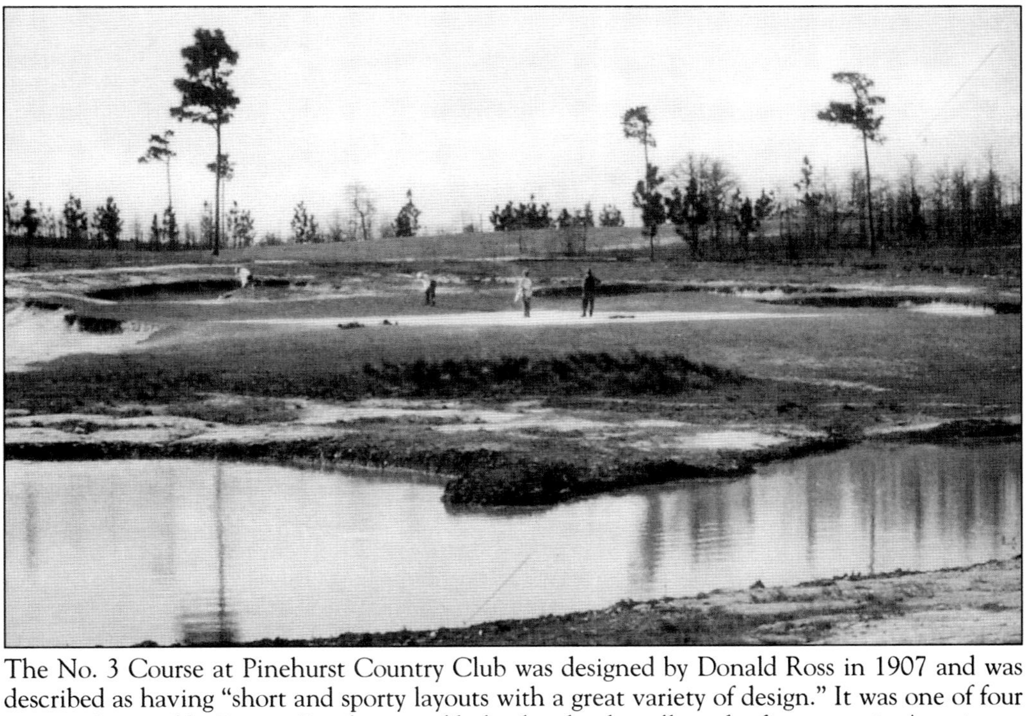

The No. 3 Course at Pinehurst Country Club was designed by Donald Ross in 1907 and was described as having "short and sporty layouts with a great variety of design." It was one of four courses designed by Ross at Pinehurst and helped make the village the first resort in America to offer seventy-two holes of golf.

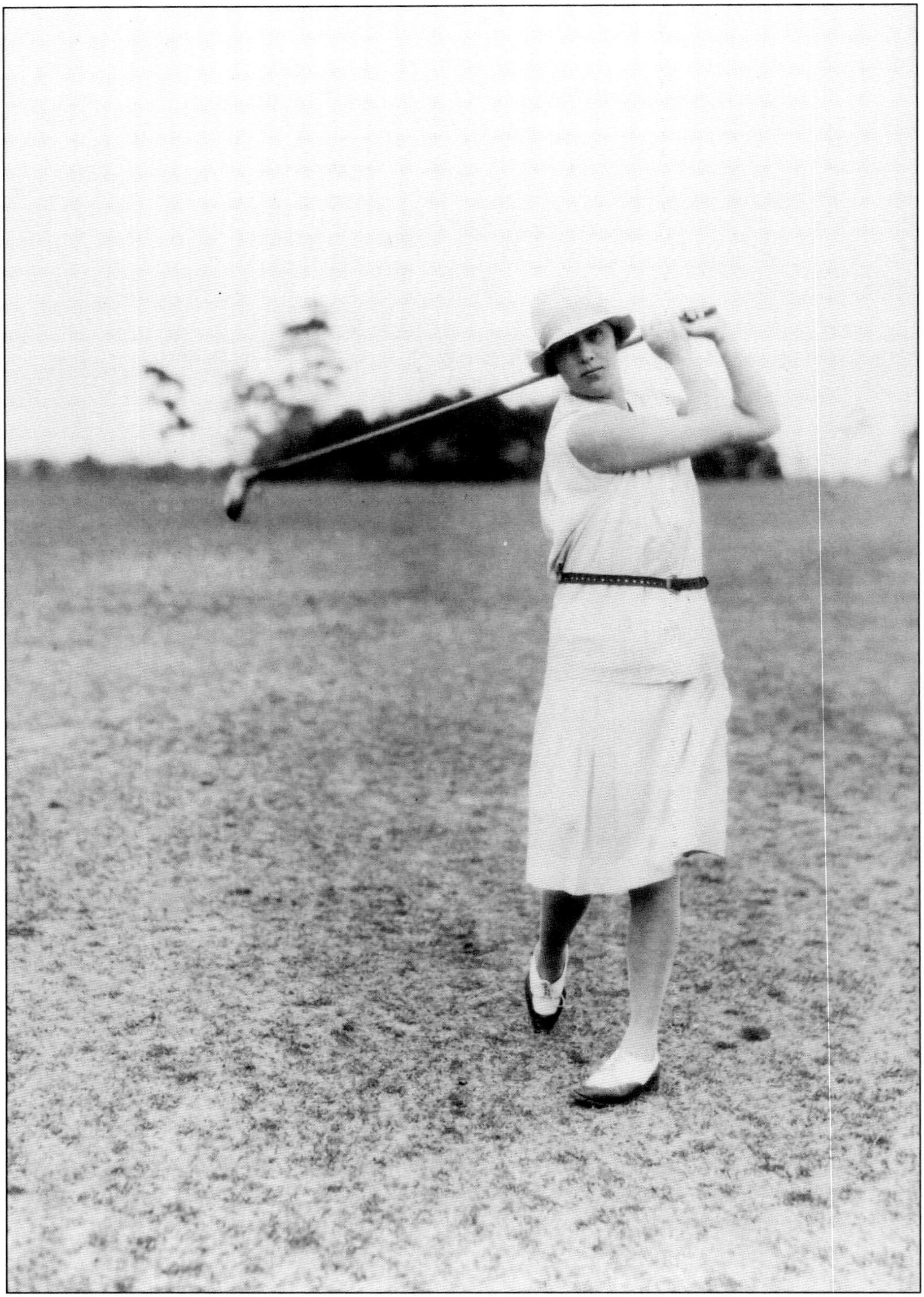

Pictured here is Glenna Collett, five-time winner of the United States Women's Amateur Golf title at Pinehurst. She dominated women's golf for over a decade and was said to have raised the level of women's golf to a new plateau in the United States. Collett was called the "female Bobby Jones of golf."

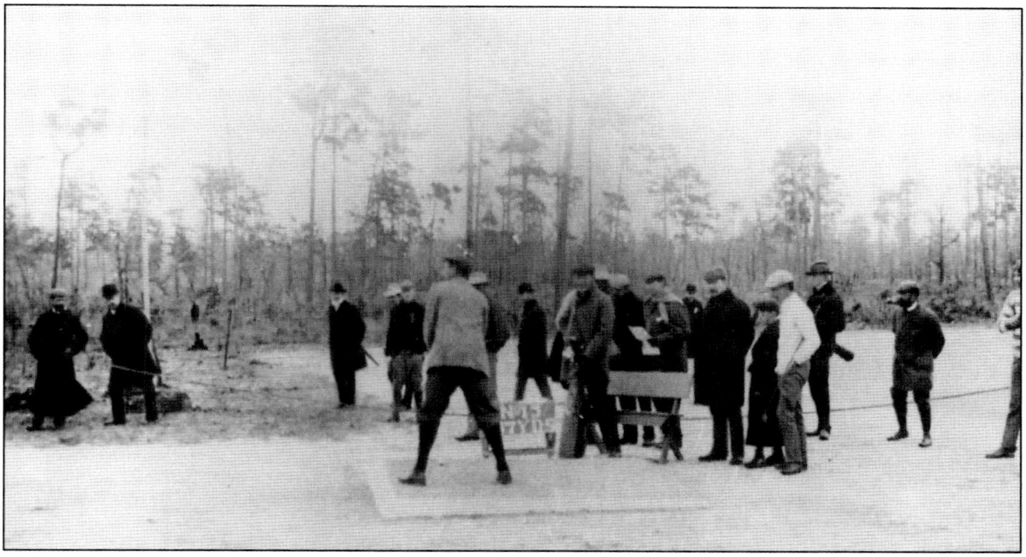

Pictured is Harry Vardon (1870–1937), who was considered one of the greatest golfers in the world, teeing off at Pinehurst's No. 1 Course in 1900. Vardon spoke favorably of the new golf course and helped to stimulate the increasing interest in the game nationwide.

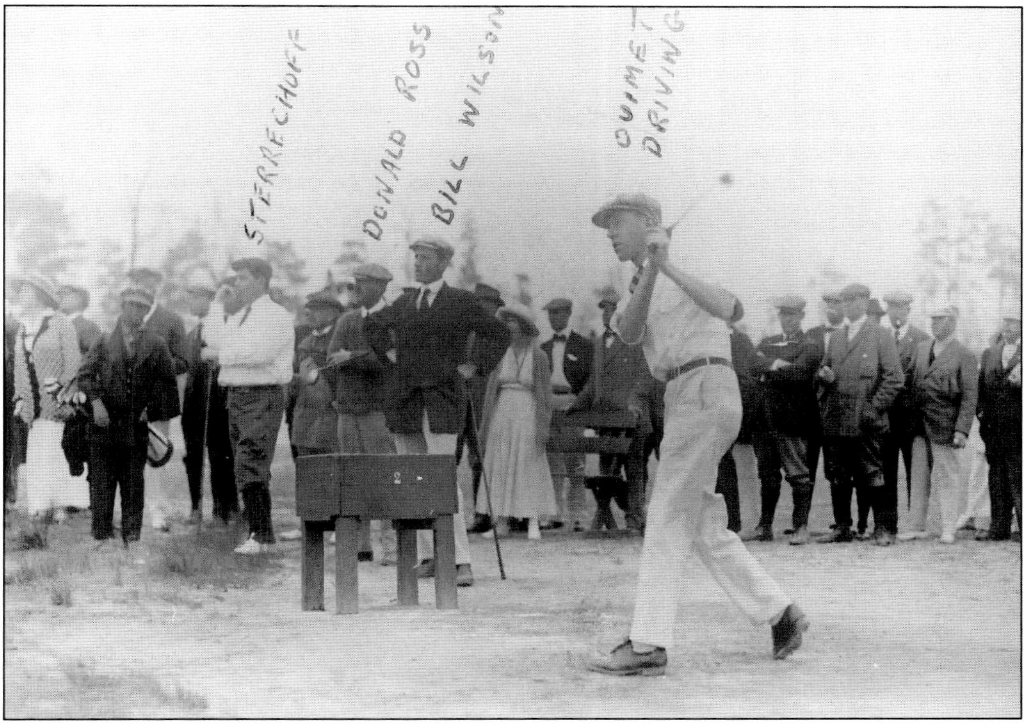

Pictured is Francis Ouimet (1893–1967), who defeated Harry Vardon and Ted Ray in a playoff for the U.S. Open in 1913. Ouimet was winner of the North and South Amateur Championship in 1920 and was a frequent visitor to Pinehurst.

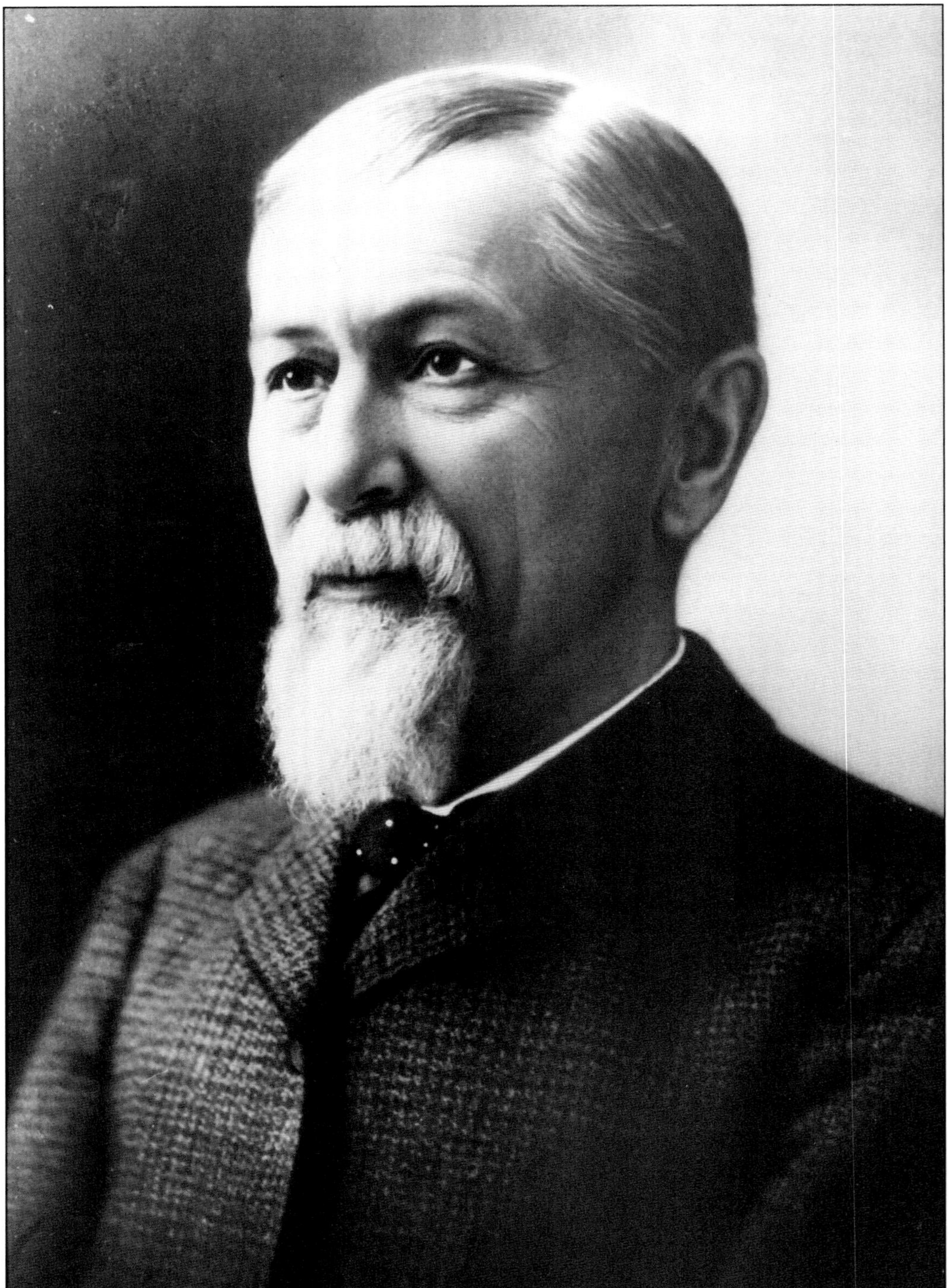

Pictured here is James Walker Tufts (1835–1902), the founder of Pinehurst.

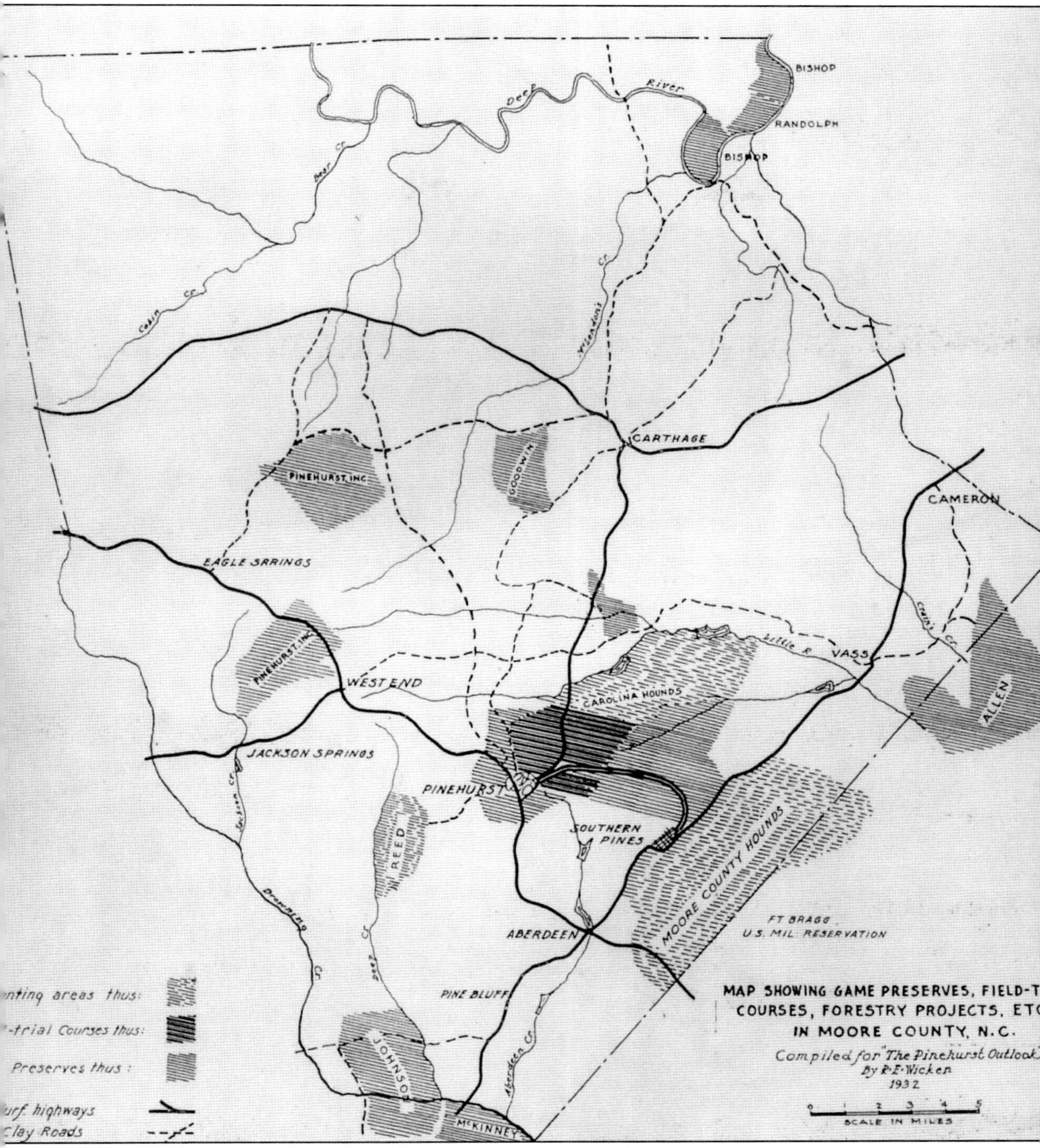

This map of Moore County shows fox hunting areas, field trial courses, and game preserves.

ACKNOWLEDGMENTS

This book would not have been possible without the assistance of Kristine Januzek and Jean Van Winkle of the Tufts Archives at Given Memorial Library in Pinehurst. Their efforts were tireless and their support unwavering. I also wish to thank Hampton Crane, Tony Parker, Richard Page, Guy V. Smith, Gladys Harris, Iris Keith, Marie Zickl, Isabel McKeithen Thomas, Harris and Barbara Blake, Virginia Walthour Moss, Sue Addor Buffkin, T. Clyde Auman, John L. Frye, Gary and Ann Kunce, Pinkie Wooten, Caesar Phillips, Robert and Lucille Hyman, Lawrence and Olive Johnson, Norris Hodgkins, Alton McDonald, Priscilla Cole, Eldiweiss Lockey, Melinda Coleman Wall, Eleanor Eddy Smith, Marilyn Hartsell, Frieda Bruton, Ann E. Dumville, Janet Cunningham, Terry Marquez and Diana Belvin of the Moore County Library, Jean Prickett of the Carthage Museum, David Sinclair of the *Fayetteville-Observer Times*, David Woronoff, Faye Dasen, and Glen Sides of *The Pilot*, and The Moore County Historical Association under whose auspices it was published.